TANTRA
AND
POPULAR RELIGION
IN TIBET

Edited by

Geoffrey Samuel, Hamish Gregor
and Elisabeth Stutchbury

INTERNATIONAL ACADEMY OF INDIAN CULTURE
and ADITYA PRAKASHAN, NEW DELHI

First published: 1994

ISBN 81-85689-68-7

Published by Pradeep Kumar Goel for
Aditya Prakashan, F-14/65, Model Town II, Delhi – 110 009
and printed at Crescent Printing Works (Pvt.) Ltd.,
P-14, Connaught Circus, New Delhi – 110 001

Contents

Introduction

Geoffrey Samuel

The papers in this collection, with one exception, originated in a session on Tibet and Himalayan Societies held at the Australian Anthropological Society conference at the University of Newcastle, New South Wales, Australia, in August 1988. Although held as part of a conference of anthropologists, the session was also open to scholars from non-anthropological backgrounds. The convenors of the session, Elisabeth Stutchbury and myself, wanted as wide a representation as possible of Tibetan and Himalayan specialists from Australia and New Zealand. Twelve papers were presented to the session. Nine contributors came from Australia and two from New Zealand, while the twelfth was a research student from the People's Republic of China working at the Australian National University.[1]

Elisabeth and I suggested that participants might choose to address a common theme, 'Tantra and Everyday Religion.' In referring to 'everyday' or 'popular'[2] religion, we meant to include both the formal religious traditions of Tibetan Buddhism and Bon as part of everyday Tibetan life and the so-called 'folk religion' (Tucci 1980:163-212). Our theme intended to suggest that Tantra formed an integral part of this whole area of 'everyday religion'.

In the event, eight of the twelve scholars who gave papers at the Newcastle meeting took up aspects of this theme. Six of these presentations, along with the contribution by Ana Marko, who was unable to attend the conference, have been rewritten to form the basis of the present book[3]. The two conveners have been joined in editing the collection by Hamish Gregor, who is responsible with myself for most of the detailed editing of the final contributions, and who also handled the preparation of the camera-ready copy.

Styles of presentation and referencing vary considerably among the articles in this collection. This in part reflects the conventions prevalent in the disciplines here represented. We have felt it better to refrain from imposing a uniform style. However, where authors have used non-Central Tibetan dialects (e.g., Ladakhi), we have attempted to facilitate comparison by supplying Central Tibetan equivalents in Wylie spelling where we are reasonably certain of them.

❁ ❁ ❁

These essays provide what I believe is a significant series of attempts to explore a side of Tibetan religious experience which is of central importance but which has remained on the sidelines of most work on Tibet. By its very nature, the topic crosses boundaries between conventional disciplines and established approaches. It proved a highly suitable theme to bring together the wide range of approaches, from the literary and textual to the ethnographic and anthropological, represented among our contributors.

Louis Dumont many years ago posed the task for the sociology (and one could equally say anthropology) of India as 'the establishment of the proper relation between it and classical Indology' (Dumont 1957). His own attempt at a synthesis, *Homo Hierarchicus* (Dumont 1970), remains controversial but there is no doubt that he succeeded in establishing his fundamental point. Neither the social sciences, with their traditional focus on the ethnographic techniques of participant observation and interview, nor Indology, with its emphasis on literary and historical materials, can provide a comprehensive picture of Indian society or of Indian religion. The two are complementary: the literary and historical material of the Indologist is given meaning and life through study of contemporary practice, while the parochial and limited focus of village ethnography is given context and depth through the Indologist's historical and textual perspective. Studies of Indian society today are coming to take this point for granted, and the best of them move freely between literary and ethnographic materials and between textual, historical, sociological and anthropological modes of analysis.

The same point can be made, *mutatis mutandis*, about Tibet, but we are only beginning to see the appearance of studies of Tibetan society which have attained this degree of sophistication. In part, this is because the historical and literary side of Tibetan studies, for all of the explosion of academic activity set into motion by the exodus of Tibetan scholars since 1959, is still at a relatively early stage. There are still many basic questions to be answered. As the outlines become clearer, we are becoming more aware how many texts have scarcely been looked at, how many religious traditions are as yet hardly studied, and how many gaps in our historical knowledge may never be adequately filled.

On the ethnographic side also, work has been concentrated in a few areas, particularly among the Tibetan frontier people in India (Ladakh) and Nepal, and large parts of the picture still remain to be filled in. Many villages and communities remain little more than names. The anthropology of Tibet has yet to be galvanised by a Louis Dumont into dialogue about a single paradigm: there are as many approaches as there are anthropologists.

The theme of our collection can perhaps help to bring some coherence into this scattered scene. Tantra is a topic *par excellence* for literary and textual scholars in departments of history, philosophy and comparative religion, but the study of tantra also demands a sensitivity to lived religious experience which goes beyond the merely textual. As for popular religion in Tibet, Tantra provides, as the word itself suggests, the continuing thread about which popular religion is woven. No understanding of Tibetan religion which fails to take it seriously into account can go beyond the superficial.

The first essay in this collection, Span Hanna's, is a remarkable personal account of one of the most spectacular and little understood components of Tibetan popular religion: the cult of *gter ma* or 'discovered objects'. *gTer ma* have been the subject of some scholarly attention in recent years (cf. Dargyay 1978, Goodman 1983, Gyatso 1986, Martin 1985, Thondup 1986) and Tibetan accounts of the finding of *gter ma* have been published (Norbu 1986:52-3, Aris 1988, Orgyan Tobgyal 1988), but as far as I know this is the first Western eyewitness account of a *gter ma* discovery. This alone makes it of considerable interest; but Hanna's seemingly straightforward account is more than a simple narrative of an apparently incomprehensible event. He leads us gently towards a Tibetan understanding of the meaning of a *gter ma* discovery. As Mangyal Lhasey Tulku told the Tibetans and Westerners present at the finding, 'the purpose of all this [...] was to encourage faith in the Dharma'. An event such as the finding of a *gter ma* has meaning and significance for Tibetans within a whole frame of knowledge and feeling which the scholar can only comprehend by careful and sympathetic study. The following six essays are all attempts from various perspectives to arrive at an understanding of this uniquely Tibetan world-view. It is for this reason that Hanna's account has been placed at the beginning of our collection.

The other essays have been divided somewhat arbitrarily into two groups: three dealing primarily with literary material, and three with a more ethnographic focus. David Templeman discusses the origins of the Tibetan connection between Tantra and popular religion in the activity of the Tantric siddhas of India, and shows how this tradition was taken up and developed in Tibet. Toni Huber deals with a genre of literature which is of great importance in the context of popular religion, the pilgrimage guide (*gnas yig, dkar chag, lam yig*); while my own contribution looks at the Tibetan epic as a source for information about popular religious attitudes.

The remaining three papers are based more on ethnography and oral history than on textual material. John Draper uses his field material to demonstrate how the differential distribution of knowledge in Sherpa society is articulated with patterns of power and inequality. Ana Marko's analysis of the great monastic and popular festival of *'cham* in Ladakh likewise reminds us that Tibetan societies have inequalities and power relations and that their modes of thinking and behaving are intimately bound up with those relationships. To argue in this way, as Draper notes, is not a denial of Tibetan spirituality, but helps us to retain an awareness of the very real human life within which that spirituality is grounded and based. Finally, Elisabeth Stutchbury provides at the same time a valuable ethnographic picture of a little-studied region (Lahul) and religious tradition (*'Brug pa bKa' brgyud*) and a reminder that religion in Tibet is not a concrete and isolated object of study but a process grounded in both Tibetan history as a whole and in the local history of the numerous little communities which make up the Tibetan region.

I have suggested only some of the themes that can be found interwoven through this collection of studies. Others will appear to the reader: the relationship between centre and periphery in Tibetan society (Draper, Stutchbury); the creation and maintenance of the 'magical' view of reality through ritual, literature and teaching (Hanna, Huber); the extent to which Tantra itself is based on a rejection of dichotomies between spirituality and everyday life (Samuel, Templeman). I hope that readers will be able to share in the excitement that was generated at our original conference and find here fruitful suggestions for further study. A collection like this is itself only a moment in an ongoing process, but it can serve to define a problem and to provide a measure of our current understanding.

This first collection of Tibetan and Himalayan studies from Australia and New Zealand also serves to demonstrate that Australasia is now a significant part of the world Tibetanist community. Tibetan studies goes back some years in Australasia. Senior scholars such as Professor J.W. De Jong, until recently at the Australian National University, and Dr Zahiruddin Ahmed of Latrobe University have made major contributions to the field.[4] As these essays show, there is now a growing and substantial body of younger scholars to follow in their footsteps.

References

ARIS, Michael. 1988. *Hidden Treasures and Secret Lives: A Study of Pemalingpa (1450-1521) and the Sixth Dalai Lama (1983-1706).* Shimla, Indian Institute of Advanced Studies and Delhi, Motilal Banarsidass.

DARGYAY, Eva K. 1978. *The Rise of Esoteric Buddhism in Tibet.* New York, Samuel Weiser.

DUMONT, Louis. 1957. 'For a sociology of India.' Contributions to *Indian Sociology* vol.1.

DUMONT, Louis. 1970. *Homo Hierarchicus: An Essay on the Caste System.* Chicago, University of Chicago Press.

GOODMAN, Steven D. 1983. *'The kLong-chen snying-thig: an eighteenth-century Tibetan revelation.'* Ph.D. thesis, University of Saskatchewan.

GYATSO, Janet. 1986. 'Signs, memory and history: a Tantric Buddhist theory of scriptural transmission.' Journal of the International Association of Buddhist Studies 9,2, 7-35.

MARTIN, Dan. 1985. 'Pearls from bones - relics, chortens, tertons and the signs of saintly death in Tibet.' Typescript.

NORBU, Namkhai. 1986. *The Crystal and the Way of Light.* Compiled and edited by John Shane. New York and London: Routledge and Kegan Paul.

ORGYEN TOBGYAL. 1988. *The Life and Teaching of Chokgyur Lingpa.* Kathmandu, Rangjung Yeshe.

THONDUP, Tulku. 1986. *Hidden Teachings of Tibet: An Explanation of the Terma Tradition of the Nyingma School of Buddhism.* London, Wisdom.

TUCCI, Giuseppe. 1980. *The Religion of Tibet.* Routledge and Kegan Paul, London; University of California Press, Berkeley.

Notes

1. Four papers were on topics outside the theme of this book and so were not included in this collection. Their authors were Jen Gibson, John Gray, Paul Ivory and Xie Guanghua.

2. I have chosen the variant 'popular religion' for the title of this book since three at least of the papers (Hanna's, Harrison's and Marko's) refer to events which, while very much part of Tibetan popular religion, can scarcely be called 'everyday'.

3. Two of the papers presented, those of Paul Harrison and Gabriel Lafitte, have been omitted from this collection at their authors' request.

4. Professor Michael Allen of Sydney University, although a Newar specialist rather than a Tibetanist in the strict sense, should also be mentioned. Three of the contributors to this collection (Draper, Marko and Stutchbury) have been students of his, and a fourth (Samuel) has benefited greatly from his advice and encouragement.

VAST AS THE SKY

The Terma Tradition in Modern Tibet

Span Hanna

IN late September 1986, I travelled to Nyingchi, in eastern Tibet, with two companions. One was an old friend named Kim, the other a Swiss woman named Tara, who had spent eight or nine years in India and Nepal studying Nyingma Buddhism and learning the Tibetan language. Nyingchi is on the main highway from Lhasa to Sichuan Province, and is well known to Tibetan pilgrims for a mountain outside the town called Bonri. This mountain is especially sacred to the Bon religion, and is a destination for pilgrims of both the Bonpo and the Buddhist traditions. The *khora* (*'khor ba*, 'circumambulation') track around Bonri is a fairly easy walk and can be done in a day and a half.

At the same time, a party of Tibetans was also present in Nyingchi, planning to do *khora*. Tara made their acquaintance and learnt that they were all Bonpos from Kham (*Khams*). The leader of the party was a woman of middle age named Khandro Khachi Wangmo, which in English means 'Powerful Lady of the *ḍākinī* Realm'. Khandro was indeed an incarnated *ḍākinī*; and furthermore was a *terton* (*gter ston*), or one empowered to find concealed objects. She was accompanied by her brother, Mangyal Lhasey Tulku, and some relatives. The father of Khandro and Rinpoche had also been a *terton*, and had revealed *terma* on Bonri in the past.

The Tibetan word *terma* (*gter ma*) literally means 'hidden treasure' and refers to sacred objects and texts which, according to tradition, have been concealed in various places by practitioners of the past. *Terma* are often associated with Guru Rimpoche (Padmasambhava), who spread the Buddhist doctrine in Tibet during the 9th century. The main reason for concealing *terma* was a fear that the doctrines would, in time, fade or become adulterated by spurious interpretations. *Terma* were concealed in rocks, mountainsides, trees, temples, images, lakes, and even in the sky. Some *terma* are concealed in the mind; and if the conditions are favourable, they are revealed in dreaming, meditation, or spontaneously. Khandro had learned that *terma* were available at Bonri at this time, and if the circumstances allowed, she would be able to reveal them.

The party which set out from Nyingchi on this remarkable mission consisted of eighteen people: Khandro, Rinpoche, Rinpoche's wife and two-year-old son, three mature women, two men (one of whom, Tagla, was Khandro's servant), Rinpoche's young servant Kunzang, a young woman of about 20 named Pema (the only member of the party to have visited Bonri before), Khandro's 19-year-old niece and her two girlfriends, Kim, Tara and myself, and a Tibetan raised in Nepal, called Lhakpa. Lhakpa spoke English fluently and was able to help us fill in many gaps, as a language barrier prevented us from finding out very much about the backgrounds of Khandro and Rinpoche. Although Tara spoke Tibetan, she was not familiar with the *Khampa* dialect which Khandro and her party used. Khandro and Rinpoche both spoke Chinese, but I only had direct communication in this language with Rinpoche. It is probable that all of the Tibetans could understand Chinese, but generally we had very little spoken communication.

The journey around Bonri took five days altogether. We proceeded at a slow pace because it was not apparent where the *terma* would be revealed. As we understood it, Khandro herself did not know if the *terma* would become available to her. Before we set out, Lhakpa impressed upon us the importance of Khandro. She was the centre of the whole enterprise, and she would have to be supported by the *khora* party during the entire trip. At all times we should maintain an atmosphere of positive feeling. No one should complain of hardships, however trivial, or bear a grudge against any other member of the party, however reasonable the cause might seem. Anything disrupting the harmony of the group would give rise to conditions inauspicious for the revelation of *terma*.

The first day of the trek covered very little ground. The Tibetans made a fire beside the river and we had a leisurely breakfast, which lasted until about midday. After leaving some gear in storage at a house in the town, we set off in the early afternoon sunshine along the track which would take us within sight of Bonri. A few minutes' walk took us to the edge of the town and across a small bridge. The land was quite open on that side of the river, and a small crowd had gathered to watch several dozen Khampa horsemen racing. Our party also watched for an hour or so and then continued, crossing another bridge and walking for perhaps three quarters of an hour before stopping to light a fire and have a tea-break. After ninety minutes or so, a tractor with an empty trailer went by in the direction we would be going, so one of the women flagged it down and persuaded the driver to carry our luggage on for us. This was a stroke of fortune, as it meant we could walk unencumbered to our proposed lodgings for that night.

On our right were the broad rushing waters of the Tsangpo (*gTsang po*), for which the little river through Nyingchi was a feeder stream. Eventually it would reach India, becoming the Brahmaputra. To our left, the mountain faces became nearer and steeper, the road following their twists and turns. Many bends of the roads were marked by small piles of stones, a common propitiation practice in Tibet. Many bushes were adorned by small tufts of wool, fragments of cloth, and prayerflags at all stages of weathering. Some of the larger boulders and occasional mountainsides were inscribed, not with the familiar *OM MAṆI PADME HŪM* we had seen so often elsewhere, but the Bonpo equivalent, *OM MATRI MUYE SALE DU.*

The party straggled out over a great stretch of this road, as it did throughout the trek. At one point we were watching Khandro, several bends back with Rinpoche and his wife and son, when an army truck slowed down and stopped next to them. Some words were exchanged, then the truck continued on its way. Soon afterwards, we reached a small village built around an army camp and found that our bags had been left for us outside the general store. When the whole party was assembled again, we were told that one of the soldiers on the truck had recognised Khandro on the road, and made the driver stop so that he could greet her. Arriving at the base in advance of us, he arranged for us to spend that night in some storage sheds, which had previously been stables. This was another stroke of luck, for it rained heavily that night, and in fact on every night of the trek.

It was a comfortable night, but we made a very early start the next morning. The Tibetans were organised and on the road well in advance of the three of us, and we had to follow as best we could in the pitch dark. As cold as it was, I soon began to feel overheated and slowed my pace. Trees and boulders gradually became bare silhouettes, until the first dawn light began to illuminate the wide grey strip of the Tsangpo and the mountains on its far side, wreathed in low cloud. Occasionally a light, misty rain fell. As the world slowly became visible, it was obvious we were quite off the beaten track. Signs of habitation were few and distant, but strangely we were meeting people on the road, sometimes singly, other times in threes or fours, pilgrims like ourselves. Several strangers stopped us and offered to carry our packs for us. At first we refused but they were insistent, for as it turned out, Rinpoche had sent them to meet us for that purpose.

When we caught up with the rest of the party, in early-morning sunshine now, we found them surrounded by a dozen or so strangers. An old lady, who spent all her time doing *khora* around Bonri, had approached Khandro and asked her to bless some object. We missed this, however, as the crowd was breaking up as we arrived. A little further on, a man approached Rinpoche and asked him to visit his wife, who was too ill to be brought to them. Rinpoche was well-versed in Tibetan medicine, but it was not merely his skill in this field which drew the attention of such people to him. He and Khandro, as we were beginning to understand, stood out to everyone as important people of high degree. If we had not met them but only seen them in the street in Nyingchi, we would probably have thought them no more than well-dressed Tibetans.

This is where I at least began to understand we were in someone else's world, and circumstances then began to emphasise the point for me. When we stopped for lunch and a lengthy break, an army truck sped by along the road, travelling in the direction from which we had come. As it passed, one of the soldiers called out and threw us a large plastic tablecloth patterned with peony blossoms. Khandro called this 'an offering of a thousand flowers'. The sky cleared as we made ready to set out again, and we walked on in full sunshine.

That afternoon, we passed a small settlement where we were stopped by a woman who, although plainly dressed in a dark gown, had the air of being well off. She wanted to invite Khandro and Rinpoche with their party into her house for some tea. After some hesitation, her offer was accepted. We were ushered into a large room on the top floor of a two-storey wooden house. Butter tea was passed around, and also hot water for those who wanted to drink coffee, and plastic jerrycans of the Tibetan beer called *chang*. Cooked rice and vegetables were also offered to us. A large crowd of local people gathered outside the door and were led in single file to prostrate before Khandro and Rinpoche and receive their blessings. Large cakes of butter and sacks of *tsampa* (*tsam pa*) were offered as gifts. This continuous demonstration of respect had to be auspicious.

The rest of that day's walk proceeded from our hostess's back garden, across fields and over turnstiles and fences. We passed the crumbling foundations of what had once been a home for the 7th Century king Songtsen Gampo and his Chinese wife Wen Cheng. We stopped briefly to rest and eat apples in an orchard, where a large black bird bathing was interpreted as another auspicious sign. Then we worked our way back towards the river, arriving in the last hour of daylight at the small riverside temple called Kongpo Jowo. This charming building was the home of a middle-aged man and a girl of about 10, who allowed us to invade their single room next door to cook ourselves a meal. That night we slept in the temple itself, stretched out in our sleeping bags under the gaze of tall, exquisitely sculpted figures who lived in the permanent fragrance of incense and butter lamps.

We arose just after dawn, and a short walk across fields and through somebody's back yard led to the point from which we finally began our ascent of Bonri. The hillside itself was well-forested, and at first the *khora* path was not easy to discover. However, it was worn by countless pilgrims and, even where other tracks crossed it, it could be distinguished by the many prayerflags which lined it. By Tibetan standards it was not a difficult path, but it was steep and hard going. Rinpoche kept saying to us, "*Man zou, man zou*" (Ch., "go slowly"). Partway up the slope we rested while the Tibetans visited a small Bonpo monastery just off the path. We were not invited to it ourselves, but we did visit a small spring nearby, which trickled over a boulder in which several Bonpo images had formed naturally. A monk and a nun joined us as we continued on.

During a break between this visit and our lunch stop, Rinpoche gave us some more advice about correct conduct during the *khora*. He stressed the advice Lhakpa had already given us, to keep a harmonious atmosphere in the group. Further, he asked us to recite mantras as we climbed. Any mantra would do, the important thing being that we generate a spirit of positive feeling and auspiciousness towards the Dharma, connection with which was the main point of the *khora*. He also said we might expect all kinds of omens, and maybe things seen in the sky. Not everyone would see things, however – it was a matter of one's merit. An apparition which Tara translated as 'like a big tent in the sky' was said to be especially auspicious.

The afternoon stretch, during which a few more unknown wanderers and the occasional dog joined our ranks, was easier than the morning stretch. The weather was good for most of the time, although the path became steeper, muddier, and more overgrown. It was necessary to use a stick. Parts of the path hugged a rock wall, and natural alcoves here contained not only prayerflags and inscribed 'mani stones' but inscribed yak skulls. Curiously notched green stalks leant against the wall in many places, and later I was told these were 'long life sticks'. Tibetans liberally adorn their countryside with offerings, so Kim and I were intrigued but not greatly surprised when we passed a large tree with many wooden boxes hanging from its branches. Later, Tara asked us if we had noticed it and explained that the boxes all contained dead babies. Tree burial is a common practice for those who die in infancy.

In the late afternoon, the rain became much heavier. We were escorted off the path to an area where a large rocky overhang gave shelter to the two dozen or so of us. It was crowded but dry and just comfortable. Two fires were going and there was no end of tea. Word went around that tomorrow would very likely be the day Khandro would find and reveal the *terma*.

The caves where we spent the night were in the vicinity of a towering natural monolith called 'Samantabhadra's Heart'. Just past Samantabhadra's Heart is a pass, from which one descends to complete the *khora* circuit. The next morning, we trekked from our caves towards this spot for some two hours, negotiating a treacherously muddy track in continual rain and hail. The vegetation and trees were thicker, and more people joined us, so that in places we were part of a long queue working its way along the *khora* track. Shortly before Samantabhadra's Heart the track opened on to a crest with a large clearing before it.

Kim and I were resting in this clearing when Tara rushed up and called us back. Khandro was standing near a large boulder, gazing around as if in distraction, now at the sky, now at the valley beside us. Tara told us she had heard Khandro say to Rinpoche that the boulder, "looked like an elephant". Khandro had apparently learnt the night before that there were *terma* concealed in 'Chinese

Elephant Rock', which meant a boulder resembling the Buddhist sacred mountain Emei Shan, in Sichuan Province. This boulder was a pretty good candidate.

We produced our offerings for a shrine which was quickly assembled about fifty yards away from the rock. Biscuits, sweets and fruit were laid out on a large cloth. At the head of the cloth were placed some pictures of deities, butter lamps, a framed photograph of the father of Khandro and Rinpoche, and Rinpoche's ceremonial dagger, the triple-bladed knife called a *phurba* (*phur ba*). At least a hundred people were gathered on the narrow path along this crest. *Torma* (*gtor ma*, sculptures made of butter, tsampa and red dye) were assembled and placed around the shrine, as a scripture was recited. This *pūjā* went on for a couple of hours, as rain alternated with hail and snow. Vultures were seen wheeling in the sky above, and this was taken to be an auspicious sign.

Then, as the weather cleared, Khandro suddenly got to her feet and began moving towards the rock. She had stripped to the waist sometime during the *pūjā*, and she was carrying Rinpoche's *phurba*. The crowd also rose, and began chanting *OM AH HUM BENZA GURU PEMA SIDDHI HUM* (OM Ā HŪM VAJRA GURU PADMA SIDDHI HŪM). When Khandro reached the rock, she struck it with the *phurba*, not violently, but as if testing it. As she turned momentarily to face the crowd, the delicate but arresting sound of a clear, small bell rang out, soft and quickly fading. As soon as it sounded, Khandro climbed a little way up the rock and began striking it again, with Kunzang taking up a position below her to support her weight.

A noticeable thrill passed through the crowd as Khandro removed a slab of stone and passed it to Tagla, who was standing nearby. This caused my stomach to drop, almost as if I were watching surgery being performed. Khandro removed several more slabs of stone, perhaps five in all. Then she reached into the cavity she had made and turned back to the crowd, holding her hand aloft for all to see. She had removed a small seated figurine, perhaps two inches high. Rinpoche, who had hurried up to the rock by this time, took it from her. As the crowd chanted with fresh enthusiasm, Khandro reached into the cavity again, this time producing a *dorje* (*rdo rje*, the 'thunderbolt sceptre') about the same size as the figurine.

It is impossible to describe the feeling which swept through the crowd then, and it was impossible not to be caught up in it oneself. For a while I don't think I really knew where I was, until the crowd about me began to swarm forward to see the two objects. Khandro held them up, one in each hand, as the crowd gathered around her. Lhakpa and some others moved into the crowd to receive offering scarves and valuables, which were replaced in the rock in exchange for the *terma*. Rinpoche opened a packet of blessing papers, which the wind took up into the sky. When all the scarves and valuables had been put into the rock, the stone slabs were also put back into position, and the cavity was sealed with the tail-ends of scarves hanging out over the rock.

Rinpoche carried the two *terma*, and a quantity of *sindhur* ('*ḍākiṇī* dust,' a kind of powder) which had also come from the rock, around the crowd to let everyone see them clearly. Then he explained what the *terma* were. The first was a figure of Amitāyus, the Buddha of Long Life. The second was a nine-pointed *dorje* with which Guru

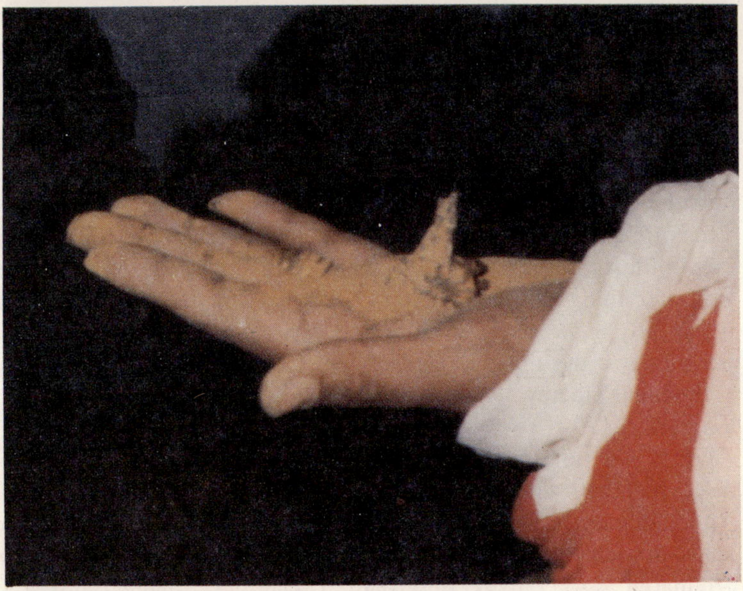

Rinpoche had formerly subdued the Oathbreakers. Although the auspiciousness of the occasion had only been 'middling', Rinpoche said, nevertheless these objects had been revealed for us. Other *terma* were concealed, but they would not be available on this occasion.

The purpose of all this, he said, was to encourage faith in the Dharma, but we could not receive the full benefit of witnessing this miraculous event except by strengthening our motivation and our commitment to work. In the future we should undertake to recite a particular number of mantras each day to maintain this commitment. In addition, we should give being as many living beings as possible their freedom. Finally, he said that the mere observation of these commitments was not in itself enough to ensure our merit. Our greatest commitment must be to practise, by meditation or any other appropriate method, and in this way develop and increase our understanding of the Dharma.

The butter *tormas* were broken up and distributed to the crowd, and a fierce rain and hailstorm set in again. We moved on to the clearing just past the rock, a fire was lit and we drank tea and ate. Kim, Tara, Lhakpa and I found much to talk about that afternoon. A lot of the time, however, I found myself standing in the continual storm, for there was no shelter, and looking down into the valley at the faraway town of Nyingchi. Apart from the occasional discussion with the others, the rest of the day was for me an uncanny condition of shock, which I mean in the clinical sense. I could not think straight, it seemed impossible to believe we had come from that town below, and I could not see how we would ever get back there.

Inevitably, one is forced to ask some questions about what was in fact witnessed on that hillside, whether or not what was witnessed was everything that took place. For myself, the question of meaning is partially answered in three ways: what we found most urgent in our minds at the time; how the event related (or seemed to relate) to the local Tibetans; and what emerges from a little sober reflection long after.

When we talked about it with Lhakpa, after the crowds had dispersed, the sound of the bell emerged as the strangest occurrence. Although it could easily have been faked, the question of this did not arise in our discussion so much as where precisely the sound originated. As I have described it, the bell sounded just after

Khandro's initial striking of the rock, and it seemed to ring just above her head. It was a very soft sound and could easily have been missed. Kim, however, is quite sure that the bell sounded when Khandro first struck the rock. Whatever the truth might be, at the time we were as sure as we could be that it was as otherworldly a phenomenon as a vision of tents in the sky might have been.

Other points we discussed were how exactly such objects were concealed in the rock; and why, if there were others there, they could not be revealed at that time. Lhakpa said that, according to the *terma* tradition, the objects are not believed to be physically in the rock, but they become physically available through the rock. Some great lama transmitted them there at some time, but since then they had been guarded by beings called *terdak* (*gter bdag*), who exist in another realm. The bell was a signal from the *terdak* that some *terma* were available. The rock then became a kind of gateway through which the *terma* could be revealed to the *terton.* Soon, he said, the *terdak* would take away the scarves and valuables which had been put into the cavity, but these things would not become *terma* themselves.

Another issue which took up a great deal of the discussion, and which surprised me at the time and still does whenever people remark on it, is why Khandro had stripped to the waist before going to the rock to reveal the *terma.* When Tara asked Rinpoche about this, he said it was to assure us that no trickery was involved. He also said that many *terton* would do this, simply because *terma* are often in places where access is difficult. When he was asked how much time would pass before the offerings in the rock were removed, he said we could go and look at it for ourselves, so long as we didn't remove anything. It is difficult to say to what extent a desire for the preservation of honesty was really behind all this, even if we had supposedly been invited along as authentic witnesses from the outside world.

Of more importance was probably the wider meaning of the *terma* revelation; that is, its significance in the context of the ethnic tradition. For the Tibetans outside Khandro's party, both at the *terma* site and all along the *khora* path, the presence of Khandro and Rinpoche was a blessing. After spending one more night on the mountain, we crossed a pass and descended to the foot, regaining the main road back to Nyingchi. What could have been a three-hour walk took a day and a half, as Khandro and Rinpoche were frequently stopped by large groups of people requesting teachings. During the three days we spent in Nyingchi waiting for the bus back to Lhasa, there was an endless procession of supplicants to their rooms in the town's solitary guesthouse. We noticed that they dealt with Buddhists and Bonpos alike, showing no religious partisanship whatever. Once, before blessing a prayer wheel, Khandro asked its owner whether he revolved it clockwise or anticlockwise. Lhakpa told me that Bonpos have no trouble accepting the Buddha, they merely see him as the fourth incarnation of the Bonpo sage Tonpa Shenrab. Tara told me that Buddhists visiting Bonri on pilgrimage circumambulate anticlockwise, as the Bonpos do. It was quite clear that the khora and the *terma* revelation were not a private matter, but something for everyone.

We were originally told that the main reason for going to Bonri in search of *terma* was to inspire faith in the Dharma. Rinpoche's explanation to the crowd immediately after the revelation of the *terma* took the form of an exhortation to practise the Dharma. After my return to Australia, I obtained and read a copy of Tulku Thondup Rinpoche's work, *Hidden Teachings of Tibet,*[1] in which he explains the *terma* tradition from the Nyingmapa perspective. *Terma* are said to have four characteristics: "maintaining the doctrine of the Buddha in the world, developing realisation in the minds of beings, satisfying the minds of beings, and being as vast as the sky".[2] They have the fourfold purpose of ensuring that "the doctrine shall not disappear, the instructions not be adulterated, the blessings not fade, and that the lineage of the transmission be shortened."[3]. In a later section of the book, we read that "the heart of the *Terma* tradition is the Mind-mandate Transmission, the transferring or transmitting of the primordial wisdom from Guru Rinpoche to the disciple."[4] It is in the

1. Tulku Thondup, *Hidden Teachings of Tibet.* London: Wisdom Publications, 1986.

2. Ibid., p. 59.

3. Ibid., p. 62

4. Ibid., p.133.

light of Tulku Thondup's discussion that I understand, objectively at least, what it was in which we took part.

The revelation of the *terma* was, for some, a kind of transmission which went through four discernible stages. In the first stage, there was an indication that powers or blessings exist to which human beings might have access. This indication is the *terma* tradition itself, which states in all traditions that Guru Rinpoche (or other figures) have given *terma* for the benefit of beings living later. To this stage also belongs the dramaturgical aspect of the *khora*, the emphasis on auspicious circumstances apparently arising from without, as well as the auspicious circumstances we create by maintaining a positive feeling toward the tradition and the terton.

The second stage was a demonstration, in which Khandro as a *ḍākiṇī* revealed for everyone present (and perhaps all who would later hear of the revelation) that *terma* had certainly been placed in the rock and were available to her. The third stage was in a sense automatic, but was certainly articulated by Lhasey Tulku as an affirmation of the tradition, a direct transmission of which had taken place through Khandro's intercession on our behalf. The *terma* were, in other words, not simply proof that once upon a time there had been great *yogis* in Tibet.

The first three stages of the transmission made clear in turn the tradition, the legacy of that tradition, and the connection with that tradition. The fourth stage, activation or motivation, is a matter for those who have received the transmission. Rinpoche explained what had to be done to ensure that all those present carried the tradition out with them to its fullest extent, through continual and committed practice. What would otherwise be estranged by historical time becomes a living present condition. There is then nothing to prevent the blessings from filling all of space.

❁ ❁ ❁

Khandro Khachi Wangmo left the human world between March and May,1987.

DOHĀ, VAJRAGĪTI AND CARYĀ SONGS

David Templeman

Introduction

WHEN we see an image of the Buddha, perhaps in some significant pose such as that of calling the earth to witness his enlightenment, we might be tempted to regard this frozen, memorialised moment as some sort of stasis point, a time and place from which he never emerged – how buddhahood was and would be for all time. Of course, this epoch-making instant comprised only one of the many deeds of the Buddha, and lest we be tempted to see the attainment of buddhahood as being an end point, a logical fulfilment of his life, we must keep in the forefront of our minds that he did indeed rise from his position under the Bodhi tree and minister at large for more than another fifty years.

How may the state of being we call enlightenment be manifested to others, and by what means might it be adequately communicated? One answer might be that it is an on-going state in which the experience of enlightenment is manifested actively in the world, but one in which that activity is not of the world. It has been said that the *siddhas*, the Buddhist practitioners *par excellence* of India and later of Tibet, moved simply within the actions themselves rather than within concepts about those actions. Through the *siddhas*' great compassion for suffering sentient beings, they were able to work with situations completely free of any sense of self-aggrandisement or partiality. Such people embodied the great mystery of the Vajrayāna, the ultimate identity of *saṁsāra* and *nirvāṇa*. Hence, like the Buddha, the *siddha* spent a considerable part of his life in teaching those who were karmically ripe to profit from such instruction. Among the modes of teaching might be symbolic instruction, a real-life demonstration of the identity of *saṁsāra* and *nirvāṇa*, thrusting the student from a "real" world of solidity into the "real" world of paradox and thereby of ultimate possibility. Such a teaching might be encapsulated in songs in which the exultance of the enlightened view, its enigmatic nature and its potential to liberate the practitioner from the constraints of dualistic thought patterns, might be expressed in pleasing style. This paper will examine three major types of tantric song and will attempt, by means of examples of these genres, to illustrate some of the ways in which the mental processes are to be re-structured to achieve the exalted state of living in the state of the absolute, authentic present.

I

It is clear from certain texts that only a few of the so-called eighty-four *mahāsiddhas* were renowned as singers of tantric songs. Indeed only thirteen have songs recorded in the great *dohā* collection, *The Rosary of Pearls.*[1] In the collection of *caryā* songs known as the *Caryāgīti*, a different group of nineteen *siddhas* is found, of whom only two or three are identical with the known *dohā* singers. According to the 16th/17th century Tibetan *savant* Tāranātha, Indian tradition ascribed various *siddhas* and their followers to various parts of India where they predominated.[2] One of these, Kṛṣṇapa, whose group, the *Caryāpas*, was predominant in Bengal, is a most renowned composer of both *caryā* songs and *dohās.* There is also a great deal of evidence from a wide range of other sources that the sect of the *Caryāpas*, which seems to have originated in the 10th-12th centuries, was still extant and a viable force as late as the 16th-17th centuries in many areas of northern and eastern India.[3] Tāranātha further notes that the main body of teachings composed by these *ācāryas* was "all in the form of *dohā* songs and pæans"; and that, as would be expected, the "compositions by the *siddhas* in manuscript form amount to but few indeed".[4] These *dohā*s, and to perhaps a greater extent the *caryā* songs which seem to have emanated from Bengal, have had a considerable influence upon later Indian religious poetry in Hindi, Bengali and Oriya, especially in metre, theme and motif. In Hindi literature, the *dohā* and *caryā* tradition was maintained by mystics such as Kabīr and the Hindu *nāth panthīs* or *nāth yogis*, as an active, vital, influence certainly into the post-World War II period, if not even into our own era.

As the *dohā* was primarily a means of direct, authentic communication between master and disciples, it had to express a spiritual truth in a way which would resonate within its listeners, rather than being understood by them at a conceptual level only. It had to fit into a wide range of folk rhythms and metres, as such songs had to travel into many cultural areas among unlettered people whose most practical way of gaining the message might well have listening to such songs. For example, Tilopa, the sesame-oil pounding *siddha*, preached in a certain town in Bengal where, "hundreds of thousands of people came to see the ācārya, and he, together with his consort, appeared before all of them, in the sky, pounding sesame. As each man questioned him the ācārya, putting his experiences into song form, replied. It is said that most of the people in the crowd realised the song's meanings and attained siddhi."[5]

One of the most potent writers of *dohā* songs, and one whose works frequently contain the most profound message in short, pithy verses, is Kṛṣṇācārya, a *siddha* and founder of the *Caryāpa* sect. He is said by some to have received his inspiration directly from Vajravārāhī. These few *dohās* are from his collection known as the *Dohākoṣa of Kṛṣṇavajra.* (Kṛṣṇavajra is also one of the common names of Kāṇha or Kṛṣṇācārya, and for the purposes of this paper I shall treat them as one and the same person.)

Homage to Vajrasattva.

Worldly people are arrogant!
They say that they have entered the realms of the Ultimately Real!
But there is only one in ten million
Who can sit in the nakedness of Reality.

Filled with authorisations to practice and mere knowledge,
Learned people are merely arrogant.
They are like bees and ripe fruit –
They make their own *saṁsāra.*"

Know that you take
Earth, water, fire and heavenly ether
As your spheres of mental activity.
The *Sahaja* state is wave-free, and in an
equipoised, natural state.
It is free of all defilements whatsoever
And neither does it contain concepts such as "virtue" or "sin".

I, Kṛṣṇa, say all this quite clearly."[6]

Saraha, the "Great Brahmin" who lived with a woman of the caste of arrowmakers, is probably the best known *dohā* singer, and certainly the only one, apart from Kāṇha/Kṛṣṇācārya, whose songs have become the subject of major studies.[7] Many of his *dohās* appear to have been aimed at those in his *milieu* who, while being no closer to realisation than a rock, were puffed up with their own self importance and sanctity. In his collection of songs known as the *Dohākoṣa-gīti*, he criticises Brahmins, *yogin*-ascetics, Jainas and various Buddhists. He says:

Homage to Mañjuśrīkumārabhūta.

To the luckless, like venomous snakes,
And to true, holy beings (I say),
Just look herein and quake with fear
So we can all laugh at the stench of sin.

As for those ignorant Brahmins
Who recite the fourfold Vedas,
Amass earth, water and *kuśa* grass,
And who sit in their homes and tend their sacred lamps,
All those purposeless burnt offerings they perform
Only serve to harm their eyes with all their smoke.

With their finely tended bodies and their one or even three staffs,
They shuffle through the *śāstras*, even having faith in them!
They think Dharma and non-Dharma are not indeed one and the same thing,
And people continue to be led astray by these lies.

Having rubbed *era* ash on their bodies,
And wearing long, matted hair on their heads,
They stay in their homes tending the sacred fire
And in the corner of the room they stay, ringing their bells.

Sitting cross-legged and with their eyes closed,
And whispering in each other's ears, thus they deceive people.
They teach widows and widowers, monks and nuns in this way
By empowering them and taking their Guru's fee.

With long nails and covered in foul-smelling clothes,
Or even naked with all their hair plucked out,
The *Digambara* (Sky-clad) Jains embody the way of harm,
And instead of giving liberation, they tuck themselves into further rebirth.

If nakedness gave liberation then
Why aren't dogs and foxes liberated?
If by plucking hairs one becomes liberated
Then all girls who do so will be liberated!

If having a tail leads to liberation

The peacock, yak and others will be liberated.
If by eating while standing up one becomes liberated
Then why are horses and cattle not liberated?

Saraha says to these *Digambara* Jains,
"Liberation will never, ever come to you!"
Becoming irreconcilably separated from the reality of Bliss
They are left only with their bodily mortifications.

As for the novices, monks and the elders,
Who have been fully ordained into the order of monks,
Some try to explain the *sūtra* collection
While others are seen clinging to uniform mental training.

Some examine the *Mahāyāna* and proclaim that
They comprise the sum total of the (Buddha's) teachings,
While others meditate solely on *maṇḍalas*,
Yet others preach on the meaning of the Fourth Stage of Bliss!

Some see it as a heavenly state,
While others act as if it is voidness itself.
Generally speaking they all disagree with each other.[8]

What sort of person, then, can embark on this path, and who can one rely on in this world where we crave security, reward and certainty in everything we undertake? Although not exactly spelling out any sort of *curriculum vitae*, Saraha tells us plainly what some of the requirements are. He says:

One who has no compassion and
Lives in a state of "voidness",
Can never reach the highest path.
If he meditates solely upon compassion
He will also not gain liberation from this state of *saṁsāra*.
Whoever is able to combine both states of compassion and voidness
Will no longer abide in either *saṁsāra* or *nirvāṇa*.

Oh ho! Get rid of all your deceits and perverted views.
Whatever is an attachment – simply fling it out!
Review things in your mind and they will all be seen to be either deceit, perversion or attachment.
No one will find things to be any different to that.

There is no religious view that does not aim at these things –
Reading texts, understanding, meditation and preaching the essence of the teachings,
But mark this – one can only hear these things from the Guru's mouth.

The Guru's words enter the heart
And it is like seeing a treasure in the palm of your hand.

A spiritually ignorant person does not see his actual state of naturalness,
And is therefore deceived. Thus says Saraha.[9]

In many of his collections of *dohās*, Saraha points clearly to the fact that mental processes or ethics or other norms of behaviour are not to be seen *per se* as aids on the path. What emerges after the quietening of mental processes, diminishing of "self" identity and other aspects of meditational praxis is the direct experience of reality as it *really* is. In this state, activity and non-activity become spontaneous. Distinctions between things (conceiving in dualities), are no longer made. That most tenacious fiction of deed and doer-of-the-deed no longer has any meaning. The following verses illustrate Saraha's outline of the state of "things as they are". The reader will not fail to be struck by the (seemingly) radical nature of a spiritual path which advocates full use of sensual pleasures and the eschewal of all ritual.

If one is not liberated from one's bonds by means of the sense pleasures,
Without meditating and without monk's ordination,
But simply by staying home with ones wives
Then I, Saraha say that that path is not at all valid.

If it has already been clearly manifested then why bother with discursive meditation?
If it is hidden away that much then you are only measuring your own ignorance.
As for the nature of co-emergence
It neither exists nor does it not exist.
Saraha continually shouts this out.

That which one takes up causes one to be born, live and die,
And by that same thing which is taken up, one gains the highest bliss.
Although Saraha speaks these secret and mysterious words
This beastly world does not even understand them.

If it exists apart from meditation, then what meditation can one possibly perform?
If it can't be spoken of, how can one possibly talk about it?
All people are deceived by the way the world manifests itself,
And nobody perceives their own state of naturalness.

Tantras, *mantras* and meditation
Are all a cause of self-deception.
Don't corrupt your mind's state of natural purity with meditation –
Stay in your own state of bliss without tormenting yourself.[10]

Much of the message of the *dohās* depends on the depth of our spontaneous reaction to their rich imagery and poetic value, but the most valuable dimension – indeed, the main key to understanding – is the actual practice of the *right* kind of meditation. This "right meditation" removes us from the vicissitudes of living at the mercy of a world of relative values and assists us in experiencing the absolute in that very same world. These deepening levels of understanding may be set out thus:

1. A state of external reference, wherein the surface aspects of mind give rise to ways of thought which treat things as though they contained some essence; i.e., the world of *saṁsāra.*
2. A deeper mental level which grounds ideas in an understanding of their emptiness, i.e., *śūnyatā*
3. A stage at which things are no longer conceived in dualities, i.e., emptiness in practical (and to a great extent, experiential) terms.
4. A transcendent stage wherein the ordinary mind is seen in its ultimately real, immaculate nature. Conceiving of things in terms of "emptiness" no longer has any meaning at all. Things are treated as they actually *are.*

Many of the Tibetans who went on pilgrimage to India in the tenth to twelfth centuries A.D. heard *dohās* such as these from their masters there. The motifs of Bengal and Orissa were of course alien in the Land of Snows, and to a certain extent the Tibetan students, now masters in their own right, had to regionalise them so that they retained their intelligibility. Some examples of the motifs commonly found in the *dohā* songs and their newly adapted Tibetan forms, might be the cow becoming the yak, the cuckoo becoming the vulture, wine becoming barley beer and the ferry-boat transforming into the leather coracle.

The Tibetan saint-poet Milarepa (*Mi la Ras pa*, 1040-1123 A.D.) exemplifies the ideal *yogin* type, and his *dohās* were liberated into a fuller song form, completely localised to Tibetan conditions. His life and songs served as a model for many subsequent generations of Tibetan yogins, and his songs bring tears of joy to Tibetan eyes to this day. The Tibetan *dohā* tradition is a magnificent synthesis of Buddhist understandings of the mental process, fused with Tibetan folk motifs and rhythms. Some of Milarepa's themes and images are drawn from Tibet's isolated and awe-inspiring natural beauty; the snow-lion on the mighty snow peaks, the wild, tempestuous rivers and the ease of the soaring vultures; but they are equally frequently drawn from the profoundly human realms of villagers seeking succour from the wonder-working hermit high on the alp above their mundane world and the yogin's struggle for isolation from a world which incessantly clamours for inspirational presence.

Later in Tibet, the form of the *dohā* was often employed in a somewhat different way, and there exist several examples wherein they have lost much of their enigmatic, challenging dimension. Instead, they appear to have become songs of exhortation, often to eminent lay patrons, encouraging them to turn a little towards the practice of religion and to attain various levels of morality and detachment from the daily whirl they faced, or even to aspire to the more elevated levels of the higher *bhūmis.* I shall adduce two such examples of this interesting genre.

Firstly, Tāranātha's *dohā* to the Mistress Nam mkha' rGyal mo, to empower her into the tenth *bhūmi* level:

Om Svā Sti.

Having travelled in the carriage of human form,
Which is particularly hard to find,
Lady, as you desire to go to the city of Liberation,
It is fitting that you embark on the path with great zeal.

Those who strenuously avoid the throng
Successfully avoid the danger of accidents and robbers.
The preconditions which are the stepping stones out of *saṁsāra*
Can't be carried away by the Lord of Death in his flood.
Who then would not embark on the path with all their energy?

The dust of a crowd of a million,
If gathered up would fill a thousand storehouses.
The person who is arrogant because he is in good health, even if he is a king,
Will find that the irresistible fortress of Yama, when entered,
Renders even an army of heroes useless.
And yet we continue to be beguiled by our bodies and our youth.

The things which are very dear to us become our great losses.
Certainly if you can transcend those things which are useless
The mind will be able to overcome those mental afflictions,
Which are in themselves are of no use to us.

Among the six classes of sentient beings
There is always love between people and their children,
Like honey bees flying around a pot.
Even the Buddha, relative of the sun, has said this.

Bliss can never be found in *saṁsāra*.
If you really desire liberation rather than *saṁsāra*
Then you must give up the grasping after existent things
And desire above all else to abide in the state of the completely real.

Confess all your sins,
And as for all your non-virtuous deeds from eternity to the present time,
Desire to confess them and to exert yourself in self-restraint,
Aided as you are by the four strengths.

If you rejoice in the deeds of others which you see and hear,
Others who have adopted the holy teachings,
Then from these actions
You will attain great virtue.

Don't be proud of yourself!
Don't be hostile to the good fortune of others!
Don't despise the poor!
Instead, make vast offerings and be liberal in your largesse to them.

Take delight in whichever teacher you might have,
And show him all due respect and reverence.
Whatever virtuous acts you may perform
The Buddha and all sentient beings will bless you.

You will never reach the limits of your Dharma practice –
This has been said by all the sages.
From all of the above you will attain skill in means and great learning.
This is what I say.[11]

The second example of a later Tibetan *dohā* style occurs in the remarkable biography of the 19th century Lama Nyima Tashi (*Nyi ma bKra shis*), the sixth incarnation of the lineage of the Traleg (*Khra legs*) Tulkus.[12] The background to the biography, which comprises mostly songs of realisation, is quite interesting. An extensive work on the Lama's life was written by a karmically unconnected disciple who challenged the Nyima Tashi saying, "You seem to have achieved no deep realisation of emptiness while your hair is still black, so what could be achieved when your hair is grey?" The biography then goes on to say that Nyima Tashi told the ignorant biographer, "You are right! Throw all you have written about me into the fire in front of you!" This the disciple did, and the superficial biography, lacking in inner understanding, went up in flames.[13] Thereafter the rest of the work consists of *dohā* songs preceded by a brief narrative section of the real-life situation which prompted them. For example, moved by the inevitability of impermanence, Nyima Tashi sang this Song of Uncertainty, to teach his unsuited disciple:

O root Guru, may I be blessed to have total revulsion towards *saṁsāra*!
The psychophysical constituents of the body, and the phenomenal world are all without essence or permanence.
All phenomena waver and crumble without any essence.
There is no essence to the things of the world; all crumbles, moves, and shakes without any stability.
Likewise, the nature of living beings crumbles and moves in an unstable manner.
The sun, moon and stars in the heavens crumble and disappear.
The broad acres of pasture, the rocks and mountains are all subject to destruction.
All that can be seen, the clouds, the high valleys, the snowy peaks, and the blue waters of the valley floor, all disappear.
To the right, the rocky summit.
To the left the flowers of the plains. All will crumble and pass.
All that can be seen and experienced, the seasons, night and day, the year and the months, by their nature change.
Whatever world we inhabit, whatever wealth we may have, children, horses, parents, weapons, power, fame and plenty as well; all are without any essence at all.
Even the status of Lama has no essence.
The lesser status of monk has no essence.
The power of Kings is prone to destruction.
The seeming certainty of enemies and friends is subject to decay.
This life is like the quickening summer sap.
Ageing is like a garland of flowers which withers, even in just one day.
Sickness is like attempting to carve a fish in sand, which is washed away in a flash.
Death is like the dewdrops burned away by the ferocity of the sun.
Close kin are like making one's bed upon thorns.
Wealth is as immaterial as a picture of a rainbow.
The next birth can no more bear fruit than can seeds at once become a crop.
All appearance is a bizarre illusion!
The pristine clarity of mind is like a rusted mirror from which all impurities have been erased.
All phenomena, being brought together adventitiously, are manufactured and are so without essence.

In short, worldly existence is impermanent, so do not get caught up in idle worldly activity.
Always act meaningfully, with purity.

Inspired by these words, Nyima Tashi's many kin gathered there to hear his teachings, and urging him to stay, asked him to teach each of them the Dharma, his heart teachings, his song of experience, before fulfilling his prophecy of departing. As they begged him, so he spoke further:

Great noble Buddha, protector of past present and future,
O sole protector, the combination of all protectors in one,
You triple protector of great kindness,
Please protect us.
Even though your house gives you bliss,
Be rid of it,
So as to wander without imposing direction.
Even though your relatives love you,
When your breath thickens, then stops,
You are bound to suffer.
Even though your life now is good,
Regaled by fascinating stories,
They won't help you, but will be harmful.
Even though your body is beautiful, and ornamented,
At the moment of your dissolution,
You will discover it is volatile and will vanish.
Even though you have so many relatives,
When the lord of death makes life fearsome, grasping at your body,
Your eyes will roll up in fright,
As the body fails, from your mouth will come only laments.
If at that time your practice has not been perfected,
Your life will end,
And you will wander endlessly.
Over and over you fritter your life away,
Your priorities are the wrong way up.
Rather than continue thus,
Always strive for happiness,
Even if you experience setbacks.
Even though right now all is well,
Renounce all non-virtue.
Even though your lifestyle is pleasant,
Be done with *saṁsāra*.
Even if your hair is grey and your body wrinkled,
And you walk with a stick,
Never give in or be downcast.
Even though you happily possess much,

It is not you but those around you who will have their use when
you die,
You die alone and alone you go on,
Without so much as the tiniest possession to take with you.
In your heart think on death.
Dharma alone is of use.
Practise it.
In a distinct, clear voice supplicate the lama,
With faith and humility go to him.
Even if your prospects are bright and clear,
This is but appearance, like a dream,
Even if you are surrounded by the loud and the flashy,
They are but empty, clear, sharp echoes.
Even if your thoughts are many,
Be done with them.
Instead seek the essential nature of mind.
I declare these words of seeming truth
To be spoken spontaneously, without thinking,
Of their own accord.
Thus are they said.

Should you find such teachings,
Which are elegantly joined together and sonorous,
Forget it!
The teachings should cut you to the quick,
And be with you ever, as is a load strapped to your back.
Welcome words are but chatter.
Even if their meaning is profound,
You fail to apprehend their meaning, and
They are but the squawking of a parrot.

These verses were spoken at Garuḍa Castle (*khyung dzong*).[14]

II

Tibetans say that whereas *dohās* are songs of joyous victory over dualistic thinking, usually sung as a means of instruction, *vajragīti* are songs whose meanings exemplify the complete understanding of the indivisibility of bliss and emptiness. *Vajragīti* were also sung and danced to in ritual performance, at *gaṇacakras*, feast-gatherings of *yogins* and their consorts at which the tantric understanding of the absolute reality of the senses was celebrated. For example, while Kṛṣṇācārya was undergoing instruction by the *ḍākinīs* in the land of Urgyen and was himself the sole "means" or male present at the *gaṇacakra*, two particularly profound vajra-songs of instruction were sung to him. The first was sung by the chief *ḍākinī* of the *gaṇa* and was intended to instruct him and to empower him on his practice path.[15]

The second song which the chief *ḍākinī* of the *gaṇacakra* sang to Kṛṣṇācārya was one of encouragement on the path in which he had by then been confirmed. She sang:

As for the karmic continent, it was Jambudvīpa;
As for the land where the teachings prospered, it was Āryavarta;
As for the site itself it was the renowned Jālandhara.
You have come here, O Yogeśvara,
With your mental doubts wavering like a swinging palanquin.
Now, you have eradicated these doubts and all those other concerns of yours.
You have great faith in the doctrine of Guhyasamāja,
But you are still one with serious doubts about your attachment to Śrī Saṁvara.
Listen with full attention to my Song of Ultimate Truth,
Which I, the chief of the *ḍākinīs*, will give to you.

The wondrous and beautiful teaching, possessed of the seven ornaments, whose
Magical activities, taught long ago, are a repository of the most profound belief
With its chapters all conjoined in due order, containing well-composed words,
Is indeed the Śrī Samāja, the King of Tantras, and the jewel of the learned.
In that Tantra's parts are sequestered secret meanings,
And you will find the core-path's breadth hard to assess.
It is not something we *ḍākinīs* can instruct you in.
How then may a learned person gain an understanding of the inner meaning of these words I have spoken?
These words have never been put into written form –
They are gathered here with me in the clear heart of the *ḍākinīs*.
In this way, to cause your direct understanding of all this to broaden,
You must perform the songs and dances of the *ḍākinī* gathering.[16]

Thereafter the thirty-seven *ḍākinīs* of the assembly taught him the unique nature of the teachings in a long and quite hard vajra song, a song which confirmed much of his life up to that point and predicted the activities he would perform after he left the *gaṇacakra*.

Often in pure verse format, and frequently in similar metre to the *dohās*, *vajragīti* often point to the absolute nature of things as they really are, using everyday examples. The following *vajragīti* use a different sort of analogy, that of *vikalpa*, 'conceiving in dualities', as a snake. Kṛṣṇapāda sings:

Homage to Mahākaruṇā.

Inasmuch as there is an "I",
By exactly that much there exists a "you".
Separating the two, "I" and "you", is *vikalpa*.
Out of the nectar-ocean a snake emerges –
Vikalpa is the thief.[17]

Nāropa sings:

Homage to the Bhagavān Mañjuvajra.

The deceitful and malicious snake of *vikalpa* grasps our minds.
Inasmuch as we have become "*vikalpa* people"
We become bound by it and have to undergo much senseless suffering.
The fool will never be freed by a follower of such foolishness.
The hero, filled with compassion, should meditate on that which is
Authentic existence.
Inasmuch as he thoroughly experiences it,
By that same amount will he be freed.
The many-headed *prajñā* snake
Devours self-identity.
It is constantly nourished by the milk of meditation.
It will kill the mongoose of *vikalpa*.
Such concepts as "Nāropa" are constantly devoured by the hundred-headed *prajñā* snake.
Who understands all that? Nāropa does and he asks the question.[18]

Tāranātha notes another interesting detail which seems to separate the natures of *dohā* and *vajragīti*. In a section of his *Life of Kṛṣṇācārya/Kāṇha* devoted to the six types of work to be undertaken by a *siddha* he says, "Although the *vajragīti* certainly came from the collection of songs in the tantras, those who were true *siddhas* expressed their experiences in the form of *dohās*, and doubtless under more conducive circumstances, later on they appeared as *vajragīti*."[19] Here it appears that the *dohā* is the basic exultation of the moment (albeit often joined together to make impressive collections), and that the *vajragīti* are the more carefully wrought works, whose contents, firmly rooted in the Vajrayāna texts themselves, are versified and made into epithetical performance pieces. At its most reduced and possibly most powerful is perhaps this tiny example, a *vajragīti* of the master Kṛṣṇapāda:

> As for Kṛṣṇapa's mental activity, whatever such a thing may be,
> It is evanescent and shifting, making everything seem a nonsense.[20]

Much of the flavour of the Tibetan genre has been captured in Stephen Beyer's translation of one of Padma Karpo's *vajragīti*. Noticeable is the pervasive influence of the *dohā* immediacy, not only in the actual content and dynamic but in the Tibetan understanding of the original source images, for example the *Dohākoṣagīti* of Saraha. Padma Karpo says:

> Mind no binding
> no binding unleash
> binding and it runs off in ten directions[21]

Saraha expresses it thus:

> When mind is bound it starts running in the ten directions
> And when it is released it stays immobile in one spot,
> Just like a camel which has little understanding.
> Thinking about it, little children, you too should see that your minds act in just this way.[22]

We know little of the melodies to which these vajra songs were sung in both India and Tibet, although each *caryā* song in the *Caryāgītikoṣa* has a *rāga* and *tāla*, which is particularly precise and useful information. However, tantric *gaṇacakras* are still held in the same manner for the same purposes as they were in early mediæval India, and research is needed into the *rāgas* and *tālas* attached to *vajragīti* as a matter of some importance. We do know from biographical records that Marpa, for example, sang a particularly beautiful *vajragīti* at a *gaṇacakra* for his Guru Kukkuripa,[23] and several of the melodies he chose for his songs are strongly reminiscent of the folkish motifs of the heroic age in Tibetan history, the so-called dynastic period. He refers to a "melody of a bee buzzing in the distance, sung at Phullahari monastery of ravishingly beautiful flowers", and to melodies of the "outstretched wings of the soaring *garuḍa*", "sparkling water" and the "whistling song of *dharmapālas*".[24]

III

More specifically localised to the delta areas of present-day Bengal and the Chittagong area of Bangla Desh, the *caryā* songs reflect much of the riverine life there. The songs' main motifs are drawn from the everyday life of the people and show much of the fishing and farming worlds, as well as offering vignettes of tribal life as it was and to a certain extent, still is today. The imagery of trees, rivers, oceans, houses, deer, elephants, cows, frogs, nets, snakes, mice, lotuses, sky, sun, moon, pots, rice, wine, arrows, silver and gold etc. are capable of being understood at either the relative (poetic) or the absolute (didactic) level. The freewheeling confidence and the ebullient language of the *caryās* perfectly complements the rustic ingenuity of the motifs. There is neither fussiness nor ceremony in these downright practical songs, but neither does their functionality make them dour or "spiritual". There is a noticeable absence of conventional tantric terminology and one finds, through the motifs referred to above, a "rustic-isation" of many tantric ideas. For example, Nairātmyā, 'lack of self-nature', the consort of the tantric divinity Hevajra, is referred to as *'yoginī'*, which has a second dimension of meaning over and above its sacred one, with connotations, even to this day, of illicit sex and outrageous, unbridled activity. Nairātmyā also becomes the outcaste *ḍombī* with all the opprobrium which attaches to that sort of person in the Indian society of the time. Per Kvaerne notes in his definitive edition and translation of the *caryā* song collection that, "by expressing the highest truth in the lowest terms, by presenting *Sophia* in the form of a whore, that *coincidentia oppositorum* is achieved which alone can express the paradox of ultimate reality."[25] He further observes that:

> ...the songs, therefore, constitute an initiation once their *essential structure* becomes apparent: *they reveal the nature of the ultimate state through the systematic ambiguity of their imagery...* it is not primarily the specific choice of images which is significant... it is their very ambiguity itself which reveals the coemergence of two modes of being... the "coemergence" of both senses corresponds to the Coemergence of saṁsāra and nirvāṇa in the state of Great Bliss.[26]

As a further paradox, the followers of this path are sometimes portrayed in hagiography as ruthless, acting without regard to sin or no-sin. They may often be a tribal people, such as Vyādali the bird hunter, who exemplifies the paradox of the holy in the seemingly unholy. Vyādali was a bird trapper whose offering to the *siddha* Virūpa was refused because of his "impure" activities. Even after eventual instruction by Virūpa, Vyādali's mind was haunted by his "evil" actions. Virūpa then taught him by paradox saying, "...although those obstructive, discursive thoughts are really hard to block out, and although you can't produce meditation, you should make bird shapes out of clay, and while cutting their throats, then meditate...".[27] It was in this very way that Vyādali attained the very highest *siddhi*. When he "manifested the miracle of killing various types of birds and eating their flesh", he was accosted by the townspeople and "all the birds he had previously killed were again revived."[28]

Purely as poetry, the *caryā* songs have to much to recommend them. Many of the folk images are admirably suited to the tantric directness of practice and view. The following example illustrates this well. In the sixth *caryā* song, Bhusukupāda says:

> Because of its own flesh the deer is its own enemy;
> Bhusuku the hunter does not leave it for a moment.[29]

When this is read with the word 'deer' glossed as the mind itself, it becomes clear that this touchingly poignant image more than adequately represents the ever-moving, restless 'twitchiness' of the mind, with its constant thought processes and divisions of what is essentially one into duality. This constant thought process denies direct experience of things as they are, in a state in which the mind is allowed to rest in its natural inactivity.

As with the *vajragīti*, *caryā* songs were set to a *rāga* and *tāla* which defined scale, mood and rhythm, and the songs were accompanied on musical instruments in much the same way as they are performed to this day by the *vajrācāryas* in Kathmandu. Although the *caryās* are quite short, consisting mostly of five verses of two lines per verse (with seven, nine or eleven syllables per line in the Tibetan), in their performance form they would have lasted a considerable time, especially after their composers had been offered laudatory pæans and the individual verses had been sung several times, further embroidered by melodic improvisation. A cycle of *caryā* songs might take more than a day to complete when the full accompanying rituals and dances were performed.

As to the order in which the complete corpus of *caryā* songs were to be performed, there is some evidence from Munidatta's commentary that the order is quite fixed, and the *yogin's* progress through the cycle constitutes a gradual unfoldment of realisation for them. This would seem to suggest that not only is the whole collection to be used as a step-by-step process, but that the songs by individual masters within the collection should also be kept in order. However, a preliminary reading of Kunga Drölchog's (*Kun dga' Grol mchog*) *Life of Kṛṣṇācārya/Kāṇha* suggests that this fixed order may not necessarily be so impervious to change. In this work, Kunga Drölchog takes the thirteen *caryā* songs of Kāṇha (including, as it would appear, the so-called "missing" *caryā* song number 24) and, instead of using them in the accepted order in which they appear, for example, in the *Caryāgītikoṣa*, he places them into the strictly narrative sequence which the *Life* itself dictates. Apart from *caryās* seven and thirteen, which remain in their usual positions, all the others have been re-ordered, with numbers ten and forty-two in ideal positions purely in terms of the narrative events.[30] Clearly, much more detailed work will be required to resolve the issue of the "correct" order of the *caryā* songs, and Kunga Drölchog's *Life of Kāṇha* will be one of the major keys in such an undertaking.

Caryā number ten, perhaps one of the best known of Kṛṣṇācārya/Kāṇha's *caryā* songs, is seen in this hagiography to have contextual meaning at the relative level of understanding, which makes sense of some of the verses (for example verses 4-7) which had hitherto been regarded as somewhat unusual. The song retains, moreover, its absolute meaning at a purely didactic level. The context of the song is that while in the demon land of Singala, Kṛṣṇācārya met with an outcaste girl, a *ḍombī*, in whom he saw all the requisite signs of an ideal tantric consort. However, as it happened, she saw him only as a glorious being – indeed as Brahmā himself – and realised that he was not a suitable person for her to consort with. Downcast, Kṛṣṇācārya made a vajra glance of indifference as to purity and impurity towards her hut and sang the *caryā*, which I have translated from the text of Kunga Drölchog. The reading of the song is not the same as Kvaerne's edition, but I use it here since I have not thus far been able to use the texts in the hagiography to form a critical edition of Kṛṣṇācārya's songs, which is effort well merited by them. He sang:

Outside the town, O *ḍombī*, lies your hut.
Touching you, touching you, goes the brahmin boy.

O *ḍombī*, I Kāṇha, will be your friend,
I, the skull-cup holding *yogin*, free from all sense of revulsion.

One is the root, but the lotus petals are sixty four.
On top of them ḍombī dances the Bapurī dance.

I myself ask you, *ḍombī*, tell me truthfully,
In which boat do you come and go?

You sell threads, *ḍombī*, and floral decorations too,
But as for you, I myself have set out the cushions.

Oh, you are a *ḍombī* and I am a *kāpālin* –
It is for your that I hold a garland of human bones.

You have caused havoc to the tank of water and ḍombī, you have eaten the very lotus beds!

Ḍombī, having taken you, I will slay all enemies![31]

Likewise, the setting for *caryā* song number forty two, (perhaps the most "controversial" of Kāṇha's *caryā* songs) occurs in the hagiography at the death-proximate time, after the failure of all attempts to get medicaments to save Kāṇha's life-strength from the malignancy of the witch Bahurī. To calm the yogins who had been tricked out of the life-preserving medicines, he sang:

The mind is co-emergent with the void and is perfected in it too.
There should be no grieving at the dissolution of the personality components.
Tell me, how can Kāṇha *not* exist?
I am always present in the triple world!
Fools seeing fixed and stable things in decay become afraid –
How can an ocean without waves become dry?

Although it exists, the fool cannot see the world as it is.
Although butter exists in the milk, the fool does not see that either.
As for that state filled with neither coming nor going
Kāṇha plays in that state of reality![32]

I would like to conclude this paper with a rendering of a *caryā* song which does not exist in the collection of *caryā* songs, the *Caryāgītikoṣa*, in either the Bengali or Tibetan recension, although Munidatta makes brief reference to it in his commentary on the collection.[33] However, a version of it does seem to occur in Kunga Drölchog's *Life of Kṛṣṇācarya/Kāṇha* at a point in the narrative where his Guru, Jālandharipa, had just bestowed the six-fold bone ornaments on him. By this act, Jālandharipa had therefore given Kāṇha permission to perform the *caryā* deeds in the twenty-three lands out of the twenty-four,[34] warning him about "opening" the land of Devīkot to Buddhist practice before its appointed time. Exultant at the gift of his Guru he

> ...adorned his body with the six-fold bone ornaments... and travelled... above the very surface of the earth. He appeared holding seven new umbrellas which multiplied themselves in number... and it was in this manner that he soared off into the heavens. Seven ḍamaru drums made of human skulls sounded by themselves... with their sound of *kar kar*, one of the mantras of the twenty four viras, and their sound filled the skies, which resounded... together with them were his retinue of seven hundred invisible followers, who flew and soared in the heavens as well as his retinue of seven hundred visible followers who attended him...[35]

In a state of joy, he sang a *caryā* song set in the *tāla* of *Vira*, the 'Heroic' rhythm:

> When the full moon shines forth
> The King of mind is stainless in its purity.
>
> The net of ignorance is cut by the Guru's teachings –
> Objects of cognition and the cognitive faculties are taught as being transformed into the heavenly realms.
>
> A seed similar to the heavens will likewise grow equal to the heavens,
> And like a forest will cover the triple world with its shadow.
> When the sun shines it clears the night away.
> So too, the faintest glimmer can clear away the gloom of ignorance from the ocean of life.
>
> Just as the swan itself cleaves the water, letting its lustre shine through,
> So too should one devour *saṁsāra* – thus says Kāṇha![36]

❀ ❀ ❀

The field of Buddhist Tantric Song is one which, it seems to me, has barely been touched. Several works, newly translated from the Tibetan,[37] seem to shed even more light on the origins, development, styles and imagery of this enigmatic form of truth communication. It is to be hoped that, through the efforts of specialists in the field from the widest range of disciplines, that interest in these unique song forms will be rekindled.

Notes

1. *Phags yul grub dbang dam pa rnams kyi zab mo'i do ha las khol byung mu tig phreng ba*, Rumtek Edition, n.d. (referred to in this paper as *The Rosary of Pearls*).

2. Tāranātha, tr. D. Templeman, *The Life of Kṛṣṇācārya/Kāṇha* (Dharamsala: Library of Tibetan Works and Archives, 1989), p. 82.

3. Tāranātha, *rGyal bu dga' byed sa skyong gi rtogs brjod*, In Tāranātha, *Collected Works* (Leh, Ladakh: Smanrtsis Shesrig Spendzod, 1985), Vol. 12., p. 688, line 7 - p. 691, line 4; p. 693, line 5 - p. 694, line 4.

Rāmagopāla (*dga' byed sa skyong*), the young prince of Tripurā, in the N.E. corner of present-day Bangladesh, lived 1566-1574. He was the rebirth of Kun dga' Grol mchog and the lineal predecessor of Tāranātha in a lineage starting with Kṛṣṇācārya/Kāṇha. The two references are to incidents in which Buddhist *siddhas* perform much the same types of deed as those of previous centuries. The second reference in particular might be traceable in historical records: it deals with Mahācarya Meghanātha, who aborted a battle between the armies of King Mukunda of Tripurā (the prince's father) and the Tajik military commander of Delhi at a site near Mathurā. As further evidence of this late *siddha* activity, I adduce the reference to the peregrinations of Tāranātha's Indian master, Buddhaguptanātha, which may be found in Tāranātha, *Collected Works*, Vol. 17. He made the arduous journey to the temple at Devīkot, said to have been erected by Kṛṣṇācārya, as well as to many other major pilgrimage spots, and according to the hagiography itself, there were many spots in India which could still be considered minor strongholds of Buddhism in the 16th-17th centuries. My translation of the biographies of both Rāmagopāla and Buddhaguptanātha will shortly be published by the Library of Tibetan Works and Archives.

4. Tāranātha, *Life of Kṛṣṇācārya/Kāṇha*, p. 45.

5. Tāranātha, tr. D. Templeman, *The Seven Instruction Lineages* (Dharamsala: Library of Tibetan Works and Archives, 1983), p. 45.

6. *The Rosary of Pearls* (see note 1), f. 113a, line 5 - f.114a, line 1; f. 114b, lines 2 - 3.

7. H.V. Guenther, *The Royal Song of Saraha* (Seattle: University of Washington Press, 1969); M. Shahidullah, *Les Chants Mystiques de Kāṇha et de Saraha* (Paris: Adrien-Maisonneuve, 1928).

8. *The Rosary of Pearls*, f. 1b, line 1 - f. 2b, line 6.

9. Ibid., f. 3a, line 2 - f. 3b, line 1.

10. Ibid., f. 3b, line 1 - f. 4a, line 1.

11. Tāranātha, *dPon mo nam mkha' rgyal mo la chos kyi 'phrin du bskur ba'o* in Tāranātha, *Collected Works*, Vol. 1., p. 830, line 4 - p. 831, line 5.

12. *mTsungs med bla ma dam pa Nyi ma bKra shis kyi mgur dang zhal gdams skye ba dran pa'i rnam thar rten gyi lo rgyus bcas phyogs gcig tu bkod pa.* Unfortunately, my only edition of this work has little or no pagination and the colophon is missing.

13. Ibid., f. 3b, line 4 - f. 4a, line 4.

14. Ibid., f. 4b, line 1 - f. 8a, line 2. I am indebted to Mr Norbu Samphel of Melbourne, Australia for his great assistance in the translation of the biography.

15. *Kun dga' Grol mChog nag po spyod pa'i rtogs pa brjod pa'i yal 'dab, The Autobiographies of Jo nang Kun dga' Grol mChog and his Previous Embodiments* (New Delhi: Tibet House', 1982) (2 vols.), f.7b - f. 8a.

16. Ibid., f. 9a - f. 9b.

17. *The Rosary of Pearls*, f. 103a, line 6 - f. 103b, line 1.

18. Ibid., f. 102b, line 6 - f. 103a, line 5.

19. Tāranātha, *Life of Kṛṣṇācārya/Kāṇha*, p. 46.

20. *The Rosary of Pearls*, f. 103b, line 1 - f. 103b, line 2.

21. S. Beyer, *The Buddhist Experience, Sources and Interpretations* (Encino: Dickenson Publishing Co. Inc., n.d.), p. 78.

22. *The Rosary of Pearls*, f. 6a, lines 5 - 6.

23. Nālandā Translation Committee, *The Life of Marpa The Translator* (Boston and London: Shambhala, 1982), pp. 20-21.

24. Ibid., pp. 102, 43, 108.

25. P. Kvaerne, *An Anthology of Buddhist Tantric Songs – a Study of the Caryāgīti* (Oslo-Bergen-Tromso: det Norske Videnskaps-Akadamie. Hist.-Filos. Klasse Skrifter. Ny Serie No. 14. Universitetsforlaget, 1977), p. 60.

26. Ibid., p. 63.

27. Tāranātha, *The Seven Instruction Lineages*, pp. 18-19.

28. Ibid.

29. P. Kvaerne, op. cit., p. 96.

30. The order of the *caryā* songs of Kṛṣṇācārya/Kāṇha in the Derge Tenjur as adduced by Kvaerne (*Op.cit.*) is as follows: *caryās* 7 / 9 / 10 / 11 / 12 / 13 / 18 / 19 / 36 / 40 / 42 / 45 //. The order of the *caryā* songs as employed by Kun dga' Grol mchog in his hagiography of Kṛṣṇācārya/Kāṇha (see note 15) is as follows: *caryās*: 7 / 24 / 40 / 9 / 12 / 13 / 10 / 18 / 19 / 36 / 45 / 11 / 42 //. Note that the *caryā* song No 24 only occurs in Kun dga' Grol mchog's edition of the songs as he incorporated them in the hagiography.

31. P. Kvaerne, op. cit., p. 4.

32. Ibid., f. 27b, lines 3 - 5.

33. See P. Kvaerne, op. cit.

34. The 'twenty-four lands' are the twenty-four places which comprise the complete *maṇḍala* of Cakrasaṁvara, the divine setting of perfection. Kṛṣṇācārya was clearly not ready to visit the most dangerous of these sites, that of Devīkot; and indeed, in the version of his life by Kun dga' Grol mchog, he is told specifically by the *ḍākinīs* in Oḍḍiyāna to avoid all places wherein the presiding deity was living on the site. His haste in ignoring the advice of both his guru and the *ḍākinīs* brought about his premature demise at the hands of the demoness of Devīkot.

35. Op. cit.

36. Ibid., f. 13b, line 6 - f. 14a, line 2.

37. E.g., P. Kvaerne, op. cit.; Nālandā Translation Committee, *The Rain of Wisdom* Boston: Shambhala, 1980); Nālandā Translation Committee, *The Life of Marpa the Translator* (Boulder: Prajñā Press, 1982); Lama

Kunga Rinpoche and B. Cutillo (tr.), *Miraculous Journey* (Novato: Lotsawa Press, 1986).

WHEN WHAT YOU SEE IS NOT WHAT YOU GET

Remarks On The Traditional Tibetan Presentation of Sacred Geography

Toni Huber

TIBETAN Buddhist pilgrimage sites have been referred to as 'power places' by some writers.[1] This is perhaps a good description of what they are, provided we take account of the fact that these places are more than just putative centres of otherworldly or supramundane power. Holy places are also a focus for human power in its various manifestations: they are centres where people are required to confront and invest in prescribed ideas and beliefs, and we should therefore treat them and their traditions accordingly.

The researcher who wishes to understand holy places as centres of power must necessarily investigate the history and process of their sanctification, and inquire into what features make them important and attractive destinations for present-day individuals to visit. These are also fundamental issues from a pilgrim's point of view, and we might ask how Tibetan pilgrims come to know of these details about their own sacred domains? How are these places presented to them in traditional sources? And by using such sources, what might they expect to encounter and experience at particular sites?

In addressing such questions we have at our disposal excellent materials in the form of the Tibetan genre of guide-book literature, generally known as *gnas yig*, *gnas bshad*, *dkar chag* or *lam yig*. A.W. Macdonald recently observed of Tibetan guide-books that although "[f]rom a literary point of view, the genre may be minor... these sources are very important for understanding not just the pilgrims but also the average Buddhist's approach to and attitude towards holy sites."[2] I think this may be particularly so if the study of such literary sources can be combined with the results of field investigations at pilgrimage sites.

Tibetan pilgrimage guide-books range from short catalogues or eulogies of particular monuments and places to lengthy and complex descriptions of pilgrimage routes and sites, covering large geographical areas. Generally they constitute a handy digest of information about aspects of both the sacred and the mundane history and geography of the places they deal with, often providing additional material on ritual performances, the benefits and merits of pilgrimage, and so forth. It is worth noting that, unlike the huge bulk of Tibetan literature, which was consumed mainly by an ecclesiastic minority, guide-books enjoyed a wide public audience in traditional Tibet. Illiteracy was no obstacle for pilgrims, as guides were often read or recited for them by monks, shrine-keepers and their literate companions at holy places. In my observation, this is still true to a limited extent in the case of guide-books used by present-day Tibetan pilgrims in India and the Himalayan zone. Written guide-books have a very significant oral dimension, and their contents are usually elaborated upon by oral traditions. They often contain, in fact, many records of oral traditions collected at sites by their authors.

It is important when working with guide-books to recognise that they are constructed and styled in particular ways in order to direct and to evoke certain responses from those who use them. When one reads various Tibetan guides, it becomes clear that they attempt to do more than simply provide interesting and convenient information for pilgrims. They actively advertise the sanctity of sites, and promote the powers and beliefs that play a significant role in controlling and shaping the lives of individual pilgrims.

In order to illustrate some aspects of the traditional presentation of a Tibetan holy place, I will give a brief description of La phyi,[3] a Central Himalayan pilgrimage site in the Nepal-Tibet Borderlands. I shall then offer a short analytical commentary on the Tibetan language guide-book[4] for the area and related oral sources.

La phyi (in Tibetan sources, *'Brog La phyi Gangs kyi Ra ba*) is the main holy place on a larger Himalayan pilgrimage circuit which traverses an area of related sites between the southern Ding ri plains, Chu dbar in Rong shar (or Brin) to the east and the gNya' nang region to the west, where the modern Lhasa-Kathmandu Highway descends to the Nepalese frontier. Pilgrims may reach La phyi via a number of routes which necessitate either crossing high snow-covered passes or negotiating the narrow Himalayan gorges which lie to the south and east. The pilgrimage requires a significant investment of time and physical exertion, and can only be undertaken easily at certain times of the year when weather conditions are favourable. Like many Tibetan pilgrimage sites, it is quite removed from major centres of human activity, and characterised by a rugged natural beauty. Pilgrims who journey to La phyi from the expansive steppes and broad valleys of the arid Tibetan plateau experience a dramatic change in physical environment as they descend deep into the heart of this Himalayan valley with its mantle of vegetation and noisy watercourses. This contrast is one that comes to mind for many Tibetans when they talk of their visits to La phyi.

The main site consists of a small monastery compound on a triangular piece of land at the junction of two steep-sided river valleys. A high, rocky mountain face rises up directly behind the monastery to the north. On this mountain side amongst the great boulders and cliffs, there are several cave temples located at intervals up the slope. Because of their mention in popular literature, some of these, such as the bDud 'dul Phug or 'Demon Conquering Cave' are as well known to many Tibetans as the major shrines of Central Tibet or India. There are numerous other smaller meditation caves here, all connected by an obscure network of precipitous trails. There are a number of individual sites at La phyi, many of which are natural formations such as rock grottos; and the few man-made constructions there, such as the monastery, appear quite insignificant in relation to the powerful landscape in which they are set.

The site is just one of many Himalayan valleys which lie along the south-western border of Tibet, populated for centuries by only a handful of yak-herders and the occasional *yogin* seeking a solitary mountain retreat. Nevertheless, despite its seeming obscurity, the name of La phyi is known throughout the zone of Tibetan cultural influence. Tibetans associate La phyi with the renowned holy places of Ti se (i.e., Kailāsa) and Tsa ri, together with which it forms a well-known trio of sacred mountain pilgrimage venues. The area is an important site for Tibetan cultural history as it is associated with two interrelated cults, those of the Buddhist Tantric cycle of *Cakrasaṁvara* and the universally popular Tibetan saint Milarepa (*Mi la Ras pa*, 1040-1123). For this reason, it has long been a desirable pilgrimage destination for Tantric initiates and lay practitioners.

The Tibetan guide-book to La phyi (LNY) was written in 1901 by the 34th hierarch of the *'Bri gung pa* lineage after his own pilgrimage to the region. It is a lengthy and detailed example of the genre, consisting of over seventy printed folios. The text is divided into six chapters, the first three of which are devoted to an account of the sanctification process of the site. They deal with what I call the 'conversion mythologies' of the cults of *Saṁvara* Tantrism and of Milarepa, with which the site is associated.[5]

In chapters 1 and 2, the original drama of the conversion of La phyi is outlined in terms of a Tibetan tradition concerning the Tantric geography of the *Saṁvara* cycle. According to this scheme, in a past aeon a violent form of Śiva, Ugra Bhairava (or Rudra), and his demonic retinue occupied La phyi, which was then identified with Godāvarī, one of the twenty-four Tantric *pīṭha* of Jambudvīpa. It was occupied first by a pair of malicious *gandharava* deities from the troupe of Ugra Bhairava, and later by Śiva himself, who manifested there in the form of a stone *linga* which is identified with the high rock mountain at the centre of La phyi. In response to the negative circumstances that arose during this occupation, the Buddhist Tantric tutelary Cakrasaṁvara, together with his consort and their retinue of *vīra* and *ḍākinī*, subdued the malignant heterodox powers in the twenty-four regions, thus converting La phyi and the other places completely into Buddhist sites. Some important points about the conquest of La phyi by Saṁvara and his retinue are summarised at the end of this legend in the text:

> In particular, they sanctified the receptacles of Mahādeva's emanation [i.e., the stone *lingas*] so that the *maṇḍala* of the emanations of the sixty-two deities of Cakrasaṁvara was directly manifest there. And, in that way, the *maṇḍala* of the emanations of Cakrasaṁvara as vanquishers was completed without abandoning the form of those to be vanquished... In brief, after the subjugation of Ugra Bhairava by Śrī-Heruka during the *kali-yuga*, the district known as Godāvarī, which is one of the eight abodes of celestial beings, was established as the realm of Cakrasaṁvara, but it should be understood that before Ugra Bhairava was conquered, it was nothing but a heap of earth and rock, or an ordinary abode of *amanuṣyas*.[6]

Using a mundane analogy, we might understand this process as being like the change of ownership of a house, where the new tenants forcefully evict the old ones. This much is clear. But how we comprehend the 'redecoration' of that house carried out by the new tenants is another matter. Exactly what does it mean for an ordinary mountain of rock and earth to become a manifestation of a Tantric *maṇḍala*? I shall return to this question shortly.

As well as demonstrating the superior powers of Buddhism over those of other systems, this 'conversion myth' also serves to legitimate La phyi as a location *par excellence* for the performance of the Tantric yoga and ritual of the *Saṁvara* cycle. It has been magically transformed not only into an abode of Heruka in his *maṇḍala*, but perhaps most importantly into a place which is easily accessible to Tibetan followers of the practice.[7]

Chapter 3 of our text details the 'second conversion' of La phyi. It is typical of Tibetan pilgrimages that they are 'opened' at some point in their early history by a great saint or lama.[8] According to the guide-book, although La phyi had previously become a Buddhist site, there were still many hostile forces in the area which made it inaccessible to ordinary folk, both pilgrims and pastoralists alike. On behalf of the people, Milarepa 'opens the door to the place' (*gnas sgo phye ba*) by overcoming the repeated harassments of autochthonous deities. As before, it is the superior powers of Buddhism, this time channelled through the Tibetan *yogin*, which lie behind the successful neutralisation and conversion of local mountain goddesses and gods. Through these stories, the present-day visitors and residents of La phyi are made to feel that it is by virtue of these earlier events that they are now able to come and meditate in the caves or herd their yaks safely in the pastures of the valley.

The way in which the Milarepa stories are used to present the sacred geography of La phyi is interesting. They provide an excellent example of Clifford Geertz's idea of a 'blurred genre',[9] in this case, one in which geography is written as theatre. The pilgrimage route is described as a stage upon which the Buddhist lama and local forces acted out important historical dramas. To illustrate this, my own impressions of a section of the pilgrimage can be compared with the description given in the Tibetan text. During July 1987, after crossing the high snow pass of Zullekang-la above La phyi, I recorded the following in my diary:

> The 5300m Zullekang la is a snow-covered pass flanked by rugged rocky peaks. Descending steeply from its summit cairn, one enters the long valley leading eastward down towards La phyi and the

Nepalese border. Some distance below the pass one comes to a large basin beside the trail, which appears to be the result of some former glacial action here. A terminal moraine wall encloses it on the downhill side. My local companions identified this as the lake-bed of Mu-dzing, or 'Demon Lake'. On the path that crosses the small moraine wall is a rock with a deep hole in it, said to be the place where the saint Milarepa drained the lake using his staff. Descending further, the path winds along the ridge of a lateral moraine, one of many that run parallel to each other down the valley at this point. They resemble a series of frozen rock wave crests. The La phyi ba call this the *Khandro ganglam* or 'Elevated Path of the *ḍākinīs*'.

In the Tibetan guide the same area is described thus:

Then the Master [Milarepa] also went towards the Zul le'i gangs pass of La phyi, and from the top of the pass the *amanuṣyas* produced spectres [to frighten him]. As soon as he reached the summit of the pass, there were violent claps of thunder and flashes of lightning, and the mountains on both sides of the valley moved, so that the mountain torrent, diverted [from its course] and churned up in violent waves, turned into a lake. At this, the Master gave a concentrated stare, took his staff and pushed it in, and the lake drained out from the bottom and disappeared. The place is known as dMu-rdzing. From there, he descended a little way, and the *amanuṣyas* stirred up waves consisting of many boulders, to the point where the mountains on both sides were thrown down. The *ḍākinīs* provided a [safe] path for him out of a hill running downward like a snake, between the sides of the valley. That 'wave-stilling' path is known as the mKha' 'gro sGang-lam.[10]

The natural topography over which the pilgrim must pass is reinterpreted and infused with a sacred significance through its association with the legendary scenarios of the past. This is indicative of the kind of presentation with which Tibetan pilgrims are equipped by guides as they approach holy places and travel pilgrimage routes. Milarepa's visit to La phyi is just the beginning of an on-going process of empowerment of the site by the presence and activities there of special human individuals. In the descriptions of the 'four great meditation caves' at La phyi given in the fifth chapter, the guide-book provides lists of the famous religious practitioners who have resided at each site over the centuries, together with details of the successful meditational experiences (e.g., *sādhana* visions, etc.) and the various spiritual attainments which they have achieved there. It is stated that these places have become 'sanctified' or 'powerfully transformed' (*byin brlabs can*, *byin gyis brlabs*) as a result of their contact with those individuals, who are considered to be enlightened, and by the great acts of religious practice they performed there. By way of offering tangible evidence of the great powers of those who once frequented a site, guide-books often enumerate miraculous features that are to be found there, such as footprints in rocks (*zhabs rjes*), self-sprung holy water (*sgrub chu*), etc.. The notion of a residual sacred power associated with these 'points of contact' is an extension of the beliefs that underlie the Buddhist cult of relics.[11] The strong belief which Tibetans have in this type of 'sanctification by association' is certainly evinced by aspects of the ritual behaviour of pilgrims at many holy places.[12]

The long fifth chapter of the text gives a systematic account of every site on the pilgrimage in the order of a large *pradakṣiṇā* circuit. The description of the main site of La phyi given here provides an example of another way in which Tibetan guides direct pilgrims to 'see' their sacred environments – that is, by referring to them in terms of the Buddhist symbol system. As one might expect, the site of La phyi is presented with reference to the esoteric symbols of *Saṁvara* Tantrism. At La phyi, one finds a rough triangle of level ground formed at the junction of two rivers. To the north, the steep mountainside which rises up directly behind this level area is the site of several meditation caves such as the famous bDud 'dul phug. To the east, south and west large mountain peaks surround the site. This is how the area is presented in the Tibetan text:

> Therefore, it is said that the central place of La phyi has the appearance of three *chos 'byung*[13] stacked one upon the other, with a triangle of sky above, a triangle of earth below and a triangle of water in between. And concerning the bDud 'dul Phug mo che and the adjacent mountain behind it, on the outside this itself has the appearance of a lifeless rock mountain soaring into the sky in lofty splendour. But inside, in the centre of a heavenly mansion constructed out of self-luminous cognition, the *maṇḍala* of the emanations of the sixty-two deities of the Bhagavan Śrī-Cakra-saṁvara is manifest there. And, in the same way, to the east of this place the divine assembly of Paramārya Mahākaruṇika [i.e., Avalokiteśvara] is to be found in the dKar po 'Bum ye mountain; to the south the divine assembly of the Lord of Secrets Vajrapāṇi is to be found in the Nag po 'Bum ye mountain; and to the west the divine assembly of the All Wise Mañjuśrīghoṣa is to be found in the

> Ser po 'Bum ye mountain.[14]

And further, concerning the level ground between the two rivers:

> Of the two plains at the foot [of the mountain], the plain between the bDud 'dul phug and Tshang leb is known as the Chos 'byung Ya thang, and the plain below the bDud 'dul [cave] is known as the Chos 'byung Ma thang, and these are present in the form of the essential *maṇḍala* of Vajrayoginī.[15]

Once again we find that mundane geography is infused with a sacred significance, this time by its identification with powerful symbols from the Buddhist Tantras, such as the *maṇḍala* palace and the *chos 'byung* (*dharmodaya*).[16] This sort of process is not uncommon in Tibetan pilgrimage traditions in general. But what is of particular interest at La phyi is the clear distinction which the tradition makes between an inanimate exterior reality – the rock mountain – and the splendid divine reality – the *maṇḍala* palace – which lies behind this. This brings us back to the earlier question of what it actually means for a rock mountain to be a manifestation of a Tantric *maṇḍala* as stated in the guide-books. Part of the answer may lie in the technical understanding of the *maṇḍala* palace as found in the Tantric commentaries of the Tibetan Buddhist canon. According to these sources the "sublime mental *maṇḍala*" of the Tantras represents the palace of the Akaniṣṭha heaven. It is the realm of *sambhogakāya* manifestations, and Tibetan commentators hold "that this sambhoga-kaya teaches only bodhisattvas of the tenth stage."[17]

Thus the very advanced practitioner who mentally constructs a *maṇḍala*, and realises it, has re-established this heavenly arrangement and has direct access to *sambhogakāya* forms such as Cakrasaṁvara. Clearly this provides a technical explanation of how those advanced meditators who practice in the caves of the sacred mountain of La phyi might come to 'see' it as a *maṇḍala* palace of Saṁvara.

The LNY confirms the idea that La phyi as a *maṇḍala* palace or pure abode is a level of reality which is the sole preserve of highly realised individuals (in the Tantric Buddhist sense). It states that while its 'true meaning' is known to perfected masters, 'ordinary' (*so sor skye bo*, Skt. *pṛthagjana*) or 'impure' (*ma dag 'gro*) people can only perceive La phyi in its inanimate, material form.[18]

An interesting explanation of this relationship between karmic purity and the perception of geographical reality is found in the Tibetan guide-book for Mount Kailāsa (Ti se), also written by the

'Bri gung Lama. Concerning the reason why the great sacred mountain appears in various ways to people of different spiritual status, he states:

> The reason is, according to the *Abhidharmakośa*, "a single substance gives rise to different states of mind." For example, it says three different ways of seeing even a single mundane element [such as] water arise for people who have or have not purified their obscurations. When seen by the gods, this water is something known as 'The River of the Elixir of Life', having a taste like honey and possessing properties such as the ability to cure illness, the ability to revive the dead and the ability to mend what is broken. When looked at by human beings, it is seen as just water which performs the function of quenching thirst and washing off impurities. When looked at by Hungry Ghosts, it is seen as pus, matter and blood, excrement and urine and so on, which performs the function of stinking and burning. And in a similar way, with regard to this snow mountain Ti se as well: to the sight of tenth stage bodhisattvas who are purified of obscurations, it exists at present in accordance with the explanations in the *sūtras*; i.e., it is made of precious substances, and has a height of five hundred *yojanas* and a heavenly mansion of the gods inside it, etc.; to the sight of mediocre people it appears as a splendoured, massive mountain and the self-created body of a deity, and so forth, and it has a covering of rainbows, etc.; to the sight of inferior people it appears as nothing but just ordinary earth and rock.[19]

What implications does this have for the 'ordinary' Tibetan Buddhists, be they lay or monastic practitioners, who go on pilgrimages to holy places such as La phyi? The fact that these sites are considered to be divine residences and so on is part of the very *raison d'être* of pilgrimages to them. Yet in presenting them, the guides simultaneously direct pilgrims to 'see' them in a certain way, and then indicate that their inferior spiritual status will prevent them from accessing this reality. In the case of La phyi, it is possible that responses to this situation are to be found in the variant oral traditions about the site. In 1901 the 'Bri gung Lama recorded an oral tradition about the form of the main sacred mountain at La phyi:

> Nowadays, some of the local occupants say it is the body of Vajravārāhī, with the rock outcrop of Ras chen as her head, the rock of Seng khyams as her belly, and the rock in front of the bDud 'dul [cave] as her knee, but this is foolish talk and should not be believed![20]

The 'Bri gung Lama's rejection of this and other oral traditions is hardly to be wondered at, as he himself was a representative of the esoteric tradition.[21] Today this same oral tradition is still found at La phyi, along with a range of others which attempt to equate landscape features with Saṁvara and his consort as they are envisaged to be sitting in their mountain/palace. When asked to describe the mountain, local residents and pilgrims indicate rock outcrops which represent the deity's head and shoulders, while ridges on either side are said to be his legs, the river that flows south from the place is said to be the stream of his urine, and so forth. These popular oral variants are pilgrim's attempts to 'concretise' or lay claim to that which the esoteric tradition alludes to but denies them.[22]

Clearly there are 'political' implications here. The status of lamas in Tibetan society depends in large part on the laity's recognition of their mastery of Tantric practices and acquisition of the powers associated with these.[23] Commonplace traditions which erode the notion of the Tibetan lamas' exclusive access to these powers, such as the perception of other realities, are therefore necessarily repudiated.

The various traditions about La phyi give us an insight into how Tibetans, and possibly other Buddhists, regard their 'power places'. In some aspects of their presentation, sites such as La phyi present problems of interpretation. For instance, are they to be understood as temporary edifices of consciousness, constructed and realised by meditators, or as some permanent projection of a heavenly or pure abode on earth, whose true character may only be perceived by a few? Their exact status is certainly a moot point. What we can say is that both Tibetan guide-books and pilgrims treat these places as being 'out there' somewhere, at real geographical locations which pilgrims must make their goal in order for their faith and practice to bear fruit.

Notes

1. See for instance K. Dowman, 'A Buddhist Guide to the Power Places of the Kathmandu Valley', *Kailash*, vol. 8, no. 3-4, pp. 183-291. 1981.

2. See the brief but important remarks on Tibetan pilgrimage and guide-books on pp. 3-5 of A.W. Macdonald, 'Points of View on Halase, a Holy Place in East Nepal', *Tibet Journal*, vol. 10, no. 3, pp. 3-13. 1985.

3. On this little known area see my 'A Pilgrimage to La-phyi: The Sacred and Historical Geography of a Holy Place in South-Western Tibet' in A.W. Macdonald (ed.), *Maṇḍala and Landscapes*, (forthcoming) Paris, 1992; and the perceptive article by A.W. Macdonald, 'Hindu-isation, Buddha-isation, Then Lama-isation Or: What Happened At La-phyi?', forthcoming in Skorupski, T. (ed.), *Indo-Tibetan Studies. Papers in appreciation of Professor David L. Snellgrove's contribution to Indo-Tibetan Studies* (Tring, 1990), pp. 195-202. E. De Rossi Filibeck, *Two Tibetan Guide Books to Ti se and La phyi* (Bonn, 1988), pp. 115-194 contains many errors and should be consulted with due caution.

4. See 34th 'Bri gung gDan rabs bsTan 'dzin Chos kyi Blo gros (1868-1906), *gSang lam sgrub pa'i gnas chen nyer bzhi'i ya gyal gau dā wa ri 'am / 'brog la phyi gangs kyi ra ba'i sngon byung gi tshul las tsam pa'i gtam gyi rab tu phyed pa nyung ngu rnam gsal*, a version of which was published in *dPal 'khor lo sdom pa'i sku yi gnas gangs ri ti se dang gsung gi gnas la phyi gangs ra gnyis kyi gnas yig* (Delhi, 1983), ff. 261-402; and my English translation in 'A Pilgrimage to La-phyi', op. cit..

5. These are the narratives of the conversion processes described as 'Buddha-isation' and 'Lama-isation' by Macdonald in his discussion of this topic, 'Hindu-isation, Buddha-isation, Then Lama-isation Or: What Happened At La-phyi?', op. cit..

6. See LNY, ff. 5a-6a.

7. In Tibetan pilgrimage traditions, the legitimation function of this narrative for Tibetan locations of the twenty-four places is important. Generally, the bKa' brgyud pa, and later the dGe lugs pa, who practised the Saṁvara cycle, patronised sites such as Ti se, Tsa ri and La phyi and subscribed to this myth. The Sa skya pa also practised the Saṁvara cycle, but have long refuted the location of the twenty-four places, and other sites, in Tibet. In his well known *sDom gsum rab dbye*, Sa skya Paṇḍita attacked this tradition, and his position has been echoed in subsequent Sa skya pa commentaries on Tibetan sacred geography. There have also been numerous bKa' brgyud pa defences of their sacred geographical traditions. I have used these sources to

deal with this issue at length in my article 'Where Exactly are Cāritra, Devikoṭa and Himavat? A Sacred Geography Controversy and the Development of Tantric Buddhist Pilgrimage Sites in Tibet', *Kailash*, vol. 16, no. 3-4. 1991.

8. On another type of 'opening' of a Tibetan pilgrimage see C. Jest, *Dolpo: Communautés de langue tibétaine du Népal* (Paris, 1975), p. 354.

9. Macdonald adverts to this dimension of the stories in 'Points of View on Halase', op. cit., p. 5. Cf. C. Geertz, 'Blurred Genres: The Refiguration of Social Thought', *The American Scholar*, vol. 49, no. 2, pp. 165-179. 1980.

10. LNY, f. 10.

11. On this subject see the excellent study by G. Schopen, "Burial 'Ad Sanctos' and the Physical Presence of the Buddha in Early Indian Buddhism – A Study in the Archeology of Religions", *Religion*, vol. 17, no. 3, pp. 193-225. 1987. In later Tibetan cultural history, it was chiefly the relics and 'points of contact' of Indian Tantric *mahāsiddhas* and their Tibetan successors which came to sanctify holy places.

12. At Tibetan pilgrimage places, one often observes ritual collection of materials such as soil, rock, water and herbs. These substances are believed to contain the residual power of the sacred environment. As portable sources of this power, they are put to a variety of magico-religious uses. See for example L.A. Waddell, *The Buddhism of Tibet or Lāmaism* (2nd ed., Cambridge, 1939), p. 309.

13. See n. 16.

14. LNY, f.26.

15. LNY, ff. 52b-53a.

16. The *chos 'byung* (*dharmodaya*) is a triangular symbol of the universal creative matrix. On its significance in the Buddhist Tantras according to Tibetans, see F. Lessing & A. Wayman, *Introduction to the Buddhist Tantric Systems* (2nd ed., Delhi, 1980), esp. p. 318, n. 7. This is a significant feature of Tibetan sacred geography, particularly at sites associated with the cult of Saṁvara. Cf. the description of Yab phu on p. 45 of L. Tsonawa, 'The Autobiography of Kyabje Ling Rinpoche', *The Tibet Journal*, vol. 8, no. 3, pp. 45-51, 1983. On the *maṇḍala* palace in the Tantras, see A. Wayman, 'Contributions on the Symbolism of the Mandala Palace', *Etudes tibétaines dédiées à la mémoire de Marcelle Lalou* (Paris, 1971), pp. 557-566.

17. See Wayman, op. cit., p. 565. For Tibetan comments on *sambhoga-kāya* perception in *Mahāmudrā* practice, see Wang ch'ug Dorje The Ninth Karmapa, *The Mahamudra Eliminating the Darkness of Ignorance* (tr. & ed. A. Berzin, Dharamsala, 1978), pp. 145-46.

18. LNY, ff.47 &70. Cf. also recent Tibetan comments on the twenty-four places of Saṁvara (Geshe Kelsang Gyatso, *Clear Light of Bliss: Mahamudra in Vajrayana Buddhism* (London, 1982), p. 24): "People with pure karma can see these outer places of Heruka as pure lands; those with impure karma see them as ordinary geographical locations".

19. See the 34th 'Bri-gung gDan-rabs, *Gangs ri chen po ti se dang mtsho chen ma dros pa bcas kyi sngon byung gi lo rgyus mdor bsdus su brjod pa'i rab byed shel dkar me long*, ff.25b-26b, also published in the Delhi edition of 1983 cited in n. 4 above; also the comments on this place in the well-known *'Dzam gling rgyas bshad* of the bTsan po Nom-unqan, see T. Wylie, *The Geography of Tibet According to the Dzam-gling-rgyas-bshad* (Rome, 1962), pp. 56-9. One might also compare the guide for Kha ba dKar po – see p. 236 of A.M. Blondeau, 'Les pèlerinages tibétains', *Les Pèlerinages* (Paris, 1960), pp. 199-246.

20. LNY, f.53.

21. See also LNY, f.71. For a brief note on the career of the 34th gDan-rabs, see my 'Drikung Kyabgon Rinpoche Chökyi Lodrö (eine kurze Biographie)', *Vajra-Klänge*, Juli 1990, p. 12.

22. One finds that Tibetans often identify landscape features with the bodies of deities. However, at any particular holy places, rather than being a casual practice, these identifications are often specific responses to what written texts say or allude to. In July 1987 I visited the meditation cave complex at Brag Yer pa east of Lhasa, the layout of which is comparable to La phyi in certain respects. Here pilgrims identify features of the sacred mountain-side with the body of the goddess Tārā similarly to their identification of Saṁvara and his consort at La phyi. These oral traditions at Yer pa are a response to the traditions set down in the Tibetan guide-book for the area: see f. 30 of the *dkar chag* for Yer-pa in *Tibetan Guides to Places of Pilgrimage* (Dharamsala, 1985), pp. 55-122. Cf. also the interesting Tibetan description of gNas Padma-bkod in South-eastern Tibet: "Sa forme, c'est la déesse «Phag-mo klu 'dul-ma»...: elle est couchée sur le dos, dans la main droite elle tient la province du Kong-po, dans la main gauche le Poyul; sa tête, c'est la montagne sainte (*çriparvata*) de rGyal-la [i.e. Gyalaperi]; son aspect extérieur, «c'est une montagne de glace qui ressemble à une tête de porc dressée vers le ciel».", see Blondeau, op. cit., p. 240; and the comments by R.A. Stein on the body

of the goddess at Dag-pa Shel-ri the holy mountain of Tsa ri in *Grottes-matrices et lieux saints de la déesse en Asie Orientale* (Paris, 1988), pp. 40-42.

23. See the comments on pp. 45-68 of G. Samuel, 'Religion in Tibetan Society: A New Approach. Part One: A Structural Model', *Kailash*, vol. 6, no. 1, pp. 45-68. 1978.

GE SAR OF gLING

Shamanic Power and Popular Religion

Geoffrey Samuel

Introduction

I have suggested elsewhere (1985, 1993) that what may be called 'shamanic' techniques have an important place in Tibetan religion. Among these techniques I include most of the procedures of Vajrayāna Buddhism in Tibet. The Vajrayāna originated in India, and probably derived in many respects from indigenous 'shamanic' practices of the Indian subcontinent (cf. for example Wayman 1961). In Tibet, Buddhism survived and prospered in large part because of its ability to supply such shamanic services to the Tibetan lay population. Over the centuries it became, in the terms I have used elsewhere, as much a 'shamanic' as a 'clerical' religion. The Vajrayāna was central to this development.

A characteristic feature of shamanic techniques is the establishment of contact with some level of reality thought to be underlying and more fundamental than the world of everyday experience (cf. Samuel, 1990). Through making contact with such profound levels of reality, shamanic practitioners undergo a process of personal transformation which enables them to perform their cultural role as diviners, healers and the like. This contact also enables them to bring about transformations in how lay members of their society, their clients, experience the world.

In Vajrayāna Buddhism, the underlying reality is conceived of in various ways. A particularly significant conceptualisation is that of the *trikāya* (lit. 'three bodies') scheme. Underlying the *nirmāṇakāya* level of apparent reality there is the *sambhogakāya* level, at which reality is experienced in terms of Tantric deities such as sPyan ras gzigs (Avalokiteśvara), sGrol ma (Tārā), Guru Rin po che (Padmasambhava) or mGon po (Mahākāla). Beyond and behind this is the underlying level of the *dharmakāya*, of Buddhahood as the ultimate ground of existence.

Tibetan Vajrayāna practitioners, and in particular Tantric lamas, encounter the world of the Tantric deities in order to pursue their own healing and integration, culminating normatively in the attainment of Buddhahood; and also in order to bring about 'magical' effects in the ordinary world. These 'magical' effects are the main aim of much Vajrayāna ritual, and typically include defence against dangerous spiritual agencies, healing, and the maintenance of the life-force. These effects can be interpreted at least in part as transformations in how ordinary Tibetans experience their life-world (including, particularly, their own bodies).

Such transformational processes have been extensively analysed in anthropological studies of ritual (e.g. Turner, 1968; cf. Samuel, 1989; Samuel 1990). There seems good reason to suppose that they can be effective, and that in this sense at least 'magical ritual' can bring about transformations in the real world. The essence of these transformations lies in their effect on how people encounter and interpret the world. They bring about an analogical shift in how the world is made sense of (cf. Wagner 1978).

To the extent that shamanic practitioners are believed able to create such transformations, they exercise a kind of power which I refer to here as 'shamanic' power. Shamanic power has some resemblance to what Weber referred to as 'charismatic authority' (cf. Weber 1978:1111-57). I refer to it as 'power' rather than 'authority', since it does not necessarily constitute a structure of authority, and may indeed be supportive of various kinds of authority in the Weberian classification.

Many societies have some indigenous conception corresponding more or less closely to shamanic power. In these societies, the use of such power is generally a matter of critical importance. It can be used for good purposes (meaning, in general, socially constructive purposes); it can also be used for destructive purposes (sorcery or witchcraft). The relationship between shamanic power and the political order is also generally a matter of considerable concern. Such societies may be stateless and relatively egalitarian, like many of the traditional 'shamanic' societies of Siberia, SE Asia or the Americas. They may also have developed state institutions, in which case the control of shamanic practitioners by the state becomes a matter of significance. This was the situation in the traditional states of South and South-East Asia.

Traditional Tibetan society cannot be adequately described as either a stateless society or a centralised state. It had elements of both, and indeed different regions of Tibet at different times were closer to one or another model. Similar patterns of oscillation have been described by Edmund Leach for the populations in the Burmese highlands (Leach 1970) and were probably quite widespread until recent times, particularly in areas on the margins of centralised states where the economic and technological basis for effective centralisation were lacking (cf. Samuel 1982). Within such societies we find a variety of conceptualisations of political authority and of shamanic power.

The Epic of Ge sar is a classical expression of the 'shamanic' Vajrayāna religion of Tibet. Unlike the technical treatises of the great Tantric lamas such as Bu ston, Tsong kha pa or Padma dKar po, however, which present a clerical and scholarly view of shamanic power and its uses, the epic gives us something much closer to a popular perspective. It is of particular interest for what it indicates about how the Tibetans viewed the proper relationship between shamanic power and political authority.

In the following three sections I introduce the epic and suggest that the view of political authority in the epic is inextricably linked with the question of shamanic power. Then, in Section 5, I suggest that the Tibetan value system implies an underlying conflict between the 'wild' (autonomous, undisciplined) and the 'tame' (subordinate, disciplined) and that Ge sar is one of a series of symbolic resolutions of this conflict. Finally, in the concluding section, I consider how far Ge sar's role in Tibetan society fits into the more general models proposed by Pierre Clastres ('society against the state') and by Gilles Deleuze and Félix Guattari ('nomadic science' and the 'war machine').

The Epic of Ge sar of Ling

The *sgrung* or cycle of epic stories concerning the life of the heroic Tibetan king Ge sar of gLing forms the principal repertoire of the so-called bards (*sgrung pa*, *sgrung mkhan*) of Tibet. The stories exist both as extemporised performances and as manuscript or printed books. Nowadays, performers often use a written or printed text.

The main centre for the epic is in East Tibet (Khams and A mdo), among the nomadic pastoralists and settled agriculturalists living in what was, until their incorporation into the Chinese People's Republic, a series of small states and chiefdoms independent of the larger Central Tibetan administration at Lhasa. These regions now form part not of the Tibet Autonomous Region of the CPR but of the provinces of Yunnan, Sichuan, Qinghai and Gansu. The epic is, however, well known throughout all parts of Tibet, as well as among the Mongols.

In the far west of Tibet, a somewhat separate (and entirely oral) epic tradition exists. It was this Ladakhi tradition which first became known to Western scholars, through the work of the Moravian missionary A.H. Francke at the beginning of the century (1900, 1901-2, 1905-9). The Western tradition includes the basic episodes of Ge sar's birth, childhood, marriage, and his becoming ruler of gLing. It also includes Ge sar's wars against kLu btsan, the demon king of the North, and against the kings of the Hor (Turkic peoples).

These episodes are common to the Eastern and Western Tibetan versions and can be regarded as forming the core of the epic. They also occur in the first Mongolian printed version of 1716 (cf. Damdinsüren 1985:593-5, Heissig 1983:3,7-9). The Eastern Tibetan tradition includes a long series of further episodes of the epic, almost all taking the form of a war between the heroes of gLing under Ge sar's leadership and the ruler and warriors of some other realm: 'Jang (Naxi), Mon (?Bhutan), sTag gzig (=Iran), Kha che (Kashmir), Sum pa, and so forth. These additional episodes do not occur in the Mongolian versions, although that has also grown from the basic core of episodes mentioned above (cf. Heissig 1983).

Some of the additional episodes are definitely quite recent. Two books dealing with the conflicts with 'Jar (?Germany) and U yan were written by the well-known bKa' brgyud pa lama Khams sprul Rin po che VIII (Don brgyud Nyi ma, 1929-80). Another contemporary bKa' brgyud pa lama, Kalu Rinpoche (1906-89), wrote a book about Ge sar and Yama, the King of Hell. Many books of the epic have been reprinted recently, both outside and within the CPR (cf. P. Tsering 1982), and there are now numerous episodes of the epic available in various editions, including a 31-volume Bhutanese edition (Tobgyel and Dorji 1979).

There has also been a considerable amount of Western research on the Tibetan versions of the epic, although they have not so far received as much scholarly attention as the Mongolian versions. After Francke's early work on the Western Tibetan tradition, the next major landmark was a summary of an Eastern Tibetan version produced by the well-known French Buddhist writer Alexandra David-Neel and her adopted Tibetan son Lama Yongden (David-Neel and Yongden 1933). This covered the core episodes as well as several of the supplementary sections.

In the 1950s, Rolf Stein published an edition and translation of three of the core episodes, following the best-known Tibetan written version, that printed under the supervision of the early 20th century rNying ma pa lama 'Ju Mi pham (1956). Stein followed this up with a study of the epic and the epic bard (1959). More recently, Mireille Helffer has produced a detailed study of the songs in the third of the episodes published by Stein, which deals with the horse-race in which Ge sar won his wife and became King of gLing. A number of episodes are also available in German versions by Matthias Hermanns (1965) and more recently by Pema Tsering and Rudolf Kaschewsky (Kaschewsky and Tsering 1972, 1987A, Tsering 1985). In addition to these studies of the Eastern Tibetan tradition of the epic, there has also been some recent work on the Western Tibetan tradition (cf. Herrmann 1987 for a review).

These scholars have taken a variety of orientations towards the epic. Helffer's very valuable study is literary and musicological in its focus, while the works of Kaschewsky and Tsering are for the most part straight editions and abridged translations of the texts, as is Stein's 1956 volume. Stein (1959, 1979) and Hermanns (1965) have speculated on the historical background to the epic. Stein in particular has traced in detail the process by which Ge sar began as a distant echo of the Emperor of Byzantium, Caesar King of Rome (= *Khrom/Phrom*), forming one of a set of four kings of the four directions, and was later adopted as an ancestor by the East Tibetan principality of gLing tshang and developed into a specifically Buddhist figure (e.g. Stein 1979, cf. also Uray 1985, Kaschewsky and Tsering 1987B).

Robert Paul (1982), in his stimulating though eccentric book *The Tibetan Symbolic World: Psychoanalytic Explorations*, has gone farthest in providing an interpretation of the symbolism of Ge sar. Paul devotes a chapter to Ge sar, and suggests that he would have liked to do more if he had had the space (1982:244). The results are disappointing, however, because Paul's main interest in the epic, as in other Tibetan cultural material, is as a source of more variations on his primal scenario of order figures, usurpers, avengers and innocent heirs, an expanded (though largely defeminised) Oedipus complex (cf. Samuel 1983).

A typical piece of Paul's analysis is his treatment of Ge sar's killing of kLu btsan, the demonic king of the North. Ge sar gains the support of kLu btsan's wife, who hides him in a pit from which he emerges to kill the demon king. 'Like Milarepa's mother', Paul comments, 'Dumo becomes the hero's ally in carrying out an act of symbolic patricide.' (Paul 1982:255) However, the parallel with Mi la ras pa is not complete:

> The pattern of emerging from the maternal womb to kill the father should be contrasted with the behaviour of Milarepa, who did not emerge from the 'womb', but spent his life in a cave with his mother's bones and his female relatives for disciples. This is the difference between a saint and a hero: Milarepa never killed his father, while Gesar did little else. [Paul 1982:255]

This kind of argument is likely to strike Tibetanists who do not share Paul's highly abstract Freudian perspective as nearly meaningless. Yet the suggested comparison between Ge sar and Mi la ras pa is not as bizarre as it may at first seem (cf. Samuel 1988). I think that there is in fact considerable mileage to be gained from seeing Ge sar as one of a range of symbolic figures, alongside the likes of Mi la ras pa, Mar pa, Padmasambhava, Tsong kha pa, and even perhaps 'Brug pa Kun legs or A khu ston pa, and exploring the contrasts and similarities among the set.

The reductionism of Paul's account nevertheless poses serious problems, as does its distance from the Tibetans' own vocabulary and symbolism. Paul is less interested in deciphering Tibetan roles than in using Tibetan material to exemplify his pancultural Freudian model. Consequently, he is unable or unwilling to consider, for example, what the precise nature of Ge sar's authority might be. For Paul, kingship is a pre-given, almost Platonic idea, grounded in his Freudian primal scenario, and the only question appears to be how well that idea is expressed in any particular body of cultural symbolism (cf. 1982:17, 36).

It would be unfair to criticise Paul for not doing what he clearly did not set out to do, but such an inflexible view of kingship is particularly inappropriate to Tibetan societies. As I have argued elsewhere, political centralisation has existed to only a limited degree in the course of Tibetan history (Samuel 1982). At most periods of Tibetan history, there have been several centres of state control, all limited in the regions over which they exercised authority and in the degree of authority they exercised within those regions. Much of the Tibetan population lay outside the effective authority of any of these regimes.

The Tibetans were, in anthropological terms, closer to the Kachin of Highland Burma, oscillating between egalitarian and hierarchical social formations (Leach 1970), than to the centralised 'galactic polities' of Southeast Asia (Tambiah 1976) or South Asia (cf. Seneviratne 1987:154; Tambiah 1987:200-01). The large estates of Central Tibet were one extreme, whether or not we choose to describe their tenants as 'serfs' (cf. Goldstein 1986). These estates undoubtedly formed part of a hierarchical polity, although the actual degree of centralisation is often exaggerated (cf. Samuel 1982, Goldstein 1971). At the other extreme, nomadic pastoralists such as the 'Go log of East Tibet formed self-governing tribal societies, and remote agricultural villages such as those of the Sherpas or the people of Dol po paid no more than nominal respect to representatives of centralised political authority.

Thus Tibetan political forms included both stateless and centralised elements, and both hierarchical and egalitarian emphases. This would suggest that the question of political authority in the epic may be both complex and well worth a careful examination. The analysis presented in the next section is preliminary, but indicates the lines along which further research might be directed.

Political Authority in the Epic

My approach to the question of political authority in the epic was in part suggested by some comments by the noted Soviet scholar Victor Zhirmunsky, speaking of another Central (and West) Asian epic tradition, that of Köroglu (Gorogli). Zhirmunsky notes how 'each of the national versions of the tale has its own character which reflects the historically determined social structure, the psychology and the social ideas of the peoples who have created it' (Chadwick and Zhirmunsky 1969:303-4). Köroglu in Azerbaijan is

> a 'noble bandit' of the Robin Hood type. Expelled from feudal society, he wages a partisan war against that society, against the khans, beys and pashas, he robs merchant caravans on the highways, performs feats of bravery on his marvellous horse Girat, penetrates in disguise to the enemy camp, and carries off beautiful young girls whom he has seduced by his songs or by his glorious exploits. In the people's opinion the djigit Köroglu is not a bandit or robber, but a brave fighter against the mighty, the rich, the powerful, and, at the same time, the protector of the unfortunate people [Chadwick and Zhirmunsky 1969:301].

By contrast, in the Uzbek version of the Köroglu epic, the hero, known as Gorogli,

> is not a 'noble bandit', but the Bek of the Turkmens and Uzbeks, of noble birth, ruler of the city and the land of Chambil, similar to the famous rulers of epic provenance - Charlemagne, King Arthur, Prince Vladimir of Kiev, the Kirghiz Manas or the Kalmuck Jangar. He is a wise and powerful sovereign and epic hero as well, the protector of his people against foreign invaders, alien khans and beks. In accordance with the democratic character of the tale, the figure of Gorogli becomes the embodiment of the popular ideal of patriarchal authority looking after the good of the people and in particular after the oppressed and unfortunate, while the legendary 'Age of Gorogli' and his state Chambil come to resemble a popular Utopia - a land where under the authority of a wise ruler the eternal popular dream of social justice comes true [Chadwick and Zhirmunsky 1969:302-3].

Ge sar of gLing in the Tibetan tradition is not quite the 'noble bandit' Zhirmunsky describes for the Azerbaijani epic. Yet he fits rather uneasily into the role of Uzbek Gorogli, or for that matter into the mould of the archetypal 'just king' of India with whom the Tibetans occasionally compare him, Rāma.

This is not especially surprising, since the epic is associated particularly with the East and Northeast Tibetan regions of Khams and A mdo where centralised authority was least in evidence. The descriptions of society in the epic are reminiscent of pastoralist tribes such as those described in Robert Ekvall's ethnographies and novels of A mdo in the 1930s (1939, 1952, 1954, 1968, 1981). The people described by Ekvall had tribal chieftains or headmen, referred to sometimes as *rgyal po*, the usual Tibetan word for 'king', and sometimes by other terms (e.g. *'go ba*). They were far from what we might normally understand by 'kingdoms', however. As Ekvall notes:

> If war is determined, levies on the economic resources are voted or decided upon by the *rgan po* ['elders'] and the *'go ba* ['chief']. If peace is made, all share in bearing the expenses of conference and treaty-making. The chief or leader derives no direct material benefit from his position except as position and influence give him unusual opportunity to amass wealth. There is no such thing as a standing army nor are there any paid public officials. Even the individuals required to handle affairs for the chief or ruler act as his personal retainers, and he may either pay them, or what is more likely, place in their way opportunities to profit in trade or war [Ekvall 1939:70].

This is the kind of social context which the epic, for the most part, would seem to imply, and it is far distant from the centralised states of South, Southeast or East Asia, or even the Dalai Lama's administration at Lhasa.

Tibetan society as described in the epic is a society of nomadic pastoralists much more than of settled agriculturalists, although A mdo and particularly Khams society include substantial populations of agriculturalists. The other surrounding societies against whom Ge sar and his followers fight are more mixed. They tend to be assimilated in descriptions to the model of the pastoralist tribe, but there is usually a central fortress (*rdzong*) whose capture, along with the death of its ruler, marks the climax of the episode. In reality, many of these societies were more or less centralised agriculturally-based states (e.g. China, Iran, Kashmir).

After capturing the fortress, the army of gLing returns home with booty from the conquest, such as medicinal herbs, magic jewels, cattle and magical treasures (David-Neel and Yongden 1933:128, 249, 275). The defeated 'tribe' does not, however, become incorporated into a centralised gLing state. Frequently, Ge sar confirms the dead king's son or minister as the new ruler. The tribe then becomes an ally of gLing, and the new king and his followers fight alongside the people of gLing in subsequent wars. Thus in the Kha che g.Yu rdzong episode, we find the people of the demon-realm of the North, of Hor, 'Jang, A grags, Sog po and Bye ri fighting alongside the people of gLing to defeat the Kashmiri invasion (Kaschewsky and Tsering 1972:367).

The epic undoubtedly contains elements referring to a more centralised and hierarchical conception of kingship. Indian concepts such as that of the *cakravartin* or 'universal ruler', and the more specifically Buddhist idea of the *dharmarāja* or 'just king', were well known in Tibet (cf. Tambiah 1976). These concepts, particularly that of the *dharmarāja* or *chos rgyal*, were adopted to some degree by the later Tibetan kings of the Yar klungs dynasty (7th to 9th centuries A.D.). Subsequently they formed part of the State ideology of Central Tibetan rulers such as Byang chub rGyal mtshan (14th century) and his successors, as of the Dalai Lamas from the 17th century onwards. It might be anticipated that they would have had some influence on the conception of kingship in the epic.

This is particularly to be expected, since we know that the story of Ge sar was used as a mythical charter for the principality of gLing tshang in Khams. gLing tshang at its height, in the 14th or 15th century, encompassed a large part of East Tibet (Khams), including most of the area which was later incorporated into the principality of sDe dge (cf. Uray 1985:542-3). Like other Tibetan states, it would doubtless have acquired some of the features of the more centralised Asian states, including a permanent bureaucracy, elaborate court ceremonial centred around the ruler's person, and elements of the *dharmarāja* and *cakravartin* ideology. It would certainly make sense for the ruling circles of gLing to visualise Ge sar as ruler of a centralised state, rather than as chieftain of a coalition of mostly nomadic tribes.

There are some signs of the *cakravartin* and *dharmarāja* concepts in the epic. The *rTa rgyugs* episode in the version produced at gLing is structured around the scheme of the seven jewels of the *cakravartin* (*cakra*, queen, horse, etc.), although its application to the story has an arbitrary air. What is striking, on the whole, is the extent to which Ge sar does not appear in this way, even in songs, such as the last three songs of the *rTa rgyugs*, which describe Ge sar's future role as ruler of gLing (Helffer 1977:347-371).

I am not suggesting that Ge sar is not seen as a Buddhist ruler - his activities are constantly referred back to the Buddhist teachings. He is an emanation of Padmasambhava, sent to earth to liberate the Tibetans from hostile forces. However, there is more than one way to be a Buddhist ruler, and my suggestion is that Ge sar's way is only to a very limited extent that of the *dharmarāja*, the just ruler at the exemplary centre of the 'galactic polity'.

The difference becomes apparent when Ge sar is compared with the historical Kings Srong btsan sGam po and Khri srong lDe'u btsan, who became the classic *dharmarāja* figures of the later Tibetan tradition. These kings lived in the early 7th and later 8th centuries. Their fame in the later tradition is connected with their role in the introduction of Buddhism, and this led to their being viewed as emanations of Avalokiteśvara and other *bodhisattvas.* Technically they are regarded as early members of the same rebirth-sequence as the Dalai Lamas, which goes back to the original monkey-ancestor of the Tibetan people (e.g. Lange 1969). As an ideological statement, this says more about the political role of the Dalai Lamas from the 17th century onwards than about the religious role of the early kings. Srong btsan sGam po and Khri srong lDe'u btsan are conceived of in Tibetan historical writings and legends as patrons of Buddhism and as just rulers according to Buddhist principles, and only secondarily as Buddhist teachers or Tantric practitioners.

This is particularly noticeable in the case of Khri srong lDe'u btsan, who was a contemporary of Padmasambhava, the great Tantric guru of whom Ge sar is held to be an emanation. In this connection, we may consider the well-known episode in Padmasambhava's legendary biography which narrates the first meeting of guru and king: on arriving at the court, Padmasambhava refuses to prostrate himself before the king; and overcome by Padmasambhava's power, the king and the entire court instead prostrate before the guru (Douglas and Bays 1978 II, 376-383).

It is, I think, significant that it is Padmasambhava's shamanic power which forces the king to prostrate before him. Had the king done so voluntarily, we would have a simple statement of the higher value attached to the Buddha than to mere worldly authority. What is in fact being said is rather different: it is that the shamanic power of the guru is greater than the secular power of the king. Khri srong lDe'u btsan subsequently became one of Padmasambhava's disciples, but the relationship between them remains essentially that of lay patron and Tantric guru.

Ge sar, by contrast, is an emanation of Padmasambhava, not a disciple; and still less a lay patron. He is, indeed, as much a Tantric guru - a lama, that is - as a king. He is frequently described as exercising power through Tantric ritual, and even as giving Tantric empowerments. He wields shamanic power in his own right, as a representative of Padmasambhava. It is the shamanic nature of the power which Ge sar exercises that marks him off most clearly from a *dharmarāja* such as Khri srong lDe'u btsan or Srong btsan sGam po. In the following section the shamanic aspects of the figure of Ge sar are examined in more detail.

The Shamanic Nature of Ge sar's Power

To begin with, it is noticeable that Ge sar has much of the shamanic trickster about him. His victories often come about more through magical illusion and outright deceit than through superior military might or through the moral authority of a legitimate *dharmarāja.*

Kaschewsky and Tsering, in the introduction to their edition of Part I of the *Kha che g.Yu rdzong*, note the absence in the epic of the kind of morality we might expect from the 'just king':

> The basic principle is to seek one's own advantage by any means available. Whether the opponent is led astray by deception, whether treachery is exploited or the other's weakness brutally made use of, scruples or any qualms of conscience are entirely lacking. If there is a basic idea that runs through the whole work it is the principle that might is right [1972:276; my translation].[1]

There is no doubt that Ge sar in the epic constantly tricks his enemies through disguises, deceptions and false prophecies, and that he shamelessly exploits their personal weaknesses. However, the matter is not so simple. In this passage, Kaschewsky and Tsering follow the tendency of Stein and others to see Ge sar as an essentially secular epic story upon which a layer of Buddhist meaning (which they go on to detail) has been imposed. The amoral behaviour of Ge sar and his associates then simply represents the attitudes of Tibetans before the more or less successful impact of Buddhism and its ethical code.

This style of analysis is tempting in part because it contains at least a grain of truth. Many plot-elements in the epic can be found in other Asian epic traditions, and doubtless they do go back in some sense to pre-Buddhist times. However, I think it is profoundly misleading to treat the Ge sar epic as simply pre-Buddhist material reworked by the lamas. Buddhism in Tibet is not imposed upon a fundamentally alien basis. It has adapted and transformed what may have been the indigenous conceptions of Tibetans in pre-Buddhist times. For Tibetans today, Ge sar cannot be a Buddhist gloss on an intrinsically anti-Buddhist hero. He is experienced as a whole, and our problem is to find out what that whole means. What can Ge sar's trickery and deviousness mean in Buddhist terms?

One Tibetan lama who has been particularly connected with Ge sar and has written on the epic is the rNying ma pa lama Tarthang Tulku, now living in Berkeley:

> ...many teachings are embedded in the stories. The external obstacles that Gesar faces are seen as outward symbols of the inner struggle for self-perfection and spiritual growth. The manner in which Gesar overcomes these obstructions is an inspiring record that can encourage our own self-confidence and awareness.
>
> King Gesar embodies a unique kind of energy, one that is open and responsive, never stuck or frozen into set patterns. He is conscious of every moment, aware through every sense, so that each of his actions is permeated with a light and positive quality. Then a situation does not implode, turning in on itself to create difficulties; instead it flows directly towards a particular goal. [...]
>
> Interpreted symbolically, King Gesar, representing freedom and liberation from the bondage of ignorance, is the King of the human mind. The Kingdom of Ling is the realm of restless experience that must be unified and strengthened. The treasure to win and protect is our own understanding. The enemies that we must conquer are emotionality and ignorance. Once these are overcome, the path of liberation is in sight, and our lives and our struggle for survival take on the character of a quest of ever-widening and enriching experience [1978:20-22].

Tarthang's mode of expression here undoubtedly owes much to its Californian context and forms part of his continuing work of conveying rNying ma pa Buddhism to a Western following. His interpretation should nevertheless be treated seriously. It may be noted that the interpretation of an epic narrative in terms of internal psychological processes has parallels elsewhere in Hindu-Buddhist Asia, for example in the *wayang kulit* of Java (e.g. Keeler 1987). Similarly, Radin's classic interpretation of North American Indian trickster narratives also points towards the plausibility of an internal psychological reading of such stories (Radin 1955).

Such a 'psychological' reading does not, however, exclude the possibility of a 'sociological' reading in which Ge sar's 'unique kind of energy, [...] open and responsive, never stuck or frozen into set patterns' becomes a style of political leadership. In fact, it may be taken to imply such a reading, since the ideal personality postulated by the epic is also that of the ideal political leader. Ge sar is undoubtedly a political figure. However, such a style of leadership is clearly not that of the ruler of a centralised state, who owes his power precisely to the existence of the 'set patterns' of authority.

The kind of energy which Tarthang is referring to is in fact that of the shaman, recast in Buddhist terms; in other words, of the Tantric lama. Here as elsewhere the shamanic nature of the Tibetan Vajrayāna emerges most clearly in rNying ma pa sources, where there is less effort to incorporate it in the rational and clerical Buddhism of the later Indian Mahāyāna tradition (cf. Samuel 1993).

The shamanic nature of Ge sar's power could be further exemplified by a detailed examination of Ge sar's behaviour in the epic. Rather than undertaking this here, I shall move on to consider the general Tibetan value-system which provides the context for Ge sar's shamanic leadership.

Tibetan Values: The Wild, the Tame and the Tamer

Christoph von Fürer-Haimendorf's early writings on the Sherpas (1962, 1964, 1967) provided the first anthropological study of a Tibetan value system. Fürer-Haimendorf portrayed Sherpa society as pervaded by a single value system deriving from the Buddhist concept of merit or virtuous action (*bsod nams* = Skt. *puṇya*). Sherpa Tibetans, like other Buddhists (e.g. Tambiah 1968), attempted to maintain a surplus of virtuous over non-virtuous actions in order to achieve a happy rebirth, or at least to avoid an unfortunate one. The system derives from the widespread South and Southeast Asian ideology of a series of rebirths linked by *karma*, in which action in one life has consequences for subsequent rebirths.

Subsequent analyses have shown that this picture is too simple. David Lichter and Laurence Epstein (1983) note that Tibetan belief in karma coexists, as we find in other Asian Buddhist societies, with the pursuit of worldly success and happiness, often by interaction with the local gods and spirits. If Tibetans are concerned about their personal stock of *bsod nams* ('merit') they are also concerned about the state of their *rlung rta* or (this-worldly) good fortune. Much of the ritual carried out by lamas (and to a lesser degree monks) for the Tibetan laity is to do with good fortune and protection from misfortune within one's present lifetime. According to Lichter and Epstein, most Tibetans try to achieve worldly success while maintaining a 'slightly ironic detachment' from a happiness which they know that they cannot ultimately hold on to (1983:257).

The writings of Barbara Aziz (e.g. 1981) and Nancy Levine (e.g. 1981) also point to a complex relationship between the normative precepts of the laws of karma and the everyday life of Tibetans. Tibetan Buddhist teachings themselves describe fear of an unfortunate rebirth and desire for happiness in future lives as the mark of a beginning practitioner. At a later stage, it is to be transcended by the desire for liberation from worldly existence, which is itself to be superseded by the *bodhisattva's* desire to attain buddhahood in order to relieve the sufferings of other beings (e.g. Berzin 1972).

A *bodhisattva* may, if necessary, act in ways contrary to the normal rules for virtuous action, while a fully enlightened being is beyond the laws of karma. These ideas are worth bearing in mind in relation to Ge sar, since they provide one line of justification for Ge sar's more devious activities, as for those of other trickster-figures such as 'Brug pa Kun legs (Stein 1972, Dowman and Paljor 1980) or even A khu sTon pa (Dorje 1975).

Elsewhere, drawing in part on the work of Robert Ekvall (1968:92-3) and Sophie Day (1986), I have suggested that the Tibetan opposition between 'wild' (*rgod po*) and 'tame' (*dul ba*) provides an indigenous way of viewing this variety of orientations (1993, chapter 11). The contrast between 'wild' and 'tame' has many ramifications within Tibetan culture, but I note in particular that 'wildness' is associated with the nomads and the pastoral life-style (and with the East Tibetan regions of Khams and A mdo) and 'tameness' both with agriculture and with Buddhism, particularly celibate monasticism (and with Central Tibet).[2] In fact the Tibetan for *Vinaya*, the disciplinary code of the monks, is *'Dul ba*, a term derived from the verbal form of 'tame'.

The opposition between 'wild' and 'tame' implies a process of 'taming', which is the work of the lama and of figures associated with Buddhism in general. The lama tames both malevolent demons and hostile forces (as in the legends of Padmasambhava) and he also tames his disciples. Here it should be remembered that the lama or guru is conceived of as 'internal' as well as 'external' to the practitioner (Guenther 1977). The external guru is ultimately only an aid to the practitioner's subduing of his or her own undisciplined thoughts and emotions. External and internal gurus, *sūtra* and *tantra* teachings, monastic vows and lay yogic practice, settled or wandering existence, all provide dimensions along which the taming process may vary.

At one ('tame') extreme can be found the process of training in the vast dGe lugs pa monasteries of Central and East Tibet, with a heavy emphasis on monastic discipline as the foundation of the path, and a scholastic curriculum lasting up to twenty years preceding serious Tantric practice. At the other ('wild') extreme the wandering yogi of the rNying ma pa or bKa' brgyud pa traditions may travel from teacher to teacher, and pursue long periods of solitary meditation. Such a yogi follows his or her own path towards enlightenment, with the external guru providing constant inspiration but only intermittent guidance.

This continuum of possibilities is closely related to the opposition I have elsewhere drawn between 'clerical' and 'shamanic' aspects of Tibetan religion. There is little doubt that secular authority in Tibet as elsewhere has preferred the 'tame' to the 'wild', disciplined and celibate monks to autonomous Tantric practitioners, although the weakness of secular authority through most of Tibetan history has meant that the non-monastic tradition has survived and, in some measure, prospered (cf. Samuel 1993).

In fact, even the dGe lugs pa tradition accepts that the attainment of enlightenment in the Vajrayāna is incompatible with the strict maintenance of the *Vinaya* (cf. Lessing and Wayman 1968:37-39). For Tibetans, monastic discipline is something one takes on, ideally at least, as part of a training which will eventually lead beyond the need for such discipline. The ultimate objective of the Vajrayāna is not to be disciplined but to be beyond discipline, however far such an objective might be from the daily reality of the life of a junior monk in a large Tibetan monastery.

It is this which opens the way for a reconciliation between the centralised and stateless poles of Tibetan society. Whatever tradition they belong to, all practitioners aim at eventually achieving the transcendent freedom from all dualities and restrictions which is implied by buddhahood. Thus the lama is not just the 'tamer', but a figure who in his own person reconciles the opposition between 'wild' and 'tame'. Symbolically, we find lama-figures in Tibetan thought who emphasise the 'tame' end of this opposition (Atīśa, Tsong khapa, the 7th Dalai Lama) and others who emphasise the 'wild' aspects (Mi la ras pa, gTsang smyon, 'Brug pa Kun legs, the 6th Dalai Lama).

If we return now to the figure of Ge sar, it may be noted that Tarthang's interpretation makes Ge sar into an image of precisely the kind of free and creative activity beyond all rules discussed above (the 'unique kind of energy, [...] open and responsive, never stuck or frozen into set patterns'). Ge sar is also pre-eminently a 'tamer', both of demons and hostile forces in general (*dgra 'dul*), and of men. As I have already suggested, Ge sar is only to a limited degree a figure of centralised authority. He is at least as much a figure of shamanic power, as is indicated by his close links with Padmasambhava. Ge sar's secular power is almost incidental to his shamanic role as a tamer of demonic forces. These demonic forces, we might note, are personified as kings, and characterised by their attachment to power over others.

This implies that in the epic, as ideally within the 'untamed' regions of East Tibet in which Ge sar's activity is centred, the role of shamanic power is not to *create* a state so much as to maintain freedom from the state. Ge sar's wars are wars of defence against hostile powers who desire to subdue and defeat the people of gLing. Frequently these powers are identified as explicitly anti-Buddhist (*mu stegs pa* or *bon*) in their religious allegiance (cf. Samuel 1991). While hostile powers tend in the epic to be assimilated to the nomadic model, their fortresses (*rdzong*) are potential centres of state power, and their defeat by Ge sar represents a successful struggle against the state.

In other words, the open and creative energy of Ge sar is specifically aimed against the development of hierarchical institutions and state power. This suggests that we might view Ge sar, cross-culturally, in the context of the arguments of Pierre Clastres, Gilles Deleuze and Félix Guattari about social mechanisms which inhibit the growth of state power. This is the theme of the final section of this paper.

Ge sar: Shamanic Warrior Against the State?

Pierre Clastres' ideas were first developed in the context of Amazonian Indian societies (cf. Clastres 1977). Their originality lay in two main features. First, as against a whole academic tradition of studying the state which still regarded stateless societies as being essentially societies where the state had not yet developed, Clastres viewed stateless societies as actively resisting the development of state organisation. As Deleuze and Guattari later observed, this meant that states and stateless societies should be seen as having developed alongside each other, with the state always implying an 'outside' to be incorporated (1987:360).

Second, Clastres analysed modes of traditional leadership within stateless societies not as incipient aspects of the state but as mechanisms which actively inhibited the formation of the state. Thus the process by which leaders and big men in Amazonian society were forced to validate their position by generosity to their followers prevented the accumulation of an economic surplus by particular individuals (an argument first presented by Marcel Mauss in relation to the potlatch), while the constant displays of fighting prowess required to maintain a reputation as a warrior led inevitably to the warrior's death and removal as a possible agent of political domination. Clastres also analyses processes of initiation in Amazonian societies as designed to impose a sense of equality upon those who undergo them.

These processes have obvious analogues, particularly among Tibetan pastoralist society. Generosity is a feature of leadership in East Tibet as in the Amazon, and few families of 'big men' maintain a significant economic disparity over their fellows for more than a generation or two, especially in the less centralised parts of Tibet. The norms of generosity to the Buddhist clergy here complement the display of generosity expected to the leader's lay following. In fact 'big men' in Tibet notoriously make large donations to lamas and temples as a way of counteracting the non-virtuous actions involved in their rise to power. While such donations may lead to the acquisition of power by lamas and monasteries, there is little doubt that they have inhibited the growth of the purely secular power of a hereditary aristocracy.

Other features reminiscent of Clastres' argument might be identified, such as the expectation, clearly expressed in the epic, that a 'big man' should constantly augment his reputation through raiding and fighting. The career of mGon po rNam gyal of Nyag rong in the mid-19th century is one of the most spectacular examples of this process (T. Tsering 1985). This local chieftain of Nyag rong in southern Khams conquered and terrorised most of East Tibet, eventually provoking a confrontation with the Lhasa regime which lead to his death. Nyag rong is incidentally one of the regions where the Ge sar epic is most popular. A modern Nyag rong author cites the proverb:

The stories of Milarepa may make
A rich man's son into a saint.
But the Epics of Gesar will surely
Impale the beggar boy on a sword (Norbu 1986:19).

An argument might also be presented for the equalising effect of Tantric initiation. Rather, however, than focusing on specific mechanisms of this kind, I should like to return to the central topic of this paper, the figure of Ge sar of gLing, and to place him in relationship to Gilles Deleuze and Félix Guattari's more general development of the work of Clastres.

Deleuze and Guattari were acquainted with Clastres' earlier work when they wrote their first joint undertaking, *Anti-Oedipus* ([1972] 1985), and it is not surprising that they took up his ideas on stateless societies with enthusiasm in its sequel, *A Thousand Plateaus* ([1980] 1987). *Anti-Oedipus* is an attack not merely on Freud's theory of the Oedipus complex but on all of the ways in which prevailing modes of thinking assume the inevitability of the state and of hierarchical power. Here Deleuze and Guattari already point to the small-scale preliterate society (the 'savage territorial machine', in their terminology) as not providing the appropriate terrain for the growth of that noxious weed Oedipus (1985:166).

Clastres' later work enabled them to go much further, and his ideas harmonise well with the non-hierarchical, 'rhizomatic' orientation of *A Thousand Plateaus.* Deleuze had already written in praise of 'nomad thought', meaning thought outside and subversive of the categories of established academic thinking; Nietzsche serves as the great exemplar (Deleuze [1973] 1985). In *A Thousand Plateaus* he and Guattari extended this idea into the concept of the nomadic 'war machine' (1987:351-423).

Historical nomads such as the Huns or the Mongols form a central image, with their capacity to destroy the hierarchical structure of the state and re-establish a smooth social universe. However, Deleuze and Guattari are less interested in nomads or in war as such than in the anti-hierarchical moment of the 'war machine', which can be expressed in all kinds of social and intellectual movements, with or without actual physical conflict, and in particular in 'nomadic', anti-State, science.

It is perhaps not going too far to assimilate the Tibetan Vajrayāna as exemplified by a figure such as Ge sar to this concept of 'nomadic science'. Nomadic science, as Deleuze and Guattari note (1987:362), is constantly subject to appropriation and transformation by State science, a process all too familiar in the history of Buddhism, as in that of other religious traditions. Whether because of the special circumstances of Tibet's political and economic history or for some other reason, that appropriation remained far from complete in Tibet. Perhaps it would be more true to say that the already-appropriated nomadic science of the Indian Vajrayāna was reclaimed in Tibet as a weapon against the State.

At any rate, Ge sar and the Vajrayāna continue to present to the Tibetans a way of being, and a form of social and political activity, capable of flowing around and beyond any kind of hierarchical structure. In a world where life is increasingly dominated by bureaucratic control, that ideal may continue to have an appeal to Tibetans and to other peoples.

References

AZIZ, Barbara N. 1981. 'Jural Friends and Buddhist Teachers.' In Mayer 1981:1-22.

AZIZ, Barbara and Matthew Kapstein (ed.) 1985. *Soundings in Tibetan Civilization.* Manohar, Delhi.

BERZIN, Alexander. 1972. 'Lam.rim.man.ngag. A standard intermediate level textbook of the graded course to enlightenment.' Typescript. [Pp.1-436 only = Ph.D. dissertation, Harvard University 1972.]

CHADWICK, Nora K. and ZHIRMUNSKY, Victor. 1969. *Oral Epics of Central Asia.* Cambridge, University Press.

CLASTRES, Pierre. 1977. *Society against the State.* New York, Urizen.

DAMDINSÜREN, Ts. 1985. 'On the New Edition of the Mongolian Version "Geseriada".' In Heissig 1985, 593-9.

DAVID-NEEL, Alexandra and the Lama YONGDEN. 1933. *The Superhuman Life of Gesar of Ling, the Legendary Tibetan Hero, as Sung by the Bards of his Country.* London, Rider.

DAY, Sophie. 1986. 'Abbot, Oracle and Witch in Ladakh.' Paper for LSE seminar.

DELEUZE, Gilles and Félix GUATTARI. 1985. *Anti-Oedipus. [Capitalism and Schizophrenia, vol.1].* London, Athlone Press.

DELEUZE, Gilles. 1985. 'Nomad Thought.' In David B. Allison (ed), *The New Nietzsche.* Cambridge, Mass., MIT Press, pp.142-9.

DELEUZE, Gilles and Félix GUATTARI. 1987. *A Thousand Plateaus. [Capitalism and Schizophrenia, vol.2].* Minneapolis, University of Minnesota Press.

DORJE, Rinjing. 1975. *Tales of Uncle Tompa: The Legendary Rascal of Tibet.* San Rafael, Dorje gLing.

DOUGLAS, Kenneth and Gwendolyn BAYS (trans.). 1978. *The Life and Liberation of Padmasambhava.* Emeryville, Cal.: Dharma.

DOWMAN, Keith and Sonam PALJOR (trans.). 1980. *The Divine Madman: The Sublime Life and Songs of Drukpa Kunley.* London, Rider.

DOWMAN, Keith (trans.). 1984. *Sky Dancer: The Secret Life and Songs of the Lady Yeshe Tsogyel.* London, Routledge and Kegan Paul.

EKVALL, Robert B. 1939. *Cultural Relations on the Kansu-Tibetan Border.* Chicago, University of Chicago Press.

EKVALL, Robert B. 1952. *Tibetan Skylines.* New York, Farrar, Straus and Young.

EKVALL, Robert B. 1954. *Tents Against the Sky: A Novel of Tibet.* London, Victor Gollancz.

EKVALL, Robert B. 1968. *Fields on the Hoof: Nexus of Tibetan Nomadic Pastoralism*. Holt, Rinehart and Winston.

EKVALL, Robert B. 1981. *The Lama Knows*. Novato, Cal., Chandler and Sharp.

FRANCKE, A.H. 1900 'Der Frühlingsmythus der Kesar Saga'; 'Der Wintermythus der Kesar Saga', *Mémoires de la Société Finno-Ougrienne*, 15, Helsinki

FRANCKE, A.H. 1901-2 'The Spring Myth of the Kesar Saga', *Indian Antiquary*, 30 (1901), 329-341 and 31 (1902), 32-40, 147-157 [Reprinted in Tobgyel and Dorje 1979, 29]

FRANCKE, A.H. 1905-9 'A Lower Ladakhi Version of the Gesar Saga', *Bibliotheca Indica*, 1134, 1150, 1164, 1218 [Reprinted in Tobgyel and Dorje 1979, 29]

FÜRER-HAIMENDORF, Christoph von. 1962. 'Moral Concepts in Three Himalayan Societies.' In T.N. Madan and Gopala Sarana (ed), *Indian Anthropology*, Bombay, pp.279-309.

FÜRER-HAIMENDORF, Christoph von. 1964. *The Sherpas of Nepal: Buddhist Highlanders*. London, John Murray.

FÜRER-HAIMENDORF, Christoph von. 1967. *Morals and Merit*. London, Weidenfeld and Nicolson.

GOLDSTEIN, Melvyn C. 1971. 'The Balance between Centralization and Decentralization in the Traditional Tibetan Political System.' *Central Asiatic Journal* 15:170-182.

GOLDSTEIN, Melvyn C. 1986. 'Reexamining Choice, Dependency and Command in the Tibetan Social System: "Tax Appendages" and Other Landless Serfs." *Tibet Journal* 11,4:79-112.

GUENTHER, Herbert V. 1977. 'The Spiritual Teacher in Tibet.' In Guenther, *Tibetan Buddhism in Western Perspective*, Emeryville, Cal., Dharma Publishing, 178-195.

HAMAYON, Roberte. 1982. 'Tricks and Turns of Legitimate Pepetuation (continued)' in Heissig 1982, pp.1-15.

HEISSIG, Walther (ed). 1982. *Fragen der mongolischen Heldendichtung. Teil II*. Wiesbaden, Otto Harrassowitz. (Asiatische Forschungen, 73.)

HEISSIG, Walther. 1983. *Geser-Studien. Untersuchungen zu den Erzählstoffen in den "neuen" Kapiteln des mongolischen Geser-Zyklus*. Westdeutscher Verlag, Opladen. (Abhandlungen der Rheinisch-Westfälischen Akademie der Wissenschaften, 69)

HEISSIG, Walther (ed). 1985. *Fragen der mongolischen Heldendichtung. Teil III*. Wiesbaden, Otto Harrassowitz. (Asiatische Forschungen, 91.)

HEISSIG, Walther (ed). 1987. *Fragen der mongolischen Heldendichtung. Teil IV*. Wiesbaden, Otto Harrassowitz. (Asiatische Forschungen, 101.)

HELFFER, Mireille. 1977 *Les chants dans l'épopée tibétaine de Gesar d'après le livre de la Course de Cheval. Version chantée de Blo-bzaṅ bstan-'jin.* Paris and Geneva, Librairie Droz.

HERMANNS, Matthias. 1965 *Das National-Epos der Tibeter Gling König Ge sar.* Regensburg, Verlag Josef Habbel.

HERRMANN, Silke. 1987. 'Stand der Epenforschung in West-Tibet.' In Heissig 1987, 406-17.

JÄSCHKE, H.A. [1881] 1968. *A Tibetan-English Dictionary with Special Reference to the Prevailing Dialects.* London, Routledge and Kegan Paul.

KASCHEWSKY, Rudolf and Pema TSERING. 1972. 'Gesars Anwehrkampf gegen Kaschmir.' *Zentralasiatische Studien* 6, 273-400.

KASCHEWSKY, Rudolf and Pema TSERING. 1987A. *Die Eroberung der Burg von Sum-pa.* Aus dem tibetischen Gesar-Epos. Herausgegeben und übersetzt.. 2 vls. Wiesbaden, Otto Harrassowitz. (Asiatische Forschungen, 94)

KASCHEWSKY, Rudolf and Pema TSERING. 1987B. 'Zur Frage der Historizität des Helden Gesar.' In Heissig 1987, 390-405.

KEELER, Ward. 1987. *Javanese Shadow Plays, Javanese Selves.* Princeton University Press.

LANGE, K. 1969. 'Über die Präexistenzen der Dalai-Lamas. Versuch einer kritischen Analyse tibetisch-buddhistische Quellen.' *Jahrbuch des Museums für Völkerkunde, Leipzig* 26:205-228.

LEACH, Edmund R. 1970. *Political Systems of Highland Burma.* London, Athlone Press.

LESSING, Ferdinand D. and Alex WAYMAN (trans.) 1968. *Mkhas grub rje's Fundamentals of the Buddhist Tantras.* The Hague and Paris, Mouton. (Indo-Iranian Monographs, 8.)

LEVINE, Nancy E. 1981. 'Perspectives on Love: Morality and Affect in Nyinba Interpersonal Relationships.' In Mayer 1981:106-125.

LICHTER, David and Lawrence EPSTEIN. 1983. 'Irony in Tibetan Notions of the Good Life.' In Charles F. Keyes and E. Valentine Daniel (ed), *Karma: An Anthropological Inquiry.* Berkeley, University of California Press, 223-259.

MAYER, Adrian C. 1981. *Culture and Morality: Essays in Honour of Christoph von Fürer-Haimendorf.* Delhi, Oxford University Press.

NORBU, Jamyang. 1986. *Warriors of Tibet.* London, Wisdom.

PAUL, Robert A. 1982 *The Tibetan Symbolic World: Psychoanalytic Explorations.* Chicago, University of Chicago Press.

RADIN, Paul. 1955. *The Trickster: A Study in American Indian Mythology.* London, Routledge and Kegan Paul.

SAMUEL, Geoffrey. 1982. 'Tibet as a Stateless Society and Some Islamic Parallels.' *Journal of Asian Studies* 41,2:215-229.

SAMUEL, Geoffrey. 1983. Review of Paul 1982. *Journal of Asian Studies* 42, 633-4.

SAMUEL, Geoffrey. 1985. 'Early Buddhism in Tibet: Some Anthropological Perspectives.' In Aziz and Kapstein 1986, 383-397.

SAMUEL, Geoffrey. 1989. 'The Body in Buddhist and Hindu Tantra: some notes.' *Religion* 19:197-210.

SAMUEL, Geoffrey. 1991. 'Music and shamanic power in the Gesar Epic.' in *Metaphor: A Musical Dimension.* Sydney, Currency Press.

SAMUEL, Geoffrey. 1993. *Civilized Shamans.* Washington and London, Smithsonian Institution Press.

SAMUEL, Geoffrey. 1990. *Mind, Body and Culture: Anthropology and the Biological Interface.* Cambridge University Press.

SENEVIRATNE, H.L. 1987 'Kingship and Polity in Buddhism and Hinduism', *Contributions to Indian Sociology* N.S. 21,1: 147-56.

STEIN, R.A. (ed. and trans.) 1956. *L'épopée tibétaine de Gesar dans sa version lamaïque de Ling.* Paris, Presses Universitaires de France.

STEIN, R.A. 1959. *Recherches sur l'épopée et le barde au Tibet.* Paris, Presses Universitaires de France. (Bibl. de l'Institut des Hautes Etudes Chinoises, 13.)

STEIN, R.A. (trans.) 1972. *Vie et Chants de 'Brug-pa Kun-legs le Yogin.* Paris, G.-P. Maisonneuve et Larose.

STEIN, R.A. 1979. 'Introduction to the Ge sar Epic' in Tobgyel and Dorji 1979, 1, 1-20. Reprinted in *Tibet Journal* 6,1 (1981), 3-13.

TAMBIAH, Stanley J. 1968 'The Ideology of Merit and the Social Correlates of Buddhism in a Thai Village.' In E.R. Leach (ed), *Dialectic in Practical Religion.* Cambridge University Press.

TAMBIAH, Stanley J. 1976. *World Conqueror and World Renouncer.* A Study of Buddhism and Polity in Thailand against a Historical Background. Cambridge University Press.

TAMBIAH, Stanley J. 1987. 'At the confluence of anthropology, history, and indology.' *Contributions to Indian Sociology* N.S. 21,1: 187-216.

TARTHANG Tulku 1978 'Gesar: Awareness through Myth', *Gesar* 5,2 (Summer 1978), 20-22.

TOBGYEL, Kunzang and Mani DORJI, 1979, *The Epic of Gesar (in 31 vols).* Thimphu, Bhutan: Kunzang Tobgyel.

TSERING, Pema. 1982. 'Neuere Ausgaben des tibetischen Gesar-Epos.' In Heissig 1982, 245-61.

TSERING, Pema. 1985. 'Die Eroberung der Goldburg von mÑa'-ris.' In Heissig 1985, 555-88.

TSERING, Tashi. 1985. 'Ñag-ron mgon-po rnam-rgyal: a 19th century Khams-pa warrior.' In Aziz and Kapstein 1985, 196-214.

TURNER, Victor W. 1968. *The Drums of Affliction: A Study of Religious Processes among the Ndembu of Zambia.* Oxford, Clarendon Press.

URAY, Geza. 1985. 'Vom römischen Kaiser bis zum König Ge-sar von Glin.' In Heissig 1985, 530-48.

WAGNER, Roy. 1978. *Lethal Speech: Daribi Myth as Symbolic Obviation.* Ithaca, Cornell University Press.

WAYMAN, Alex. 1961. 'Totemic beliefs in the Buddhist Tantras.' *History of Religions* 1,1:81-94.

WEBER, Max. 1978. *Economy and Society.* Edited by Guenther Roth and Claus Wittich. Berkeley, University of California Press.

Notes

1. 'Grundprinzip ist, mit allen Mitteln den eigenen Vorteil zu suchen. Ob ein Betrug den anderen irreführt, Verrat aus Opportunismus angewandt wird oder eine Schwäche des anderen brutal ausgenutzt wird, Skrupel oder gar Gewissensbisse fehlen völlig. Wenn es einen Grundgedanken gibt, der das Ganze durchzieht, so ist es das Prinzip, dass der Stärkere Recht hat.' Roberte Hamayon has commented in similar terms on Mongolian epics (1982:2).

2. Cf. the range of meanings given for the verb *'dul ba* in Jäschke's dictionary (1968:278): to tame, to break in (of horses); to till, to cultivate; to educate, to convert, to discipline.

LAMA KNOWS

Religion and Power in Sherpa Society

John Draper

Introduction

IN the first part of this paper, I review the ethnography of religion in South and Southeast Asia, with particular reference to the question of the relation between what Mandelbaum has called 'transcendental' and 'pragmatic' aspects of Asian religion (Mandelbaum, 1966). In the second, I examine the ramifications of a theoretical model of Sherpa religion which I developed in my M.A. thesis: there I asserted a dialectical structural relation between what I referred to, following Mandelbaum and others, as 'transcendental' and 'pragmatic' orientations. Here I explore, on the basis of my subsequent fieldwork, how meaningful such a model is for the Sherpas themselves; what such a model says (or rather, doesn't say) about the distribution of various forms of religious knowledge and power; and what this in its turn says about the relations between tantric, shamanic and orthodox conceptions and practices. I thus focus in particular on exorcism rituals and the various understandings of the nature and function of demons within these rituals. This approach provides a basis to explore more fully – and perhaps less idealistically – the relations of power within Sherpa society as a whole and the way in which religion serves, at least in part, as an instrument of social control.

My central thesis is that the increasing control by the monastic establishment of the means of production and distribution of legitimate spiritual knowledge and power has marked a significant decline in the relative status and power of tantric, married, village based ngapa banzin* ('lamas', cf. Tib. *sngags pa*) and lhawa-minung ('shamans', cf. Tib. *lha pa mig thong*), and has resulted in a widening cleavage between the religious elite as a whole and the laity.

---

* In this article, bold type denotes a Sherpa term for which the editors have been unable to identify a Tibetan orthography with any certainty.

Sherpa religion may not be composed of distinct competing traditions, but neither is it a homogenous static system equally accessible and satisfying to all. To the extent that models of structural interdependence and unity ignore or mask this cleavage and the unequal and changing distribution of knowledge/power which it represents, such models require review.

This is not to say that lay Sherpas have no access to spiritual knowledge and power, that they do not benefit from the presence of monasteries in their communities, or that tantra and shamanism are locked in an inevitably fatal struggle with the orthodox monastic establishment. Nevertheless, my analysis draws attention to the important relation between knowledge and power and, by extension, between religion and society. In so doing, it also draws attention to the nature of the analysis itself and how text-based models which mask relations of knowledge/power as they are experienced in day-to-day life are themselves products of relations of knowledge/power and have potentially powerful consequences.

Models of Religion in South and Southeast Asia

The source of much of the interest in – and confusion about – the relationship between different religious conceptions, practices and practitioners in Southeast and South Asia religions derives, I would suggest, from questions surrounding the existential nature and status of gods and supernaturals within these religions. In particular, the erroneous view that Buddhist doctrine does not allow for a belief in the existence of such supernaturals[1] has led to the portrayal by Durkheim, Weber and others of two separate religions, that of the Buddha and that of the supernaturals, coexisting only because they are fundamentally opposed.[2] This dichotomisation is founded on Tylorean and Frazerian contrasts between magic and religion, as well as on Durkheim's own opposition of the profane and the sacred. It has spawned such perennial models as the 'Great Tradition / Little Tradition' thesis (e.g., Marriott 1955 and Srinivas 1955), as well as the contrast between *nibbānic* and *kammatic* religious structures (e.g., Ames 1964 and Spiro 1971), and betweeen transcendental and pragmatic traditions (e.g., Mandelbaum 1966 and 1970).

Few religious systems exhibit such a rigid separation in practice. What is held 'sacred' in one context may well be – indeed, as I shall argue in the Sherpa case, must be – 'profane' in another, and *vice versa*; and what is transcendental in one context may well be pragmatic in another. While the Sherpa gods (lha), demons (dui, cf. Tib. *bdud*) and supernaturals (shrendi, cf. Tib. *srin bdud*) of various forms may not be considered 'real' at the level of theological formulations of the absolute, they are nevertheless thought of as sharing the same existential status as humans (i.e., they are locked into the same endless cycle of death and rebirth to which all *saṁsāric* phenomena are subject). For the laity at least, consequently, they serve very important functions at the phenomenal level of day-to-day experience and practice. Analyses which focus on the differences between levels of 'reality' rather than the relationships between them often, in practice, assert attitudes and beliefs which are more representative of the religious elite than of ordinary villagers, and ignore the significant variety of such attitudes and beliefs in the community.

The most popular approach in the ethnography of religion in South East Asian Theravādin communities is the identification of two or more traditions within a single religious 'field', but a great diversity of approaches is found within this framework. Spiro (1967, 1971), for example, speaks in terms of a rigid separation in Burma of 'philosophical Buddhism' (the religion of the *virtuosi*) from 'practical religion' (popular religion).[3] He justifies this 'two religions' thesis in three ways. Firstly, attempts to achieve this-worldly goals through the propitiation of *nat* ('spirits') are a denial of karmic law and involve behaviours which contravene the precepts and ethos of pure Buddhism. Secondly, there is a clear separation of practitioners, places of worship, days of worship and modes of worship. Thirdly, the Burmese themselves – or those to whom Spiro talked, at least – see the two religions as distinct.[4] According to Spiro, Buddhism enjoys primacy over the *nat* cults by virtue of its relative purity (i.e., its lack of contamination through involvement with low order *nat*), its access to a literate tradition, its links with political power at both local and state level, and the way in which it is affirmed as ultimately superior through exorcism rituals. As we shall see, a very similar relationship can be posited between the monasteries and the tantric lamas and shamans in Sherpa society.

Yet Spiro's analysis fails to account for a number of problems raised by his own data. How can a devout Burmese monk also be a renowned *weikza* magician? How is the 'opposition' between monk and shaman mediated? How and why is the ascetic *nibbānic* soteriological system reproduced if Burmese have, as Spiro asserts, a psychological need to move towards the more pragmatic and accessible *kammatic* soteriological system?

Spiro's distinction between these two systems is similar in a number of respects to models of Sinhalese Buddhism developed by Ames (1964) and Yalman (1964). In Ames' model, however, there is an important interdependence between Buddhism and what he calls 'magical animism,' the latter providing temporary relief from worldly anxieties, while the former provides more enduring relief from existential anxieties. The two traditions are separate in theory, perhaps, but complementary in function and fused in everyday practice. More importantly, the different orientations which they imply are found within each tradition. My own approach to Sherpa religion has its beginnings in this model, and consequently differs in important ways from Spiro's more rigid 'two religions' thesis.

The ethnography of religion in India appears to be especially influenced by models emphasising dichotomy, particularly the 'Great Tradition / Little Tradition' thesis, which asserts an essential division between, on the one hand, an allegedly universalised, centralised, highly intellectualised philosophical system founded on religious texts and communicated through a specialised religious hierarchy; and, on the other, a more localised, parochial, oral-based and relatively unstructured system of beliefs and practices found more commonly in rural villages.[5] Implicit is the assumption of movement from the latter to the former (e.g., Srinivas 1955 and Singer 1972) and a resulting consolidation of caste ranking (e.g., Cohn 1959 and Kolenda 1964). Lewis (1958) quotes Dube as saying in 1955 that:

> Clearly Hinduism as it is practiced in the village is not the Hinduism of the classical philosophical systems of India, for it possesses neither the metaphysical heights nor the abstract content of the latter. It is a religion of fasts, feasts and festivals (1958: quoted 250).

A number of ethnographers, however, particularly those with a structuralist bent, have been highly critical of the 'Great / Little Tradition' model, its lack of precision,[6] and its failure to account for the co-operation and interpenetration of traditions. Dumont calls it a 'destructive dichotomy' (1959:57),[7] and even Srinivas in his later analyses (1966) portrays a far less rigid separation than in his earlier works. Srinivas blames his original emphasis on separation on his own high caste socialisation and bias towards the superiority of the Brahman. Ironically, Dumont's (1980) portrayal of the structural unity of the caste system appears to be heavily influenced by the same high caste theological conceptions that Srinivas has attempted to shed. The result is a static, 'Brahmanised' idealisation of the caste system which neglects the fluidity and context-specificity of intercaste relations, the different but equally important conceptions and practices of other castes, and the very real inequalities which Brahmanic conceptions help to sustain.[8]

Mandelbaum (1966, 1970) has attempted to overcome the rigidity of the 'Great / Little Tradition' model by distinguishing not between traditions but rather between transcendental and pragmatic orientations and practices. Different orientations may correspond with different traditions and different gods but, as in Ames' model, may be found *within* a single tradition as well. Yet Mandelbaum is still more concerned with differences than with similarities. He is thus unable to account for transformations of local gods into universal deities, shamans possessed by local gods and universal deities simultaneously, or shamans who are Brahmans. The fluidity and dynamism of Hinduism are still betrayed by an over-emphasis on differences.

In the ethnography of religion in Nepal, the notion of disjunction between traditions is less pervasive. Campbell (1978) for example, in his study of religion in Jumla, emphasises the complementary and interpenetrating relation between patrifocal, hierarchical Brahmanism on the one hand and a filiafocal, more egalitarian, 'oracular religion' on the other. Although the former is dominant and encompassing, the latter remains vitally important. Moreover, both high caste and lower caste *Pabais* utilise both, and rebel against both.[9] We may note also Peters' (1981) conclusion in his discussion of the Tamangs: 'the concepts of Great Tradition and Little Tradition are not applicable in Nepal' (1981:67).

Earlier writers on Tibet, on the other hand, often portrayed a culture deeply divided between Buddhism (or "Lamaism") and the more shamanic *Bon* tradition. Hoffman (1961), for example, claims that:

> The internal situation of Tibet may be said to turn on a polar reaction between a luminous dynamic fructifying and historical

> element on the one hand and a sombre, static and fundamentally unhistorical element – the ancient Tibetan religion – on the other (1961:14).

Snellgrove (1957), on the other hand, rejects notions of division between traditions and, in a later work (1967) on the *Bon* tradition, suggests:

> Thus there is probably no such thing as pre-Buddhist Bon, for from the start the followers of Bon were anxious to accept and readapt religious teachings and practices of all kinds... The development of Bon and Chos [orthodox Buddhism] were parallel processes (1967:20,21).

Stein (1972) quotes an excerpt from the *bLon po bka' thang*: 'Basing oneself on the field of the religion of men, the religion of the gods (Buddhism) will grow there as fruit' (1972:192). And Zwalf (1981) comments that 'Nyingma...has significant features in common with Bon... it is legitimate to think of one national Tibetan religion with many aspects' (1981:37-38). Similarly, Tucci (1980) writes:

> The mountain preserves undiminished its sacredness as the ancestral deity. The powers of the underground, the prehistoric cycles of myths, the duties of the atmosphere and of the storm, are directly experienced in all their feared presence, but on the other hand they appear side by side with the Buddhas... Thus is confirmed for us in a continually repeating manner the indissoluble coexistence of Buddhist and non-Buddhist traditions, which through their combined action produce the religious experience lived by the Tibetan... the religious expectation of salvation infuses everything with sacredness and so integrates this apparently disunited world into a total picture (1980:208).

Studies of Tibetan Buddhist communities in Nepal present a similar picture. Cartier's (1975) study of the overlap between *Bon* and *Sa skya* followers in Dhorpatan, and the intermingling of Bon and Buddhist symbols, texts and paraphernalia in an exorcism in Tarakot, concludes that 'The shamans of Tibet have become vehicles of Buddhist philosophy and they are an integral part of this syncretic religion' (1975:140). Similarly Holmberg (1980, 1984) traces the relations of interdependence and interpenetration between the tantric lama, **lambu** ('exorcist') and **bombo** ('shaman') in West Tamang religion, arguing that 'these aspects are not conceivable as separate religions' (1980:5) and that 'no aspect of Tamang religion is isolable from the others; each derives its meaning from its position within a superordinate system' (1984:2).

The complementarity between religious traditions is a common theme in the ethnography of the Sherpas. Samuel (1978), for example, has suggested that the Sherpas, like other Tibetans, must be Buddhists so as to keep the spirits under control, but must simultaneously acknowledge the spirits so as to provide a *raison d'ètre* of Buddhism. He writes:

> *[B]oth* the beliefs in local gods and malevolent spirits, *and* the lamas and monasteries with their practice of the literary tradition of tantric Buddhism, are essential parts of religion in Tibetan societies... [i]t is precisely *because* the Sherpa believe in... spirits... that the lamas and their monasteries have such a central place in Sherpa and in Tibetan society (1978:111-112).

Compared to Southeast Asia, 'a much higher proportion of the total ritual field in Tibet is carried out under Buddhist auspices' (Samuel 1975:210).

Similarly, Paul (1979) says that Sherpa religion 'has embraced and included within itself many practices and functions which in Theravādin societies find expression in extra-Buddhist traditions' (1979:274). There is no split, according to Paul (1970) between "'high religionists' and "low religious" practitioners as there is in many other Buddhist societies" (1970:500): 'Many... different strains coexist in the same sect, in the same doctrine, and even in the same person' (1970:396).[10]

Von Fürer-Haimendorf (1955), in a preliminary article on Sherpa religion, also noted the 'coexistence and partial integration of two heterogenous ritual systems' (1955:49). In 1964 he wrote:

> Sherpa society embraces the laity as well as the many men and women who choose the religious life, and the one part is incomplete and incomprehensible without the other... there is no cleavage between the Buddhist doctrine practised in the monasteries and the religion of the ordinary villager. Both have their roots in Tibetan religious traditions, and the worship of local deities foremost in the religious thought of the untutored layman is not excluded from the ritual performances of the monasteries (1964:126).

This emphasis on unity within Sherpa religion is consistent with his portrayal of egalitarianism, communality and harmony in Sherpa society more generally, which he sees as due in part to the significance of cooperation in the harsh physical environment, and in part to Buddhist ethics, morals and values (1967). The result is an internal emphasis on hospitality and gift exchange, a lack of centralised formal political organisation, and an emphasis on co-operation and compassion.

Ortner (1978a), on the other hand, reacting against von Fürer-Haimendorf's rather Durkheimian functionalist account, stresses instead the individualism, hierarchy and conflict which she sees as characterizing Sherpa religion and society. Ortner (1970:38) says that, contrary to Paul's assertions (1970:500), the disjunction between 'high' and 'low' pervades both religious and social life, and parallels the disjunction in every Buddhist society between Buddhism and 'popular' cults, 'whose content is not only different from but often actually contradictory to Buddhism' (1975:51). Theravāda Buddhism, according to Ortner (1978a), in fact allows a closer interdependence between monastery and village than occurs among the Sherpas, and is more social in orientation than Sherpa religion. Through rituals (kurim, cf. Tib. *sku rim*),[11] the high gods reproduce their dominance over the low gods and supernaturals by maintaining their separateness and thus their purity, 'keep[ing] their hands clean and enter[ing] the party only after their underlings have dealt with the messier issues' (1978a:131).

Funke (1969) has also drawn attention to the cleavage between high and low religion and is particularly concerned to distinguish shamanism from the monasteries, arguing that 'the basic beliefs of Sherpa religion drawn from the Bon religion can still be clearly distinguished' (1969:289). 'The institution of the *minung* ['diviner'] has always stood in marked contrast to the prescriptions of the Tibetan Buddhism' (1969:291).

Is Sherpa religion different from Mahāyāna Buddhism elsewhere in the Tibetan Buddhist world? The historical development of Sherpa religion, and the sociopolitical, cultural, economic, environmental and other factors influencing day-to-day Sherpa life, may limit the applicability of generalizations which apply to other Tibetan Buddhist communities. However, as Gombrich has commented, 'academic boundaries are artificial; the realities are the problems. Problems have a way of crossing these boundaries' (1971:13). We should be wary of assuming or reproducing static boundaries where none may in fact exist.

Prior to the introduction of celibate monasticism early this century,[12] the Sherpas relied on married, village-based tantric ngapa banzin lamas and shamans (lhawa-minung) for contact with the supernatural world. Each ngapa lama was free to develop different religious interpretations and practices according to the needs of different clients. The result was a fairly personalised and direct system of contact with the supernatural world.

The introduction of the potato in the late 19th century, together with increased trade with Tibet and Nepal and the growing wealth and political power of the pembu ('tax-collectors', cf. Tib. *dpon po*) appointed by the Rana regime in Kathmandu, signalled the creation of an economic, social and political base which could support celibate monasticism, and which encouraged a more controlled and centralised religious system. Wealth became increasingly important for the support of sons in monasteries and thus for the acquisition of both religious merit and social status.

These changes are associated with the expansion of the political influence of Tibetan celibate monasticism into the Himalayan border region.[13] Increased trade with Tibet in the 1940s and the influx of thousands of Tibetan refugees following the annexation of Tibet by the Chinese in 1959 further strengthened the influence of celibate monasticism. While still *rNying ma*, the new monasteries placed increasing emphasis on *'Dul ba* (Skt. *Vinaya*) and *mDo* (Skt. *Sūtra*) as against the tantric practices of the banzin lamas. They also emphasised Buddhist deities such as *'Phags pa sPyan ras gzigs* (Skt. *Ārya Avalokiteśvara*), whose cult is not necessarily Tantric, as against the unambiguously tantric Padmasambhava (*Guru Rin po che*); and stressed transcendental, spiritual pursuits by means of ascetic individualistic practices as against the more worldly concerns of illness, material prosperity and social conflict traditionally dealt with by the banzin lamas and lhawa-minung. The result was an increasing separation between the celibate, orthodox Buddhist elite and the banzin and lhawa-minung, and also between the religious community as a whole and the laity. The banzin in particular suffered a loss of status relative to the celibate monks (tawa, cf. Tib. *grva pa*) and reincarnate lamas (Tib. *sprul sku*) in the monasteries.[14]

Nevertheless the banzin and lhawa-minung remained popular with the laity and continued to be responsible for the ritual manipulation of the lower gods (Tib. *lha*) and supernaturals (shrendi) which was necessary to day-to-day worldly concerns such as illness. Funke (1969) and Frerkes (1982), indeed, describe these practices and practitioners as the core of Sherpa religion, although von Fürer-Haimendorf, Ortner and Paul do not place so much emphasis on the 'control of invisible forces' (von Fürer-Haimendorf 1964).

By the mid 1970's, the monasteries appeared to be facing something of a crisis, with only a third the number of monks previously active at Tengboche remaining in the monastery and concern being freely expressed in the community about the standard of scholarship and religious practice in the monasteries (von Fürer-Haimendorf 1975:102). There were a number of cases of reincarnate lamas being admonished by their wealthy lay patrons for involving themselves in secular affairs (Paul 1977 offers a particularly telling case of this); and indeed of some reincarnate lamas leaving the monasteries altogether. Interestingly enough, both Ortner (1978a:32) and Paul (1976:141,147) reported a corresponding decline in the status of banzin and lhawa-minung as well.

By the 1980's however, there was a resurgence of support for the monasteries (von Fürer-Haimendorf 1984). During the period of my fieldwork in 1986-1987, community-wide monastery-based festivals such as bumtso (cf. Tib. *'bum tsho*), mani rimdu (cf. Tib. *maṇi ril sgrub*) and dumji (cf. Tib. *sgrub chen*) were attended in large numbers.[15] Donations to the monasteries and to individual monks were considerable.[16] Many new lhang ('private chapels', cf. Tib. *lha khang*), mani-stones and kani ('entrances to monasteries') were constructed. The demand for the services of monks to perform domestic rituals in the village, including exorcistic kurim, is now such that monks complain they have no time to attend to their own religious pursuits.

Significantly, there is also clear evidence of continuing support for lhawa-minung (and, to a lesser extent, banzin lamas) as well, despite the assertions of Ortner and Paul. In 92% of the 400 or so episodes of illness on which I collected data in the Thame valley, at least one traditional healer was employed, and in 53% of cases between two and four such healers were consulted.[17]

There is, furthermore, evidence of a significant degree of co-operation between the celibate monastic elite and the banzin and lhawa-minung. The legitimation of a 'calling' by the gods (*lha*) to become a lhawa ('shaman', cf. Tib. *lha pa*), and instructions as to how to manage it either through direct empowerment (tsalam betup) or with blessings (kaku) are provided by high lamas and *sprul sku* (see e.g., Samuel 1978:103). Lamas and shamans occasionally prescribe each other's rituals (e.g., Paul, 1982:84) and, at least in Solu, sometimes work alongside each other, as in the case of funerals (see e.g., Downs, 1980). Tantric *mantras* are often used by shamans to give extra power to their activities (see e.g., Funke 1969), and all shamanic rituals commence with invocations to the high orthodox deities. Both exorcistic kurim and offering rituals (kangsur, cf. Tib. *bskang gsol*) use a similar arrangement of *gtor ma* ('dough effigies') on their altars, combining *gtor ma* of high orthodox deities with tantric and lower local shamanic deities. Many lhawa-minung like to consider themselves lamas, especially as they grow older (see e.g., Paul, 1984). Lay people will often employ the services of a shaman, lama and monk simultaneously, if they can afford to do so, and a similar pattern of cooperation has been observed throughout the Tibetan Buddhist world.[18]

Clearly, then, the introduction of celibate monasticism has not signalled the disappearance of tantric and shamanic practitioners, even if the latter's status has suffered somewhat. In fact, there is considerable evidence for the view that, in a rapidly changing environment, Sherpas are actively seeking out the lhawa-minung, and even banzin, in an effort to reconstruct their sociocultural identity and reactivate their links with local sources of power.

A Structural Model of Sherpa Religion

At this point, it will perhaps be useful to summarise my earlier model of Sherpa religion (cf. Draper 1985). There I identified and described an asymmetrical but nevertheless dialectical structural relation between 'transcendental' and 'pragmatic' orientations and practices, *both* of which are present, to varying degrees, in the celibate monastic, tantric and shamanic strands of Sherpa religion. What is important about this relation, I suggested, is that it is mediated by the tantric encompassment of oppositions. One tradition is not wholly opposed to or eclipsed by another, but rather different orientations and practices intersect and reaffirm each other in different ways in different contexts.

While the more determinate theories of *karma* (Tib. *las*) enjoy high status, they are not necessarily understood by the laity and, in any case, coexist alongside more indeterminate notions of causation such as luck and supernatural interference. Certainly, an acceptance of the notion of the interconnectedness of all phenomena and the inevitability of effects deriving from all actions does not preclude the possibility of forestalling or in some other way manipulating these effects through ritual activity. While the passive and remote orthodox deities are accorded a higher existential status in orthodox

Buddhism than the local, more active and capricious *yul lha* ('earth gods'), *klu* ('serpent deities', Skt. *nāga*) and so on, they are no more 'real'. Indeed, for the average lay Sherpa, it is these lower deities and spirits who are more 'real,' in the sense that they are more important in understanding and dealing with day-to-day concerns and events. Even young educated Sherpas who claim to be less affected by the spirits because their relations with them are more tenuous as a result of Western knowledge and neglect of ritual nevertheless complain that, for this very reason, they are unable to control them and call upon their assistance when it is required.

To sum up, a convincing case can be made for structural unity within Sherpa religion. Such a case provides an important counter-balance to assertions of division deriving from models founded in the Cartesian intellectual tradition. And there is something very satisfying about arguing that Sherpa religion is indeed a religion of inner logic, consistency and harmony. But does my model really overcome the problems of dichotomisation? Does it in any way represent the views of Sherpas – in particular lay Sherpas – themselves? And does it help to illuminate the link between religion and society and relations of power more generally? These were some of the questions which began to concern me as I set off to commence fieldwork.

Lessons from Field Work

> Some tourists say that mani rimdu [a famous Sherpa festival] is about the Buddha and some say it is not. Some say it is a *cham* [*'cham*, 'dance-drama'] and some say it is just for drinking *chang* ['beer']... (laughter)...]. Some stay for the *tse ong* (*tshe dbang*, 'life-empowerment') and *jinsak* [*sbyin sreg*, 'rituals'] and others just go off trekking. But they don't come into the kitchen... How [then] can they understand what mani rimdu is? Even we lawa ['hosts for the festival'] don't really understand. But lama knows.
>
> - A Sherpa friend.

Field work has a remarkable capacity for blowing theories and models apart, and bringing 'experts' down to earth. The questions I had left unanswered in my earlier model of Sherpa religion soon became more significant than the 'answers' which had provoked them. The more I harrassed my Sherpa friends about their understanding of the structural unity of Sherpa religion, the infinite reification of Buddhahood made possible through my model, the encompassment of opposites achieved through tantra, or the fluidity of the existential status of supernaturals, the more I realised I was speaking a foreign language. My theoretical insights suddenly appeared uninteresting and irrelevant. In fact, rarely did lay Sherpas offer me any interpretation at all of religious ideas and practices, and this was not just because I wouldn't have understood it if they had. The response to my inquiries was so often a smile and the advice: 'Go and ask the lama. Lama knows'. What was particularly interesting was that even Lama sometimes didn't know, or was not willing to let on that he knew (or perhaps I was unable to recognise that he knew).

Paul (1970) apparently also had this experience:

> One unexpected problem I ran into in trying to collect data on explicit religious symbolism was the constant practice of lamas whom I interviewed to assure me that the details were of no importance, that all concrete symbols, such as specific conceptions of individual gods etc., were only ways of approaching the Truth...(1970:278).[19]

On one occasion in the Khumbu, a reincarnate abbot said to me that the 'how' of religion is more important than the why; that only trouble comes from monks who engage in theological debates with interested Westerners. Moreover, it is a common view among Sherpas that such Westerners inevitably get it wrong.[20]

Considerable pressure was applied on me to write 'correctly,' i.e., in accordance with the (Tibetan) texts in the possession of the Lamas) For the same reason, my first tentative inquiries to one well-respected Lama resulted not in answers but in the gift of a tanga ('rosary', cf. Tib. *'phreng ba*) and the teaching of the Zhembiyang (*'Jam dpal dbyangs*, Skt. *Mañjuśrī*) rigpa (*mantra*, Tib. *rig pa*), and the exhortation to practise before thinking. Said the Lama:

> You cannot understand cho [religion, Tib. *chos*, Skt. *dharma*] by talking about it. Tomorrow it will be different. If you sit somewhere else it will be different. If you drink *chang* it will be different. If you stop talking and start saying the rigpa it will be different.

The same Lama used to bewail my impatience for new information, likening me to a demon with a distended stomach and tiny mouth, and consequently always hungry.

Sherpas, both lay and lama / monk, do not reject religious doctrine[21] so much as the importance of elaborate theological interpretation and argument, preferring to maintain a direct link between the words themselves, their textual vehicles and spiritual power. For most Sherpas, religion is something done, something lived, something that simply *is*, rather than a structural relationship between various traditions, or a body of complex theories and doctrines. Furthermore, for most Sherpas, spiritual knowledge is something given, something self-constituted and axiomatic (even if it is inaccessible to most), rather than a commodity, something to be produced, dissected and analysed, or in some other way questioned. What, then, is glossed so readily as 'Tibetan Buddhism' in the literature is, I suggest, quite foreign to most Sherpas.

This speaks either of significant inequalities in the access to and control over spiritual knowledge and discourse within Sherpa society (and, by extension, the whole Tibetan Buddhist world), or of radical differences in the form and content of such knowledge and discourse, or both. Such issues cannot be treated as merely interesting political epiphenomena to studies of religion, but rather must become a central focus of attention. We must be wary of analyses which fail to explore such differences and inequalities, which reflect the relatively static and often reductionist intellectualisations and interests of indigenous professors of theology, the orthodox ruling elite, or our own academic disciplines rather than the complex, sometimes apparently contradictory and often changing views of the community as a whole.

I shall now explore some of these issues further in the context of my fieldwork experience. In the first few months, I elicited many of the familiar, more or less predictable responses to my inquiries, supporting the view of a harmonious egalitarian society founded firmly on Buddhist principles of compassion and co-operation. As I became increasingly immersed in the day-to-day realities of village life, however, and became increasingly part of the all-important network of relations of hospitality and exchange, I also became increasingly aware of the pervasiveness of conflicts, both overt and more subtle and suppressed, within and between villages, within and between monasteries, and even between villages and monasteries.[22] This should hardly have been surprising, of course, for Sherpas are as human as the rest of us. Ortner (1978a) observes that:

> Just as the absence of political and economic power structures does not mean that a Sherpa community is egalitarian, so the absence of systematic dispute-settling mechanisms does not mean that a Sherpa community is at all times peaceful and harmonious. While many disputes occur over real material resources, others are often expressions of status rivalry that seize upon some material factor as an excuse for an argument. The Sherpas recognize, and lament, the fact that envy over wealth differences is rife in the community, and status competition and rivalry chronic (1978a:77).

My direct questioning about conflicts got me nowhere, as a rule, but specific details of conflicts were often readily forthcoming in the course of more general conversations over a glass of chang.

The significance and pervasiveness of socioeconomic inequalities also became increasingly apparent. Differences in wealth, although not necessarily displayed in terms of differences in standards of living, are nevertheless fundamental to differences in social status, political power, the ability to throw lavish status-raising parties, the ability to take advantage of market opportunities and the ability to hedge against inflation. Furthermore, they are fundamental to differences in access to opportunities to accrue religious merit (*bsod nams*), for example through the sponsorship of family members as monks, direct donations to the monasteries, the construction of *maṇi* walls, the purchase of empowering religious texts and paraphernalia, the holding of lavish funerals for deceased family members, the commissioning of the more expensive (and thus more effective) healing rituals, or simply through being able to devote time and energy to religious pursuits rather than to material survival.[23]

As a consequence, wealth promises a better life *and* a better rebirth (although, as we shall see, it does not guarantee it), while the poor are destined to suffer even further because of their need to focus on material survival rather than on spiritual development. While I was in the Khumbu, two widows died in pathetically poor circumstances and I was surprised to discover that they did not receive the funerary rites so important to a favourable rebirth because their children could not afford them. Of course, wealth is also somewhat problematic (contrary to Ortner's account of wealth in Solu) in that it is sometimes considered evidence of worldliness and greed. Also, increasing wealth generally implies increasingly onerous gift exchange obligations (larke). What is important, however, is that inequalities are more or less accepted, because concepts of karma and hereditary luck (ngulkile, cf. Tib. *dngul kyi las*) offer a powerful explanation for differences in wealth.

Closely related to differences in wealth is the pervasive influence of differences in status, expressed, for example, through rules of commensality, hospitality etiquette and seating arrangements at parties. Members of the original Sherpa clans enjoy higher status over what Oppitz (1975) calls 'pseudo-clans' (including Chhetri and Rai immigrants arriving in the 19th century), more recent Tibetan immigrants ('Khambas') and various classes of social outcaste groups, referred to variously as gyakhamba, kachar, khamendeu, yemba and so on.[24] The latter are subject to taboos of intermarriage with Sherpa clan members, are debarred from drinking from the same cup (a significant handicap, given the importance of sharing the same cup for the maintenance of reciprocal gift, labour, and hospitality exchanges) and are debarred from attaining lama status.[25]

The division of the cosmos, environment and social world into high/low, inner/outer, white/black (cf. Ortner 1978b) and so on is not a mere symbolic construction of the ethnographer. High-low differentiation in particular (cf. Ortner 1970:38) is expressed, for example, in differences within such diverse categories as cosmic realms (sanggye, Tib. *sangs rgyas*, 'buddha'; and nyela, 'heaven and hell'), deities (lha) in general, the tutelary deities of shamans (lhawa), serpent deities (*klu*), demons (*bdud*), temple architecture (Paul 1976), beer and food (Ortner 1970), villages, life-empowerment rituals (*tshe dbang*), prayer/offering scarves (*kha btags*), people,[26] occupations, language, cremation grounds and, as we shall see, exorcistic kurim rituals. Living day-to-day with Sherpas who do not necessarily enjoy the benefits of a high status makes one very conscious of how pervasive the high-low theme is.

Differences in status between religious practitioners are also fundamentally important. The lhawa, for example, is considered more powerful than the minung, for the latter can only point to and interpret a cause, while the former, through possession (lhabeu, cf. Tib. *lha 'bab*), *becomes* the cause. The art of lhabeu is monopolised by the lhawa. There is no concept (or evidence) of lay possession[27] and certainly no evidence of possession serving as an 'oblique aggressive strategy', a response to deprivation, or an expression of gender inequalities.[28]

The qualified monk, however, enjoys higher status than either minung or lhawa. This is demonstrated in a number of areas, such as the fact that his spiritual power (*dbang*) comes from a higher source than the *sngags* of the lhawa-minung; that he can reject a religious calling (unlike the minung and lhawa); that he is led in his rituals by sacred powerful texts (and thus his rituals are unassailable); and that he controls the highly significant funerary rituals (and thus the process of rebirth).

Furthermore, the qualified monk is considered capable of performing all rituals performed by the lhawa-minung, although he will seldom do so, because they are considered 'low' and polluting. The hereditary banzin lama can acquire *dbang* through training and tsam ('retreats', cf, Tib *mtshams*) but the reincarnate lama (*sprul sku*) is *dbang* embodied. The Sherpas respect the power of a possessed lhawa, but they literally worship the *sprul sku.* As a reincarnate, the *sprul sku* is, at least in theory, both all-knowing and all-compassionate, and thus cannot be criticised on either religious or social grounds. The power of the banzin, by contrast, is far more arbitrary, and the banzin now occupies, according to Paul, 'an anomalous and somewhat absurd role' (1970:585).

The status and role of the lhawa is even more anomalous. On the one hand, the lhawa responds to real and important concerns of the laity, including the fear of physical weakening and sickness, increasing vulnerability to shrendi. The lhawa responds to these fears by strengthening the body-spirit connection, while the monastic establishment regards the body as a source of attachment and suffering and thus seeks to separate the spirit from the body (see Ortner 1978a:119). On the other hand, the lhawa's activities are not directed by an unbreakable written code, as are those of the monastic establishment: the lhawa's power is dependent on being possessed, is not, therefore, classed as *chos* and does not bestow *bsod nams* ('merit'). Paul (1976) notes:

> Sherpas often say you cannot trust a shaman because you never know whether what he sees when possessed are really the gods or only his imagination. But a lama chanting from a book cannot possibly make a mistake for the letters themselves contain truth (1976:140).

Lhawa themselves (and their families) often complain about the low status, dangerous nature, physical exertion and small rewards of their occupation, saying they would not practise as lhawa if they had an option. One minung in Thame who had been blamed for creating social tensions as result of one of her divinations decided to risk the wrath of the gods and not practise again. Many lhawa-minung divest themselves of their shamanic paraphernalia (chopa) and pursue the life of a banzin as they become elderly.[29]

There is, of course, an important hierarchy of status within the monastic establishment itself, reflecting different roles, levels of training and vows undertaken. Only 'low' monks, for example, will assist in the shetu ('funerals', cf. Tib. *zhi khro*) of 'low' laity or at 'low' exorcistic kurim because of the likelihood of tip ('pollution', cf. Tib. *sgrib*) through contact with the 'low' shrendi ('supernaturals') attracted to such shetu. High lamas and monks, on the other hand, monopolise the shetu of high (i.e., the more pious, relatively 'pure,' and often wealthy) members of the community. The monastic establishment as a whole, of course, is not exactly uninterested in wealth, status and material concerns. Paul (1970) writes:

> ...despite their supposed lack of interest in the things of this world, monks and also village lamas are, both empirically and by general Sherpa consent, *more* rather than less concerned with material possessions and status than are other people (1970:564-5).

The establishment and maintenance of a network of 'good' relations and exchanges between people, but also between people and the gods, and between people and the natural environment is fundamental to Sherpa existence. Even such highly idealised values as generosity, co-operation, hospitality and compassion, for which the Sherpas are justly famous, have meaning and come into play only within a framework of social relations. If a person is unable to establish and maintain such relations, the result is often social isolation, and in such a harsh environment such isolation may mean death. After some months in the village, I began to hear of and see a number of cases of Sherpas who had suffered greatly from such isolation.[30]

At the same time, I became very conscious that even a network of 'good' relations can be problematic. Privacy, agency and individual autonomy are highly prized by the Sherpas. The need for co-operation for successful agricultural activity in a harsh environment, for example, is balanced by the preference for autonomy and individualism which pervades animal husbandry and trading activities. As one friend remarked: 'The rongpa [non-Sherpas living down in the valleys, cf. Tib. *rong pa*] live together like animals but we Sherpas live alone like men [*sic*]'. Insofar as karma is not wholly determinate for the Sherpas, human existence involves many effects deriving from unknown causes, and unknown effects of known causes. There is an ongoing tension in Sherpa society between a remote but powerful cognitive ideal emphasising interconnectedness, and a culturally disvalued but emotionally powerful interest in individual autonomy.

Relations are never static, never given. They are experienced in different ways, at different times, by different people. The responsibilities involved in maintaining relations can sometimes be very onerous: one friend, for example, was able to enumerate over twenty various debts and obligations arising from membership of a larke ('gift exchange') group. Giving is idealised, but is often more motivated by the desire for status and individual merit than by pure altruism. Hospitality and the giving of *chang* (of which there are at least sixteen different ritual varieties) are fundamentally important, and detailed and mental notes are kept of all such exchanges. The giving of apsa (i.e., *chang* from one's own glass) in particular establishes a close relationship, although it is never offered to high lamas or monks because of the potential for pollution, and the affront this would imply to their higher status – such lamas and monks are offered the highest foods, the highest seats, and are spoken to in the high 'respect' form of language.

Hospitality among the laity is even more problematic. It is a major source of illnesses resulting from pem (i.e., the unconscious projection of feelings of envy, hurt or greed between people who are closely related, cf. Tib. *dpa'mo*).[31] Hospitality is also a major source of tuk ('poisoning') and kyukto ('a form of pollution resulting from infractions of commensality rules'). Even slight breaches of etiquette by either host or guest can cause 'bad' relations. In fact, the closer the relations are, the more likely that they will cause problems. In some cases of illness, even close kin will be refused hospitality and entry to the house (dulchi dambup) – the only occasion on which this is permitted – because of the likelihood that shrendi, attracted to the illness, will attach themselves to the visitor and complicate the illness.

To the extent, then, that relations are a significant and pervasive influence in Sherpa culture and society, there is an emphasis on gift exchange, on communality and co-operation, on hospitality, on acceptance of the notion of *karma*, and so on. To the extent, however, that relations are problematic and flexible, a variety of other forces and phenomena are also engendered, such as an emphasis on individualism, on the nuclear family and neolocal residence, on entrepreneurial activity and commodity exchange, on the concentration of status and power among the wealthy, on the ritual manipulation of karma, and so on. While it is important to recognize the significance of relations in Sherpa society, it is equally important to recognize that they are also inherently problematic.

As time went on, I became increasingly conscious of the differences in the nature of secular exchanges on the one hand, and spiritual exchanges (i.e., between the laity and healers, the monastic elite, and through them the gods and supernaturals) on the other. While the former are based on relatively direct transactions and allow a significant degree of agency (subject to control of the appropriate resources, including knowledge of market forces, and material and labour resources), the latter are based on what I shall call exchanges of 'equivalences': e.g., the offering of food and hospitality in return for revelation of the causes of illness and misfortune, promises by demons and other supernaturals to desist from causing such things, or spiritual power from the gods to overcome them. The value of what is exchanged in these cases is determined not by the transactors in direct negotiation as much as by healers and the religious elite who control access to the supernatural realm. Often, in the case of sickness, the patient will not even be present at the exchange through which healing is sought, and will be socially isolated. It soon became apparent to me that although wealth facilitated these exchanges, it did not guarantee their success. That is, the successful manipulation of exchanges with the gods and supernaturals is determined not so much by control of material resources *per se* as by control of the means of production and distribution of knowledge concerning the relation between the material and spiritual realms, and how to access supernatural assistance and spiritual power.

Prior to the introduction of monasticism, this knowledge lay in the hands of the relatively accessible banzin lamas and lhawa-minung. The past is considered by the Sherpas to be samen lemu ('good era') because the distance between humanity and the gods was not so great, and all things were more closely interrelated. People are thus said to have lived longer, healers were stronger and more readily accessible, assistance from the gods was more immediate and powerful, the causes of illness and misfortune were more readily observable, there was more control over the environment, less division of labour between religious specialists, and more emphasis on personal, clan and local deities. Agency and power in both material and spiritual exchanges required the maintenance and active manipulation of familial and social relationships.

With the rise of celibate monasticism however, access to spiritual knowledge increasingly required *separation* from such relations. Paul writes that:

> Among Sherpas, it is common to decry the passing of bygone days when almost every self-respecting citizen of the village was also a practicing *[sic]* lama... (1970:412).

and that

> Whereas religious virtuosity may once have coincided with magical power or charisma... today it corresponds to obedience to a high number of moral regulations (1976:149).

The more the laity involved themselves in worldly activities, and the more profitable these activities became, the more this wealth was directed towards supporting an institution which took control of spiritual matters, thereby permitting the laity to pursue worldly activities. But such activities dispossessed them of direct access to spiritual knowledge and power, for according to the monasteries, worldly activities are a source of pollution and ignorance. The monasteries could have their cake and eat it too, while for the laity, increasing agency in secular exchanges gave rise to decreasing agency in spiritual exchanges.

This is not to say that worldly knowledge has no bearing on spiritual matters, but the two are clearly distinguished. The laity are even prepared to override the monasteries on certain secular matters (e.g., the control of forest resources) but would never question them on spiritual matters. Social transgressions (e.g., shamden, an endogamous sexual relationship) have consequences quite distinct from religious transgressions (e.g., lou, a sexual relationship with a monk or nun). The laity's knowledge of socially-caused illnesses (e.g., tuk, poisoning, and pang, a form of postnatal depression arising from inadequate care from one's husband during pregnancy), as well as of diet-caused illnesses, is far more elaborate and uniform than their knowledge of supernaturally-caused illnesses (e.g., tak kiup, the sudden and unexplained vomiting of blood, and zakin, a form of epilepsy). Knowledge of social relations and conflicts is in fact sometimes claimed by healers to be distracting to the eliciting of knowledge about the supernatural causes of illness.[32]

For a similar reason, Western medical knowledge, despite its acknowledged efficacy in dealing with symptoms, has low status because it is not divinely inspired and therefore cannot assist in the identification and treatment of the supernatural causes of illness. Similarly, Western education, though much sought after because it is fundamental to a successful career in tourism, is nevertheless seen as lower in status and less 'powerful' than a monastic education.[33] As one Sherpa commented: 'the reason for schools is jobs, not religion. Sir Edmund Hillary provides schools but not a better rebirth; and not even jobs'.

The disjunction between secular and spiritual knowledge does not mean, either, that the laity have no knowledge of spiritual matters. In fact, even young children appear to know at least the basic elements of many religious rituals. But this kind of 'technical' or factual religious knowledge should not be confused with the ability, and/or the right, to generate and communicate *interpretive* knowledge about spiritual matters. Few lay Sherpas understand, or at least claim to understand, such notions as 'voidness' or 'mindfulness' or the contingency of reality.[34] Fewer still are prepared to explain them openly. No lay Sherpa in Thame was aware that Tulshig Rimpoche (*'khrul zhig*), the abbot of Tubten Choling (*thub bstan chos gling* monastery in Solu), is recognized as the *sprul sku* of the Tibetan monk who assassinated the evil King Langdarma through the use of illusion (and is thus, literally, the 'destroyer of illusion' and master of mani rimdu). Few Sherpas have even heard of Dudjom Rimpoche and Khyentse Rimpoche, the late reincarnate heads of the *rNying ma* lineage. When the Buddha's birthday passed unnoticed, the response from a lay friend to my question 'Why?', was, 'Which Buddha?' When I said 'Gautama Buddha,' he replied, 'That's Nepali'.

There is much variation among Sherpas with regard to terminology for the conceptual domain corresponding to the English 'mind', 'soul', 'spirit', etc. (e.g., she, *sems*, *la*, nasam, *tshe*, *khams*). There is much apparent confusion (or is this mine?) regarding various forms of power, such as *sngags*, *dbang*, *gzungs*, and so on, as well as regarding various forms of 'black magic'. There is much difference of opinion as to what constitues namdok ('demerits arising from transgression of religious rules', cf. Tib. *rnam rtog*); and there is much variation between Sherpa and Tibetan concepts of omens.[35]

Similarly, in the healing system there is considerable variation among the laity in knowledge of the supernatural causes of illness, although there is more concern about this relative to knowledge of symptoms, because it is believed that symptoms will not disappear until the causes have been satisfactorily dealt with.[36] This uncertainty is reflected in a number of ways, such as the laity's tendency to multiple choice of healers, as well as in variations in therapy management, compliance patterns, determination of efficacy and explanations for the lack of success of curing rituals. In the latter case, it is rare for the healer to be blamed, for the healer is merely a vehicle for divine power. This is particularly so where the healer uses texts, for the knowledge contained in the texts is inherently powerful, and cannot be wrong. Removal of symptoms, or even death, does not therefore conclude the healing process, for untreated causes will merely manifest themselves elsewhere, and perhaps in a more insidious form because the supernaturals are angry.[37]

A lack of understanding, intention, or even awareness of causes will not prevent an effect, and failure to deal satisfactorily with causes – even with repeated attempts – will inevitably result in further effects. Yet the correspondence between cause and effect is in no way fixed, and different causes will have different effects at different times among different people. Furthermore, all illnesses have multiple causes and the successful resolution of one or more of these does not guarantee healing. Where an offender's ngulkile ('luck') is favourable, the consequences of his or her actions may pass on to others less lucky, including children and animals.

There is thus much uncertainty and even fear of illness among the laity. There are very few home remedies, and little or no self-healing – this is partly because self-healing does not involve an exchange between the patient and the gods, on which healing is based. In fact, patients remain dependent on others for all aspects of the illness and healing experience. They are dependent on family members for the choice of healers and for care; and they are dependent on healers for the divination of causes, the management of causes, and the determination of efficacy. Patient-healer negotiation is minimised: there is no pressure on healers to 'sell' themselves or explain the 'logic' of their activities. Access to the healing profession is restricted to those who are 'called' by the gods to become healers, and relations between different healers are cordial and co-operative,[38] despite the lack of formal intraprofessional organisation. Patients, as we have seen, are often socially isolated and sometimes are not even present when divination and curing take place.[39]

Few lay Sherpas – or, for that matter, healers – appear able to explain *how* illness or healing occurs. However, they do not see this as particularly important. No lay Sherpa has any extensive knowledge of the Tibetan medical system, and even Sherpa amji ('Tibetan doctors', cf. Tib. *am chi*) have little knowledge of some of its major branches such as psychiatry. Many monks do not claim any special healing expertise either. However, they claim not to be affected by many of the illnesses suffered by the laity because they are 'above' the supernaturals that inhabit the villages. In any case, they have direct access to the powerful healing provided through the Rinpoche's chilap ('empowered blessings', cf. Tib. *byin rlabs*) and cho ('texts', cf. Tib. *chos*).

Women are especially reticent about discussing religious issues and rarely take any part in rituals, even if they are their object. Women claim to have little knowledge even of childbirth, as this is an activity highly susceptible to supernatural interference. As a result, there are no traditional midwives and birthing is very much a private affair. Women have virtually no opportunity to be incorporated into the spiritual lineages through which spiritual knowledge is transmitted, legitimated and empowered. There is virtually no knowledge of the Tibetan *ḍākiṇī* cults, and deities and supernaturals associated with femaleness (e.g., *klu*) tend to be accorded an increasingly low status. This gender division with respect to religion is very significant given the high status of Sherpa women in social and economic affairs relative to Hindu women elsewhere in Nepal.[40]

The Sherpa laity has few of the opportunities for direct spiritual empowerment enjoyed by Tibetan Buddhists elsewhere, such as annual displays of 'high' *thang ka* ('religious paintings'); revelations of *gter ma* ('hidden treasures'); the sacralisation of objects, places and people; the production of *rnam thar* ('biographies of spiritual masters'), and so on. There are few universally known myths and legends; and those which are known to the laity are not considered to be of great significance, perhaps because of the low status of the oral tradition in which they are transmitted. If Turner (1969) is correct when he says that the production of myth is a significant expression of 'communitas,' then the relative insignificance of myth in Sherpa society might suggest the dominance of 'structure'.

Relative to the oral tradition, the literate tradition, of course, enjoys almost unassailable authority. The Sherpa word for religion (cho, cf. Tib. *chos*) is also often used to mean 'text'. Texts have a vast variety of forms ranging from *maṇi* stones and shunga ('talismans') to lungta ('prayer flags', cf. Tib. *rlung rta*) and chilap (printed medicines, cf. Tib. *byin rlabs*), as well as the *Kengyur* (*bKa' 'gyur*), *Tengyur* (*bsTan 'gyur*), *Bum* (*idem*), *Domang* (*mDo mangs*) and many other books. The spiritual power embodied in these texts is absolute, and recitations are directed toward releasing this power through the action of vocalisation, blowing, ingestion, wearing, or simply reading, rather than to communicating ideas or meaning. For this reason, the more monks – and the 'higher' the monks – one can commission to recite texts, the more merit will accrue, not because the texts are read faster or are better understood, but because merit accrues from the physical process of the reading of each copy of the text. Even the divinations revealed through texts such as the lhamu gyezu or dadu may not be entirely understood. Nevertheless divination through texts is considered a higher and more accurate form of divination than that through dice, rosary, rice grains, or dreams. Furthermore, textual divination performed by monks and lamas (sungdakshop) is considered to be higher and more accurate than that of minung (tsilhap). One Sherpa friend (perhaps familiar with Lévi-Strauss) commented to me how books, when read by monks and lamas, are transformed into spiritual power just as food is transformed into a more edible and higher form when cooked.

Gifts of texts hence represent an exchange very similar to that achieved through hospitality, and are even more highly valued. Thus, one successful Sherpa entrepreneur gave the entire set of 160 folios of one of the texts to his local monastery as a parting gift when he relocated to Kathmandu, a gift designed to offset the possible karmic effects of his activities and of his move to an alien environment. The ownership of texts, which is almost exclusively the right of religious officiants, is fundamental to access to and control of the power and status which they embody. A wealthy monk will have more texts, and thus can perform more rituals and enjoy greater wealth and higher status (and thus have access to more texts and so on). The laity on the other hand – and poor or illiterate monks – are denied such opportunities. Clearly, then, the written word has a power in the Khumbu which even our enslavement to the discourse of the text would be hard pressed to match.

For the laity at least, then, the meaning contained in texts cannot be separated from the power of the written word itself, and even the monks find the question of meaning somewhat irrelevant. As one astute monk noted, 'if we were supposed to understand the books, they would be written in Sherpa'. But they are not – they are in Tibetan, the language of 'high' religion, and the medium of all orthodox rituals. In any case, less than a third of adult men, and considerably fewer women and children, can read Tibetan at all. The laity do not discuss, certainly cannot write and rarely even try to read for themselves the texts which represent such a significant source of spiritual knowledge and power. Even Sherpa itself incorporates a 'high' sociolect which must be used in conversations with high lamas and monks and on certain more formal ritual occasions. Many Sherpas – particularly women – do not fully understand or at least use this sociolect, and so are hindered in their communications with such personages, and in participation in such rituals. They are therefore also hindered, of course, in acquiring access to the means by which spiritual knowledge might be interpreted and shared.

In addition to the high sociolect used by high lamas and monks, the lhawa-minung have a 'language' or code of their own used when summoning and communicating with their tutelary deities and other supernaturals. This 'code' is taught to them directly by the gods during a calling, and cannot be taught or explained to the laity. This, of course, provides another important means of control over access to the profession and to healing knowledge. There is value, I suggest, in distinguishing between the different languages of the various religious practitioners and the language of the laity in terms of Bernstein's (1971) distinction between 'elaborated' and 'restricted' codes.[41]

Any attempts by the laity to 'produce' new spiritual knowledge (and I recorded no such cases) are punished by social isolation and religious condemnation, and are considered to be the source of significant misfortune, in both this life and the next. Thinking – or rather 'too much thinking' – is commonly adduced to explain such illnesses as shroklung, (cf. Tib. *srog rlung*) and too much thinking about religion in particular is considered a principal source of psychosis.[42]

Many religious specialists claim, of course, that interpretive spiritual knowledge, as opposed to technical worldly knowledge, is something which they do not 'produce' so much as 'express'. Worldly knowledge is subjective, and thus the source of illusion and pollution; while spiritual knowledge is absolute, axiomatic, inherently virtuous and powerful, and ever-present. It is revealed only when appropriate and remains inacessible to the laity only because of their worldliness, material attachments and ignorance. Learning is by rote, by modelling, or by divine inspiration; but with the occurrence of the latter, of course, one ceases to be a layperson.

The gods become bigger and higher as a result of lay religious activity, but therefore more remote, increasing the laity's dependence on monks and lamas. There are many ways to the gods but they all rely on the mediation of the religious elite. There are no 'mad saint' heroes (see Ardussi and Epstein 1978) as there are in Tibet, no subversive healing cults or other similar vehicles for expressing opposition to the monasteries. There are no lay political groupings such as a lay gerontocracy which might challenge the authority of the religious elite. And there are no significant lay rites of passage which might create such groupings. The primary rites of passage remain birth, death and entry into a religious occupation (i.e., events that signal the transition to and from a lay status).

To sum up, there is a major division in Sherpa society between the religious elite and the laity. This division is based on the control exercised by the religious elite over the means of production and distribution of knowledge about the relation between the material and the spiritual realms. Given the importance of spiritual knowledge even to secular activities, this control represents, I would suggest, the primary axis of inequality in Sherpa society, from which other inequalities flow and are legitimated and reproduced. The control of spiritual knowledge is thus fundamental to the exercise of power and the reproduction of social structures and cultural values, and thus the maintenance of order and social control more generally. Indeed, in a very real sense knowledge is power in Sherpa society. Any significant change in Sherpa society – or rather any empowering change – will be dependent on changes in the control of knowledge, and in the relations of power that such control represents.

Towards a Power-centred View of Sherpa Religion

I do not wish to argue that Sherpas have no access to spiritual knowledge, but rather that lay Sherpas do not control the means of production and communication of this knowledge. At this point, then,

I want to suggest that to be a passive recipient, or, as it were, a consumer of spiritual knowledge rather than an active producer of it may in fact be more disempowering than not having access to knowledge at all. It is one thing to 'know', but it is quite another to be in control of how and why one knows some things but not others, and what the consequences of this might be. Knowledge is power only to the extent that one controls how this knowledge comes into being and is legitimated, how it might be subjected to critical reflection, and how it might be consciously used to effect empowering action. Foucault once wrote that 'people know what they do; they frequently know why they do what they do; but what they don't know is what what they do does' (quoted by Ortner 1984: footnote P.157). This, according to Foucault, is the real source of oppression and exploitation.

In the case of the Sherpas, the laity often do not even know why they do what they do, or at least feel compelled to refrain from discussing why; and very rarely do they explore, at least publicly, the wider sociopolitical causes and consequences of their actions. Ortner (1978a) has argued that 'the general religious tendency [is] to desocialize all affective problems, to see them as matters of individual private urges having nothing to do with social relations' (1978a:180, n.11). And yet:

> [Buddhism's] power as a psychological theory... is inextricably related to its social theory: The endurance of spirit as a psychologically comforting notion is linked to a moral system in which some spirits endure (are reincarnated) in better forms (social positions) than others. In order to avail oneself of the orthodox solution to the problem of fear and death... one must also bow before the justness of unequal distribution of wealth and privilege (1978a:127).

Through ritual activity, the supremacy of the Buddhas is reaffirmed, but this also represents

> ...the triumph of the big people and the reestablishment of the social hierarchy. The transcendence of spirit over body, the highness of the big people, and the triumph of the gods are all rendered homologous. Divine protection, personal immortality and social inequality are all experienced as part of the same package (1978a:127).

Through the depoliticising effect of the religious elite's control of interpretive knowledge of both day-to-day and more existential concerns, the subjective political nature of inequality and its causes and its consequences are masked, thus facilitating their legitimation and reproduction. In other words, the religious elite achieves its separation from and power over the laity not through the use of overt force but rather through the lack of it; through the establishment and maintenance of covert relations of knowledge-power which remain masked and unchallenged.

This, of course, fits in with the absence of formal centralised political structures more generally in Sherpa society. For the Sherpas, the exercise of overt political power, either by individuals or by groups, is considered somewhat crass, an unnecessary admission of worldly attachments. Never is overt force used, except in the almost ritualised fighting which occasionally takes place at parties and festivals. In secular affairs, responsibility for the hosting (lawa) of village festivals is rotated, as are other responsibilities for the control of grazing (naua) and forest management (shing naua). The Nepalese Government's *panchayat* system carries little practical significance, at least for Thame Sherpas. The courts are openly distrusted, and Sherpas will virtually never refer a conflict which might have a supernatural implication (e.g., a case of poisoning) to the police, no matter how serious it is. Furthermore, the monasteries are expected to refrain from involvement in secular, political and economic affairs which might compromise their religious purity.

This is not to say, of course, that there is no leadership, political organisation or exercise of power in Sherpa villages. But it is to say that such power is of a very different kind to that found in Kathmandu, or Lhasa (or even, for that matter, in nearby D'ing-ri). In fact, it is the very absence of formal centralised political structures which gives such weight and significance to the power of the religious elite, exercised through its control of knowledge and discourse. If this is so, then the assumption of uniformity within Tibetan Buddhist communities is clearly problematic. A focus on power will clearly be of assistance in illuminating the various differences – and similarities – between these communities.

Following Lukes (1974), Foucault (1975) and Bourdieu (1977), I would suggest that power, in the sense of a general theoretical construct, is best understood not as a property, something overtly exercised by someone over someone else through the use of force or coercion, but rather as a relation – asymmetrical and changing, but a relation nevertheless – between those forces which serve to reproduce structure and those which provide the opportunity for agency. Although not directly observable, the relation in the case of the Sherpas is such that the varying degree of agency promised individual actors winds up reproducing structures, albeit imperfectly, without the actors being aware of it, or particularly concerned about if it they are. What is important, however, is that the relation remains a dialectical one: structure exists only insofar as it is animated, and reproduced, through agency, and agency remains constrained by the structures it serves to reproduce.

The impression that Sherpas have the opportunity to choose from multiple therapeutic alternatives, for example, masks the fact that such choices are inevitably shaped by, constrained within, and even devalued through the limits set by the structure of social relations and a system of authority which is legitimated and reproduced primarily through its control of knowledge. The very notion of 'choice' is misleading if an agent is not aware that she or he does not have access to the knowledge and discourses (not to speak of good relations or wealth etc.) which will ensure that the choice is available at all, and – if it is - that it is an empowering one. Choices do not necessarily maximise self-interests, as decision theory so often suggests, because of the impact of the structure of socio-cultural relations, including the control of knowledge, in which such choices are inevitably embedded. The apparent availability of multiple therapeutic systems encompassing the spiritual and social dimensions of sickness as well as the physical does not of itself guarantee a more efficacious, accessible or equitable healing system. Through its control of access to the supernatural realm, and thus of spiritual knowledge and power, the Sherpa healing system serves as a fundamentally important instrument of social control. What is particularly interesting, however, is how few Sherpas – and even ethnographers – appear prepared to acknowledge or discuss such a possiblity.

Demons, Exorcisms and Intellectualisations

Let us now explore some of these ideas further in the context of what are perhaps the most common, and – for the lay Sherpa – most significant religious rituals, namely exorcistic **kurim**. I have already discussed Ortner's (1978a) proposition of a structurally and functionally complementary relation between the **dodzongup** and the more orthodox **gyepshi** rituals, and have proposed a reworking of that relation in terms of a dialectic between transcendental and pragmatic orientations. That discussion was based on the assumption that exorcistic kurim are concerned primarily with the removal and/or transcendence of evil, as expressed through demons, and the inevitable tendency towards negativity in the cosmos. But are they? What would Sherpas make of this assumption? What is the existential status of demons for the laity, and what might this tell us about exorcistic kurim?

Demons are in many ways the *raison d'ȅtre* for Tibetan Buddhism. It was the influence of demons in Tibet which led to Indian tantric exorcist Padmasambhava (*Guru Rimpoche*) being invited to Tibet to transmit the teachings and practices necessary to keep the demons at bay. Tantra is regarded as a particularly effective system for overcoming the evil represented by demons. This system is based on the strategy of revealing the ultimately illusory nature of demons and the arbitrary nature of their power. One of the many myths surrounding the historical conflict between tantric lamas and demons tells of Guru Rimpoche overcoming a particularly recalcitrant demon in a cave by urinating on him. Another myth concerns a demoness who set out to challenge the piety and power of the religious elite. First, she confronted a monk and forced him to break one of his vows by presenting him with the options of drinking a bottle of *chang* she was carrying, killing a goat she had, or sleeping with her. The monk chose the 'orthodox' rather than the tantric approach: he drank the *chang*; but then, influenced by the alcohol, he killed the goat and slept with the demoness. The second episode reveals much about the tantric approach to overcoming evil. The demoness, filled with confidence, then sought out a tantric lama and presented the same options, although, recognising that he would be more difficult prey, she produced two bottles of *chang* instead of one. The lama responded immediately, drinking the *chang*, and then, in a drunken ecsctasy, slept with the goat and killed the demoness. The lesson is clearly that evil is most effectively overcome when it is confronted head-on, rather than through efforts to avoid it through piety and rule-governed behaviour.[43]

The Khumbu was first made inhabitable when Guru Rimpoche exorcised the demons who ruled it. The monasteries, according to the monks, merely continue these teachings and practices. However, if the monasteries succeeded in destroying those demons altogether, their continuing *raison d'ȅtre* would be lost. Thus, according to Ortner (1970, 1973, 1978a, 1978b) and Paul (1970, 1982), the monasteries teach a notion of the demonic aspect of human nature, which ensures that the exorcism of demons remains problematic. The real point, then, of the dodzongup and gyepshi rituals, Ortner suggested, was to expose demons as illusions; as projections of the 'low,' ignorant, polluted, 'evil' side of human nature which is first made manifest and then subjugated through the power of the buddhas, rather than as objective entities in their own right. In other words, despite its social consequences, exorcism is designed, according to Ortner and Paul, as a psychological process, for the victory over demons requires an enlightened mind able to break through the duality of good and evil and perceive the underlying oneness of reality. As such, however, the victory is neither total nor permanent, for enlightenment is a process rather than an exchange of one perception of reality for another. To this extent, demons are also 'real'. Ma gcig lags (*Ma gcig sLab gron*), a twelfth-century tantric *ḍākiṇī* spoke of this dual aspect of demons:

> Listen my son, I will teach you about the nature of demons: what we call a demon is very huge and coloured all black. Whoever sees one is truly terrified and trembles from head to foot – but demons don't really exist! The truth of the matter is this: anything whatsoever which obstructs the attainment of liberation is a demon... the greatest demon of them all is belief in a self as an independent and lasting principle.[44]

Put another way, demons exist (insofar as their effects can be felt), yet are not real (from the point of view of their objective existential status). And yet according to tantra, any such distinction between existence and reality is itself ultimately an illusion.

As we have seen, early students of religion – including Durkheim, Weber and Freud – found such existential flip-flops difficult to digest. Ortner deals with the conundrum in the following terms: on the one hand, 'demons are a sort of catch-all *social* projective system for any category or group that is threatening or problematic' (1978a:101, Ortner's emphasis). This applies particularly to the poor. That is, the concept of demons legitimates and reproduces socioeconomic inequalities. On the other hand, however, there is also the psychological notion of a demonic self. According to Buddhist doctrine, says Ortner:

> Everyone should strive to be pure, that is, to diminish the physical and demonic tendencies of the self, and to enlarge and render dominant the spiritual tendencies. But in lay life, it is difficult to

> avoid experiences that exaggerate either the physical or the demonic tendencies. Hence, the aim is not so much to eliminate or demolish those aspects of the self, but to keep them in an integrated balance... (1978a:104).

By tolerating the less orthodox dodzongup ritual, which gives form to the demons, the monasteries acknowledge the laity's need for a tangible, direct means of dealing with demons in a way it can understand. Yet in so doing, it clearly identifies an opponent and sets the stage for the final victory of orthodox Buddhism over demons through the gyepshi.

This victory is achieved not through the connecting of body and spirit, but through a separation. Ortner says that:

> The religious view of the proper relationship between spirit, body and demons may be seen as just the inverse of the lay view. The lay view... involves fear of physical weakening, in turn creating the condition for departure of spirit, and hence leaving the self prey to the attacks of demons from without. From the religious view, however, spirit *must* be able to dissociate itself (metaphorically) from body... because the body is destructible... [Thus] the religious attempt is to weaken the spirit/body connection... hence in fact strengthening spirit, and creating the condition for "defeating" the demons by realising their integration with the self (1978a:118).

Ortner recounts how one lama justified this cleavage between religious and lay conceptions as follows: '[The laity] are ignorant. In the book it doesn't say to do that, but they don't understand. They think the tiger is a demon, and they can kill it and it will never come back' (quoted by Ortner 1978a:98).

But the Lama knows better. Demons cannot be killed by such means, and thus they must keep coming back. What this means, of course, is that they must be regularly exorcised. The more they are exorcised, the more their existence is confirmed; and the more their existence is confirmed the more they must be exorcised. Food offerings may temporarily placate the demons, but also make them stronger and hungrier. The supremacy of the monasteries is achieved, according to Ortner, by the idea that no layperson can totally or permanently exorcise demons, let alone his or her demonic self.

Now all this, of course, confirms what I have already said about the division between the religious elite and the laity. It represents, I believe, an improvement over analyses which imply that Sherpas as a whole hold to a uniform view of demons as either wholly objective, pragmatic entities or as wholly transcendental projections of the self. Given the frequency and significance of exorcistic kurim in the day-to-day lives of the Sherpas, the division between the religious elites and the laity's knowledge and understanding of demons is profoundly important and cannot be ignored. But immediately we are confronted with a further problem. Do Sherpa monks and lamas really hold to the more intellectualised view of demonic tendencies in the human psyche as assumed here? Or rather do *all* monks and lamas hold to this view? Is there really a neat cleavage between those who do and do not understand the true 'meaning' of demons and exorcisms?

The first point to make is the tremendous variety of interpretations surrounding the subject of exorcism within both the laity *and* the religious elite. The Sherpas commission a vast variety of kurim, some regular (e.g., dumji, chozin) and some spontaneous (e.g., lali, srine); some public (e.g., sabjipumba, yum) and some private (e.g., kyekur, tanak); some concerned with death (e.g., tanak) and some with life (e.g., yerngu [cf. Tib. *g.yang 'gugs*], dodzong); some performed by high lamas and monks (e.g., mani rimdu, bumtso) and some by low banzin (e.g., tsendo). Most of these have some exorcistic content. In theory, all kurim are classified as distinct from shamanic rituals (a generic term for which is zozong) no matter how similar they may appear, but in practice a shamanic seance will often be referred to as a kurim.

Within the kurim category there are a number of possible classifications, for example between doa and the higher and more elaborate gyewa, or between those which involve the destruction of an effigy (*gtor ma*) and those which involve the more passive propitiation of evil through the provision of offerings (*bskang gsol*) purification (*bsangs*) and prostrations (shawa). Some Sherpas say that a kurim is necessary after the performance of a zozong while some say it is not. Some Sherpas say that kurim are preventative, some say that zozong are curative, and others say that they are both. Some say that the many kinds of do exorcisms (e.g., gyaldo, tsendo and kyekur) should be commissioned only at funerals but others regard these as 'household luck' rituals. Some explained that dumji is a big funeral for the legendary Lama Sanga Dorje while others had no knowledge of this connection, or the relation between dumji and the chozin rituals performed immediately afterwards at the nearby Kyerok gonda.[45]

Similarly, there is much difference of opinion as to the nature of demons. A few more religiously-inclined Sherpas were able to distinguish between de (Cf. Tib. *'dre*, a particularly low form of demon partial to devouring corpses), gyaptak (or negative 'shadow' influence), *btsan* (which some call the 'masters' of demons and others call the servants) and dui (a more generic term), but many Sherpas found it difficult to separate these from dhu ('spirits inhabiting rocks') and other forms of shrendi. Others again explained to me that demons 'cause' people to interfere in other people's karma (e.g., tuk and pem) and are 'behind' the activities of shrendi (e.g., nerpa, who cause sickness in order to alert living beings to attacks by dui). For some, this means that demons are more important than shrendi, but for others that they are less significant.

Responses to my questions concerning the function of kurim were just as varied. The most common was simply that 'the shrendi are sent away'. Others said that 'it is to put the demons and shrendi in their correct place'. A rising *sri*, for example, requires a srine to 'put it back down,' just as a lowered *lha* requires a lhachetu to raise it, and an intruding nerpa requires a tanak to remove it to the land of the dead. A few of the monks, and even some laymen, were familiar with the notion of demons as psychological projections but were unable (or unwilling) to elaborate on it, and appeared to attach little significance to it. As one lay friend remarked: 'maybe the demons do not bother them up there in the monastery, but why then do they spend so much time doing kurim?'.

One monk referred me to the *gtor ma* ('effigies') used in kurim, suggesting that: 'there would not be any point in making the *gtor ma* of the shrendi if they weren't real'. In the do class of kurim, for example, the various *gtor ma* (done) appear to have a common underlying form. Offerings (sane) are placed in front to attract the shrendi, followed by the flags (gyangbu) and the shrendi themselves. The changbu ('pieces of dough into which the shrendi are drawn while being rubbed across the body') are placed next to the shrendi. Behind this is the trap (*nam mkha'*) to ensure the shrendi do not escape, followed by the drum (nga) to send the shrendi away. The done is eventually carried out into the night by a peshangba ('a ritually low-status figure') and destroyed, to the accompaniment of shouts of victory.[46] Each done however, and each do appears to vary considerably according to the audience, the officiants, and the circumstances, and few lay Sherpas were able (or prepared) to explain the underlying symbolism of the done in the way described above.

Western interpretations of kurim as representing an attempt to overcome evil tendencies within oneself, and linked with this interpretations of such festivals as mani rimdu as reflecting a battle between 'good' and 'evil,' or between Buddhism and Bon[47] are met with some bewilderment, if not bemusement by the Sherpas. As the lawa ('host') of one mani rimdu said to me: 'Because you and I have good relations, you were invited into the kitchen and I gave you *chang.* And you were also invited to the "inside" *tshe dbang* [empowerment ritual] and Rimpoche gave you tu [holy water]. That is mani rimdu. The rest is just dancing'. As time went on, I began to suspect that the very notion of the transcendence over 'evil' might be a relatively recent import in Thame (as is mani rimdu itself), especially where 'evil' is conceived as a state of 'mind' rather than objectified in the form of a demon. Such a notion appears to have coincided with the rising influence of the orthodox celibate monasteries, and is somewhat out of step with the rest of Sherpa religion.

What is particularly important is that there is a wide variation of knowledge and understanding of demons and exorcisms within the religious elite as well, between individual monks, banzin lamas and shamans, as well as between different classes of practitioners. A number of lay Sherpas have commented to me that: '...some lamas say this and some lamas say that. Who to believe?' The lhawa-minung of course are seen as even more divided in their knowledge and understanding of demons. Rather than asserting a neat opposition, then, between the religious elite and the laity – which would, as it were, be a cousin of the Great/Little Tradition dichotomy – it is perhaps more accurate to think of Sherpa religion as a continuum of knowledge along which various religious practitioners and laypersons fall according to their status, wealth, religious training and role, and so on. That the religious elite tend to fall at one end of this continuum and the laity at the other is an important phenomenon, and has a variety of important implications extending well beyond the field of religion itself, but it is something which must be demonstrated through analysis rather than assumed in analysis.

A brief look at two exorcistic kurim in particular will further illuminate some of the main themes raised in this discussion. In Thame, I witnessed the performance of a sabjipumba exorcism (literally, 'offerings for the earth deities'). The ritual was led by a highly revered lama (who was also an amji) according to the prescriptions of a text which only he possessed, and with the assistance of monks only, in order to avoid tsokpa, a form of religious pollution which might be contracted from lower, less 'pure' religious practitioners. During the preparation of the offerings, which included samples of as many 'high' substances as possible (including a stone from the top of Mount Everest!), one monk from a nearby *dGe lugs* monastery claimed that the *rNying ma* Thame monks were not preparing the offerings correctly because they had not studied the texts carefully enough. The same monk however, broke one of the *bum pa* ('vase of offerings') while filling it, causing one of the Thame monks to remark with much amusement that 'the *dGe lugs pa* might claim to have more "knowledge," but they aren't very good with the "practice"'!

Once the offerings were ready, the public rituals themselves were performed. The rituals on the first day consisted of lengthy prostrations before the lama, presentation of *kha btags* ('offering scarves') to him, and a seemingly endless procession of gift giving, first between the monks and lama, then between the monks/lama and the laity, organised according to the status of those involved, and the relative values of their gifts. (The 'highest' of these included texts.) Following this was a *tshe dbang* ('life empowerment ritual'), followed by three days of recitations of the text, during which the laity presented further gifts to the lama and received his blessings. On the seventh and last day, after the performance of a serkhyim (cf. Tib. *gser skyems*, invocatory offering ritual) and a teaching by the officiating lama, the biggest *bum pa* were ceremoniously placed at auspicious points around the village and nearby environs. The rest of the *bum pa* were then distributed among the more wealthy and important families.

Some villagers explained to me that the ritual had been commissioned to subdue the demons and shrendi that had been causing illness in the village. Others said it was intended to 'keep the ground strong and quiet' and prevent the breaking of a glacial lake above the village.[48] The Rimpoche, on the other hand, later explained the ritual to me as engendering 'mindfulness' among villagers in the face of samen kokpu ('bad era'). When I asked how such variant explanations might be accounted for, one friend simply shrugged and said, 'What does it matter? It's all *cho* [religion]'. When I asked about the meaning of the teaching offered at the ritual, another friend replied

'I don't know. It was in Tibetan. Even the monks don't understand. Ask the lama'. When I asked about the absence of so many of the villagers, another friend explained to me: 'There was a gyewa [funeral feast] for A.T. today in Namche. Whoever went there got two *manas* of rice and Rs. 30'. Finally, when I asked about the presence of so many young children at the ritual, the same friend replied: 'They couldn't go to Namche. But they came to take home some tu [holy water] and *ril bu* [pills blessed by the lama] for their parents who went to Namche instead.' The presence of young children suggests that Sherpas do not attend kurim just to increase their awareness of the demonic side of their personality.

The second exorcistic kurim I want to describe briefly is the srine (cf. Tib *sri gnon*), whose purpose is to 'send back down' the very 'low' *sri* that causes a family's female members to lose their first born children. Unlike the relatively 'high' sabjipumba, where interpretations of the nature and function of the kurim varied considerably, there is a greater uniformity among Sherpas as to what a srine is. Only two high lamas and the Rimpoche are considered qualified to perform this kurim because of its 'dangerous' and potentially highly polluting nature. For this reason, however, the Rimpoche and the more orthodox (and celibate) of the lamas are never asked to perform it ('because they would be embarrassed'). The lama who does perform it in this instance (because of kinship obligations) is assisted by five monks, including one who is 'low' (who will take the *gtor ma* outside). A number of women, including the beneficiary (who is some months pregnant), are present but take no active role other than to serve as hostesses. The kurim costs some Rs. 500 to commission, plus the costs of the various offerings (all samples of 'low' substances) and the costs of food and *chang* for the officiants and guests. Because of the expense involved, it is assumed that the ritual will be effective; but because of its dangerous nature, it is important that it should be performed correctly to avoid its becoming counterproductive.

Once the offerings have been collected and the various *gtor ma* prepared, a hole is dug outside the house at dusk on a site that has been previously purified, and adjacent to a rock whose dhu has already been placated. After several rounds of *chang* for all men present, the recitation of the appropriate text begins, interrupted occasionally by refills of *chang* and discussions about who will sleep with whom after the ritual has ended. Around midnight, the lama puts on his *papier-maché* 'black hat' of the Tibetan *sngags pa* tradition and attempts to put on his multicoloured cloak. (Finding it no longer fits him, he suggests that maybe he is the pregnant one!) All males present are daubed with a black soot mixture to prevent the *sri* and other shrendi from harming us. Then, to the accompaniment of crashing cymbals and horns and more refills of *chang*, the lama throws the various offerings into the lokpar,[49] ('a 'low' and 'ugly' *gtor ma* built on a tripod, which serves as the 'jail' for the *sri*). A black calico bag containing a yak's horn filled with black sand, blood and various other offerings is then pierced with small wooden arrows[50] and all men present place a wax mark on it as witnesses to the *sri*'s incarceration. During this rather serious and dramatic event, the lama farts loudly and comments that if the offerings don't satisfy the *sri*, his farts will (i.e., it is difficult to argue that the creation of a serious spiritual ambience with psychological impact is particularly important in Sherpa rituals). The lokpar, black calico bag and other low *gtor ma* are then taken to the hole outside. After more recitations, *chang*, serkhyim and *'cham* ('dances'), the *gtor ma* are ceremoniously thrown into the hole with red hot coals, three stones, and quickly covered up with earth. Dinner, more *chang*, and the presentation of gifts and fees follows, just as dawn approaches.

One of my particular concerns in this kurim was to explore the nature and function of the various *gtor ma*. There was common agreement that the different kinds of *gtor ma* were for different gods, but beyond this, interpretations varied considerably. The officiating lama explained to me on one occasion that the *gtor ma* were the gods. On another occasion, however, he explained that the kinggur ('the highest gtor ma on the altar') represented the household head, with the lower *gtor ma* representing his wife and children, and the lokpar representing the *sri* that was bothering them. On another occasion again he referred to the *gtor ma* as the 'houses' of the gods, some more ostentatious than others because of differences in the worldliness of the gods. (These houses were necessary for the gods to be given form through the ritual.) The lay members present, however, were more inclined to see the different *gtor ma* as representing different foods for the different gods,[51] just as one serves different foods to human guests of different status. The lama rejected this however, reminding me that the high gods are not hungry and therefore cannot be tempted with food. A similar theme was that the *gtor ma* represented human bodies, offered to the gods as a form of worship and to get the gods to 'live in us'. One of the more interesting (and probably less traditional) interpretations was that the *gtor ma* was the cassette player and the god the cassette.

The point here is simply that there are multiple interpretations of religious ritual and symbols according to the context and the person asked (and the person doing the asking). It would be inaccurate and, indeed, to miss the whole point, if one were to provide only one of these interpretations as somehow definitive, representative or even illuminating. Not only do multiple interpretations tell us more about the ritual itself, they also tell us much about relations of power more generally, and the importance of the control of knowledge in establishing and maintaining these relations.

Some Implications

Before concluding, I would like to return to the question of what relevance a study of Sherpa religion might have for the study of Tibetan Buddhism more generally. Snellgrove (1957:216), von Fürer-Haimendorf (1964), Paul (1970, 1982), Samuel (1978) and even Funke (1969) have all stressed the correspondence between Sherpa and Tibetan Buddhism, and draw freely from the one to explore the other. Samuel in fact comments that: '...if the Sherpas are not really Buddhists then neither was anyone in Tibet' (1978:108). In a later article however, Samuel (1982) draws a sharp contrast between societies in the centre and on the periphery of Tibetan Buddhist influence, and suggests that 'a Sherpa-centred view of Tibetan society is in an important sense more representative than one centred on the Dalai Lama's regime at Lhasa' (1982:216). He argues that lamas in peripheral societies 'developed their autonomous political role because there was a power vacuum' (1982:221). Similarly, Aziz (1978) in her study of the people of nearby D'ing-ri, suggests that the differences between D'ing-ri and central Tibet are more significant than the similarities. She draws attention, for example, to the relatively insignificant, alien and almost wholly secular influence of the central 'government' monasteries vis-a-vis the village *ser khyim* monasteries. What applies, then, in Lhasa may well be irrelevant to the D'ing-riwa, or Sherpas, and vice versa.

And yet, it must be recalled that in the Khumbu – contrary to the experience of the *ser khyim* of D'ing-ri – the banzin lamas have lost much of their status as result of the increasing influence of celibate monasticism. This has coincided with a reduction in the influence of family, clan and local mountain deities. Clearly, an awareness of the differences between central and peripheral societies, while representing an advance on assumptions of uniformity in the Tibetan Buddhist world as a whole, must remain wary of assuming uniformity between peripheral societies. Furthermore, as I have tried to show in this paper, any assumption of uniformity within such societies is problematic, at best.

How significant, then, are the differences in religious knowledge, attitudes and practices between Sherpas and other Tibetan Buddhists? And how important are these relative to the differences within the community? If the Sherpas really are so different, is it enough merely to take note of the Sherpa case as an interesting exception, and continue to speak of the unity of Tibetan Buddhism more generally? If not, then perhaps we need to reexamine exactly what we mean by a study of Tibetan Buddhism. More attention to the variation in and distribution of spiritual knowledge, and the relations of power which this reflects and reproduces both within and between communities will, I suggest, provide valuable additional material with which to mount comparisons, and pursue such a reexamination.

I would like to mention briefly two further implications of my discussion, both of which bear on more theoretical ideas associated with Ortner, but whose significance extends well beyond the Sherpas. The first is Ortner's allegiance to the Geertzian doctrine that religious symbols are profoundly important in providing a sense of order and solution to the 'problem of meaning' in the face of disorder and suffering, and that such symbols must therefore first be analysed as systems of meaning before their relation to social structural and psychological processes is examined (Geertz, 1975). As Asad (1983) and others have argued, however, the central problem is not the meaning of symbols *per se* but rather how (and why) certain symbols and their various meanings (and not others) become established, how (and why) they are changed, and how (and why) the consequences of such symbols and meanings are recognised (or misrecognised) and rendered subject to control by an elite. For knowledge-power theorists, there are no 'natural' symbols: all symbols are social constructions – hence Geertz's celebrated two-stage formula for the study of symbols must be collapsed into one.

It is somewhat ironic – though perhaps now understandable – that Ortner has focused attention on the cleavage between the religious elite and the laity in Sherpa society without illuminating the way in which the religious elite controls the means of production and distribution of symbols and spiritual knowledge, thereby masking and thus reproducing this cleavage. She shows how the exorcism of demons – as a projection of the evil, negative side of the self – reaffirms the ultimate supremacy of orthodox Buddhism over more pragmatic rituals (1978a), yet fails to show how the very notion of demons and exorcism varies considerably, how the notion of the demonic side of the human persona is fuzzy at best for most lay Sherpas, and how the very inequality of access to such notions reflects and reproduces the religious-lay cleavage at an even more profound level. Similarly, she explains the increasing remoteness of the high gods in terms of their decreasing relevance to the laity's worldly concerns (1978b:285), yet fails to explore their decreasing accessibility for some Sherpas (and not others); how and why this has occurred, and its consequences. As Ortner (1978a:5) suggests, we may not know what ritual does until we know what it says. However, I suggest that we will not know what ritual says until we know what it does; until we have explored how the symbols of which it is composed are produced and distributed within a community; until we know how and why symbols do what they do without the laity being aware of it. Symbols disguise reality as well as reveal it, but this aspect remains hidden if we merely reproduce the intellectualisations of those who control the symbols, and for whom the meaning is clear.

The second issue I wish to raise is that of tantra's appeal to the ultimate oneness of 'natural' or worldly knowledge (over which the laity has some control) and 'divine' or spiritual knowledge (which is considered absolute and is controlled by the religious elite). In an influential discussion of gender relations, Ortner (1974) has argued that women's subordinate social status has been achieved by relegating women to a 'nature' category (by focusing on women's reproductive and nurturing capacities and roles) while men have assumed a 'culture' category (i.e., responsibility for the production and reproduction of ideas). There is, of course, much evidence for and utility in such a contrast, including among the Sherpas, where the clearest demarcation of gender boundaries is in terms of access to spiritual knowledge and power.

But there is a real danger that the nature-culture dichotomy, as Ortner has formulated it, winds up reproducing that very categorisation which gave rise to the subordination of women in the first place. This is because the dichotomy – itself a construction deriving from male-stream anthropology – gives legitimacy to the existence of 'nature' as an objective entity or 'fact' in its own right, apprehendable independently of the socially constructed meanings derived from and ascribed to it. Yet as the 'new physics' has shown us in the case of 'science,' as contemporary feminist anthropologists have shown us in the case of gender dichotomies, and even, perhaps, as tantra seeks to demonstrate in the case of the perceived distinction between the noumenal and the phenomenal (see Part 1), no such categorisations are independent of socially constructed meanings, if only because all such categorisations must be constructed through language, which is an inherently social phenomenon. That is, all meanings are ultimately produced and distributed according to relations of power/knowledge.[52]

No meaning, or knowledge, or symbol is 'natural'. Thus so-called 'natural' or worldly knowledge is not necessarily either more or less a social construction than 'divine' or spiritual knowledge, even though the two are significantly different. The failure of analytical models to recognise this may mask the tendency of such oppositions to wind up legitimating and reproducing the very inequalities they seek to explain and overcome.

Tantra, of course, has not been particularly successful in revealing the essential unity of such oppositions to today's Sherpas. Perhaps it never was. Or perhaps the increasing currency of oppositions in Sherpa discourse is due to the declining influence of tantra today. Or perhaps it is because tantra has been appropriated by, and now serves the interests of, the ruling monastic elite. Whatever the case, Sherpas as a whole continue to make an important distinction between *chos*, or religion, and worldly knowledge and activity. To the extent that they accept without question the relative objectivity, 'truth' and divine power of *chos*, they wind up legitimating and reproducing the division between the religious elite and the laity, and thus the very foundation of the structure of relations of power in contemporary Sherpa society more generally.

Conclusion

In this paper, I have developed the case for a power-centred approach to Sherpa religion, i.e., one which focuses on the relation between structure and agency, and the ways in which this relation is influenced by the religious elite's control of the means of production and distribution of spiritual knowledge and practice in day-to-day life. I have argued for the rejection of structural-functionalist, relatively static models distinguishing between 'Great' and 'Little' Traditions, or between 'nibbānic' and 'kammatic' systems. But in so doing, I have also rejected models portraying internal harmony and homogeneity or implying universal coherence and accessibility. Alternative models must remain vitally concerned with exploring differences in access to, understanding of, and benefit from any alleged single system of spiritual knowledge and power. The ethnographer must be careful not to represent the ideology and practice dominant within centralised Tibetan societies as being in any way necessarily indicative of those of more peripheral communities.

Furthermore, the ethnographer must be careful not to represent the knowledge and discourses of the religious elite within these communities as being in any way necessarily indicative of those of the laity, and certainly not of all the laity. The important differences within the laity in access to spiritual knowledge and power, e.g., between the rich and the poor, men and women, old and young, and so on, should not be ignored. Nor should differences within the religious hierarchy, e.g., between the banzin lama and lhawa-minung, the *sprul sku* and the monk, or the monastic establishment as a whole and tantric, married, village-based lamas and shamans. The control of spiritual knowledge represents, I suggest, the principal dimension of inequality in Sherpa society today.

Now what this suggests, of course, is that the ethnographer must be particularly sensitive to the way in which the knowledge and discourse contained within his or her own analyses may themselves be social constructions reflecting relations of power/knowledge in the Western academic world as much as in the community analysed. To the extent that these relations are masked, mystified, or perhaps reified through analysis, such constructions might be more accurately thought of as MISconstructions. Lobsang Lhalungpa recently commented that: 'We [Tibetans] have been able to read for ourselves, always with amusement and sometimes with concern, the degree of misrepresentation that exists in many Western accounts of our religion and culture' (1981:9).

Awareness of the possible consequences of these misconstructions, both for the community studied and for the nature of ethnography itself, should serve to qualify the idealism of an over-emphasis on *either* internal structural unity *or* division.

Yet such awareness should not render us impotent, silent or inert. Indeed, the opportunity to be self-reflexive represents one of the great strengths, I suggest, of the ethnographic endeavour. If we have added to our awareness of the subjective, arbitrary, sociopolitical nature of our own knowledge and discourse through recognising that of our friends and informants, then why reproduce idealism through embarrassment about confronting the subjective, arbitrary, sociopolitical nature of the reality we seek to describe and understand? As one of the sūtras says: 'Action divorced from appreciative discrimination (*prajñā*) is a fetter; but appreciative discrimination divorced from action (*upāya*) is also a fetter. Action endowed with appreciative discrimination is freedom' (quoted by Guenther, 1976:52). There is still much to be gained, I suggest, from an analysis which – in exploring the variation in and distribution of spiritual knowledge – reveals more about that knowledge, about relations of power more generally in Tibetan Buddhist communities, and about our own experiences and responses, as privileged observers of these rich and vibrant communities.

References

AMES, M.M. 1964. 'Magical animism and Buddhism: A structural analysis of the Sinhalese religious system.' In Harper 1964:21-52.

ARDUSSI, John and Lawrence EPSTEIN. 1978. 'The saintly madman in Tibet.' In Fisher 1978, 327-338.

ARIS, Michael and AUNG SAN Suu Kyi (ed). 1980. *Tibetan Studies in Honour of Hugh Richardson: Proceedings of the International Seminar on Tibetan Studies, Oxford 1979.* Warminster, Aris and Phillips.

ASAD, Talal. 1983. 'Anthropological conceptions of religion: reflections on Geertz.' *Man* (N.S.) 18.

AZIZ, Barbara N. 1976. 'Reincarnation reconsidered – or the reincarnate lama as shaman.' In Hitchcock and Jones 1976:343-360.

AZIZ, Barbara N. 1978. *Tibetan Frontier Families.* New Delhi, Vikas.

BABB, Lawrence. 1975. *The Divine Hierarchy: Popular Hinduism in Central India.* New York, University of Columbia Press.

BERNSTEIN, Basil. 1972. *Classes, Codes and Social Control.* London, Routledge and Kegan Paul.

BERREMAN, Gerald. 1964. 'Brahmans and shamans in Pahari religion.' In Harper 1964.

BEYER, Stephan. 1973. *The Cult of Tārā: Magic and Ritual in Tibet.* Berkeley, University of California Press.

BOURDIEU, Pierre. 1977. *Outline of a Theory of Practice.* Cambridge University Press.

BROHM, J. 1963. 'Buddhism and animism in a Burmese village.' *Journal of Asian Studies* 22.

BURGHART, R. 1978. 'Hierarchical models of the Hindu social system.' *Man* N.S. 13.

CAMPBELL, J.G. 1978. 'Consultations with Himalayan gods.' Ph.D. thesis, Columbia University.

CARTIER, R. 1975. 'Syncretism in a Sanskritic religion.' Ph.D. thesis, Rice University.

CHOPHEL, Norbu. 1983. *Folk Culture of Tibet.* Dharamsala, HP, LTWA.

CLIFFORD, Terry. 1984. *The Diamond Healing: Tibetan Buddhist Medicine and Psychiatry.* Weelinborough, Aquarian Press.

DAVID, K. (ed) 1977. *The New Wind: Changing Identities in South Asia.* The Hague, Mouton.

DE SILVA, L. 1980. *Buddhism: Beliefs and Practices in Sri Lanka.* (2nd edition). Wesley Press, Columbia.

DRAPER, John. 1985. 'Transcendence and pragmatism: a study of Sherpa religion.' Unpublished M.A. thesis, Australian National University.

DRAPER, John. 1986. 'Nagas.' *Contributions to Nepal Studies.* Vol. 13, No. 2.

DRAPER, John. 1989. 'The Sherpas "transformed"? Towards a power-centred view of change in the Khumbu.' *Contributions to Nepal Studies.* Vol. 15, No. 2.

DRAPER, John. Forthcoming, a. 'Beyond medicine: sickness, healing and order in Sherpa society.' Ph.D. thesis, University of Sydney.

DRAPER, John. Forthcoming, b. '"Disease" vs. "illness": the case for a healing.'

DRAPER, John. Forthcoming, c. 'Power and health seeking in a Sherpa society.'

DUMONT, Louis. 1980. *Homo Hierarchicus: An Essay on the Caste System.* Chicago, University of Chicago Press.

EPSTEIN, L. 1977. 'Causation in Tibetan religion'. Ph.D. thesis, University of Washington.

FISHER, James F (ed). 1978. *Himalayan Anthropology: The Indo-Tibetan Interface.* The Hague, Mouton.

FOUCAULT, M. 1975. *The Archaeology of Knowledge.* London, Tavistock.

FOURNIER, A. 1978. 'The role of priest in Sunawar society' in FISHER, J. 1978.

FRERKES, F. 1982. *Khumbu Himal.* Innsbruck, Universitätsverlag Wagner.

FUNKE, Friedrich W. 1969. *Religiöses Leben der Sherpa.* Innsbruck and München, Universitätsverlag Wagner. (Khumbu Himal, 9.)

FÜRER-HAIMENDORF, Christoph von. 1955. 'Pre-Buddhist elements in Sherpa belief and ritual.' *Man* 55.

FÜRER-HAIMENDORF, Christoph von. 1964. *The Sherpas of Nepal: Buddhist Highlanders.* London, John Murray.

FÜRER-HAIMENDORF, Christoph von. 1967. *Morals and Merit.* London, Weidenfeld and Nicolson.

FÜRER-HAIMENDORF, Christoph von (ed). 1974. *Contributions to the Anthropology of Nepal.* Warminster, Aris and Phillips.

FÜRER-HAIMENDORF, Christoph von. 1975. *Himalayan Traders: Life in Highland Nepal.* London, John Murray.

FÜRER-HAIMENDORF, Christoph von. 1984. *The Sherpas Transformed: Social Change in a Buddhist Society of Nepal.* New Delhi, Sterling.

GEERTZ, C. 1973. *The Interpretation of Cultures.* New York, Basic Books.

GOMBRICH, R.F. 1971. *Precept and Practice: Traditional Buddhism in the Rural Highlands of Ceylon.* Oxford, Clarendon Press.

GORER, Geoffrey. 1939. *Himalayan Village: An Account of the Lepchas of Sikkim.* London, Michael Joseph.

GUENTHER, H.V. 1976. *The Tantric View of Life.* Boulder, Shambhala Press.

HARPER, E.B. (ed), 1964. *Religion in South Asia.* Seattle, University of Washington Press.

HITCHCOCK, J.L. and Rex L. JONES (ed). 1976. *Spirit Possession in the Nepal Himalayas.* Warminster, Aris and Phillips.

HOFFMAN, H. 1961. *The Religions of Tibet.* London, Allen and Unwin.

HOLMBERG, D. 1984. 'Ritual paradoxes in Nepal: comparative perspectives on Tamang religion.' *Journal of Asian Studies* 43: 697-722.

JERSTAD, L.G. 1969. *Mani Rimdu: Sherpa Dance-Drama.* Seattle and London, University of Washington Press.

JONES, R. 1967. 'Shamanism in South Asia: a preliminary survey' in *History of Religions.* 7 (2).

KIRSCH, A. 1977. 'Complexity in the Thai religious system: an interpretation' in *Journal of Asian Studies.* 36 (2).

KOLENDA, P. 1964. 'Religious anxiety and Hindu fate' in Harper 1964.

LEACH, E. R (ed). 1968. *Dialectic in Practical Religion.* Cambridge University Press.

LEWIS, O. 1958. *Village Life in North India.* Illinois University Press.

LUKES, S. 1974. *Power: A Radical View.* London, Macmillan.

MANDELBAUM, David G. 1966. 'Transcendental and pragmatic aspects of religion.' *American Anthropologist* 68:1174-91.

MANDELBAUM, D. 1970. *Society in India.* California University Press.

MARRIOTT, M. (ed), 1955. *Village India.* Chicago University Press.

MORRIS, J. 1938. *Living with Lepchas.* London, Heinemann.

MULLIN, G. 1984. *Essence of Refined Gold.*
NEBESKY-WOJKOWITZ, René de. 1956. *Oracles and Demons of Tibet: The Cult and Iconography of the Tibetan Protective Deities.* The Hague, Mouton.
OPPITZ, M. 1974. 'Myths and facts: Reconsidering some data concerning the clan history of the Sherpa.' *Kailash* 2:121-132.
ORTNER, Sherry B. (= S. Ortner PAUL.). 1970. 'Food for thought: a key symbol in Sherpa culture.' Ph.D. dissertation, University of Chicago.
ORTNER, Sherry B. 1973a. 'On key symbols.' *American Anthropologist* 75:1338-46.
ORTNER, Sherry B. 1973b. 'Sherpa purity.' *American Anthropologist* 75:49-63.
ORTNER, Sherry B. 1974. 'Is female to male as nature is to culture?' in M. Rosaldo and L. Lamphere (eds) *Woman, culture and society.* Stanford University Press.
ORTNER, Sherry B. 1978a. *Sherpas Through Their Rituals.* Cambridge University Press.
ORTNER, Sherry B. 1978b. 'The white-black ones: The Sherpa view of human nature.' In Fisher 1978, 263-86.
ORTNER, Sherry B. 1984. 'Theory in anthropology since the sixties.' *Comparative Studies in Society and History* 26:126-66.
PAUL, Robert A. 1970. 'Sherpas and their Religion.' Ph.D. dissertation, University of Chicago.
PAUL, Robert A. 1976. 'Some observations on Sherpa shamanism.' Hitchcock and Jones 1976:141-51.
PAUL, Robert A. 1977. 'The place of truth in Sherpa law and religion.' *Journal of Anthropological Research* 33.
PAUL, Robert A. 1979. 'Dumje: paradox and resolution in Sherpa ritual symbolism.' *American Ethnologist* 6:274-304.
PAUL, Robert A. 1982. *The Tibetan Symbolic World: Psychoanalytic Explorations.* Chicago, University of Chicago Press.
PAUL, Robert A. 1984a. 'Recruitment to monasticism among the Sherpas.' MS.
PAUL, Robert A. 1984b. 'Fire and ice: the psychology of a Sherpa shaman.' MS.
PETERS, L. 1981. *Ecstasy and Healing in Nepal.* Malibu, Undena.
PIGNEDE, B. 1966. *Les Gurungs.* Hague, Mouton.
REDFIELD, R. 1955. *The Little Community.* Univeristy of Chicago Press.

SAGANT, P. 1976. 'Becoming a Limbu priest' in HITCHCOCK, J. and JONES, R. (eds) 1976.

SAMUEL, Geoffrey. 1975. 'The Crystal Rosary.' Ph.D. dissertation, Social Anthropology, University of Cambridge.

SAMUEL, Geoffrey. 1978a,b. 'Religion in Tibetan society: a new approach.' *Kailash* 6:45-68 and 99-114.

SAMUEL, Geoffrey. 1982. 'Tibet as a stateless society and some Islamic parallels.' Journal of Asian Studies 41:215-229.

SCHMID, T. 1967. 'Shamanism in North Nepal' in EDSMAN, C. (ed) 1967. *Studies in Shamanism.* Stockholm, Almquist and Wiksell.

SIERKSMA, F. 1966. *Tibet's Terrifying Deities.* Hague, Mouton.

SINGER, M. 1972. *When a Great Tradition Modernises.* N.Y., Praeger.

SNELLGROVE, David L. 1957. *Buddhist Himalaya.* Oxford, Bruno Cassirer.

SNELLGROVE, David L. 1967. *The Nine Ways of Bon: Excerpts from gZi brjid.* London, Oxford University Press. (London Oriental Series, 18.)

SPIRO, Melford E. 1967. *Burmese Supernaturalism: A Study in the Explanation and Reduction of Suffering.* Englewood Cliffs, NJ, Prentice-Hall. [Expanded edition, 1978, Philadelphia, Institute for the Study of Human Issues.]

SPIRO, Melford E. 1971. *Buddhism and Society: A Great Tradition and its Burmese Vicissitudes.* London, Allen and Unwin.

STABLEIN, William G. 1976b. 'Mahākāla the neo-shaman – master of the ritual.' Hitchcock and Jones 1976:361-75.

STEIN, Rolf A. 1972a. *Tibetan Civilization.* London, Faber.

TAMBIAH, Stanley J. 1970. *Buddhism and the Spirit Cults in North-East Thailand.* Cambridge, University Press.

TERWIEL, B. 1976. 'A model for the study of Thai Buddhism' in *Journal of Asian Studies.* 35 (3).

TRUNGPA, C. 1973. *Cutting Through Spiritual Materialism.* Boulder, Shambhala.

TUCCI, Giuseppe. 1980. *The Religions of Tibet.* Translated by Geoffrey Samuel. London, Routledge and Kegan Paul.

WADDELL, L. Austine. 1958. *The Buddhism of Tibet, or Lāmaism.* Cambridge, W. Heffer & Sons.

YALMAN, N. 1964. 'The structure of Sinhalese healing rituals' in HARPER, E. (ed) 1964.

ZWALF, W. 1981. *Heritage of Tibet.* London, British Musuem.

Notes

1. Techniques for the propitiation of supernaturals are found in both the Mahāyāna and Theravāda canons, and many are attributable directly to Gautama Buddha. See Gombrich (1971), and de Silva (1980), who quotes von Glasenapp as saying 'There is no doubt whatsoever that Buddha and all his adherents believed in the concrete existence of gods... It is an unpardonable mistake for a historian to assume that only later tradition has incorporated them into the teaching in order to pander to the masses' (1980: quoted 180-181).

2. Note also Southwold's (1978) argument that Buddhism cannot be classified as a theistic religion because gods are 'profane' within Buddhism.

3. This distinction, of course, derives from Leach (1968); but Leach is careful to point out that both orthodox and folk religion embody both philosophical and practical elements, and both are used by both monks and the laity.

4. There are, however, many instances in Spiro's analysis where he appears to contradict this (e.g., 1971:275).

5. The division derives from studies generated by the Chicago school of anthropology of the influence of urban cultures and economies on rural or 'folk' peasant communities. Redfield (1967:25) and Kroeber (1948:284) before him spoke of peasant society as a 'half society' and peasant culture as a 'half culture'.

6. The model is used variously to refer to differences between literate/Sanskritic and nonliterate/vernacular traditions, between universal and local religions, between Brahmin religious virtuosi and the masses, between Brahmanism and shamanism, between doctrines and practices, and so on.

7. See also Babb (1975), Berreman (1964). It is notable, however, that these critics of the Great/Little Tradition model nevertheless make extensive use of other dichotomies.

8. See Beteille (1969), Tambiah (1972), and the papers by Lynch, Berreman and Cohn in David (1977). Burghart (1978) argues that in Nepalese Hindu communities there are three 'incongruent yet coexisting and intersecting codes of hierarchy', each of which is acceded to by the others according to the context and purpose at hand. Says Burghart: 'by analysing social relations in terms of three hierarchial models instead of one, the unity of the traditional social system becomes not an

assumption in analysis but rather an observation to be analysed' (1978:519).

9. Campbell writes: 'The different levels and aspects... are part of a single religious system... the Great and Little Traditions are in a very real sense only different manifestations of One Tradition and merely express the same structure on different levels' (1978:501). Similar analyses, emphasizing the structural complementarity of traditions, have been provided by Fournier (1978) on the complementarity of the Sunwar *naso* ('priest') and *puimbo* ('shaman'); by Pignede (1966) on the Gurungs, and Jones (1968) and Sagant (1976) on the Limbus.

10. It is noteworthy, however, that Paul emphasises distinctions more in his later publications, perhaps because of his increasing preoccupation with Freudian interpretations. In 1982 he comments that 'far from being a neatly organised and integrated mechanism, [the Sherpa religion] is the precipitate of complex historical and social processes and reflects as much conflict and opposition as it does complementarity' (1982:83). Even in 1970, Paul wrote that 'local gods are somewhat inconsistent with the larger Buddhist scheme of the cosmos' (1970:371).

11. Kurim is a generic term for ritual, including both invoking and making offerings to the gods, and exorcizing demons with aid from the gods. Ortner suggests 'rites of protection' as a general gloss. A sub-class of rituals, such as the dodzongup and gyepshi, is more narrowly concerned with the exorcism of demons (Ortner 1978a:92-8 and 179 n.1).

12. I discuss in some detail the history of Sherpa religion and society and more recent responses to change in Draper 1989 and in Draper forthcoming, a.

13. The first celibate monastery in the Khumbu was established at Tengboche in 1923 by Lama Gulu, a member of a wealthy Khumjung family (later recognised by the abbot of Rongbuk monastery as a reincarnation of the father of Lama Sanga Dorje, one of the first settlers in the Khumbu).

14. Aziz (1978) notes that the *ser khyim* of nearby D'ing-ri, who are the equivalent of the Sherpa *banzin*, never enjoyed a particularly high status in D'ing-ri.

15. The 1986 bumtso at Tengboche attracted nearly 1000 Sherpas, a third of the total population of Khumbu. In 1987, donations enabled a high reincarnate lama from Kathmandu to be flown in by helicopter for the occasion and nearly 1500 people came to receive his blessing.

16. Nearly Rs. 200,000 (US$13,000) was collected to enable the bumtso to be held at Tengboche. Household expenditure patterns in Thame show that an average of nearly 20% of income will be devoted to monastery-related activities, with a further 18% spent on domestic religious activities.

17. See Draper, forthcoming, a.

18. See e.g., Schmid (1967) on the Sherpas of Helambu, Holmberg (1984) on the Tamangs, Morris (1938) on the Lepcha of Sikkim, and Nebesky-Wojkowitz (1976) on Tibetans in India.

19. Snellgrove (1957) also acknowledges that few lamas were able to explain to him why particular deities are invoked on particular occasions and not others.

20. There is considerable dissatisfaction, for example, with von Fürer-Haimendorf's recent re-study of the Sherpas (1984). See Draper 1989. A number of Thame Sherpas commented to me later in my fieldwork how half truths and half answers were often given to Western researchers 'because they asked half questions'.

21. Sierksma (1966), I think, misses the point in suggesting that '...the Tibetan people never attached full credence to that strange religion from India, which taught that the world perceived by the senses... is nothing but a fleeting illusion...' (1966:14). The point is surely that lay Tibetans did not have the choice as to whether to attach credence or not to such ideas because few had any real understanding of them.

22. See my Ph.D. thesis (Draper, forthcoming, a). One conflict involved the reincarnate abbot, a particular monk, and a resident woman and her children, and resulted in the expulsion of the monk and the woman from the monastery, the death of one of the children, and the abbot's threat to leave the monastery altogether.

23. See also Ortner (1978a:112).

24. See also von Fürer-Haimendorf (1964).

25. The status of Westerners is somewhat problematic. One friend explained that Sherpas are 'high' like *lha* ('gods'), living spiritual lives but remaining poor as a result, while Westerners are 'low,' like *klu* ('serpent deities'), living more materialistic lives down in the valleys but enjoying wealth as a result. Monolingual Australians and Americans are considered by some to be 'lower' than the bilingual Europeans who, like the Sherpas, have a high language (their own) and a low language (English).

26. Paul (1970:70) refers to 'inside people' and 'outside people'.

27. On the other hand, there *is* the condition known as tomik, which can be described as a temporary ability to 'see' the shrendi.

28. This, of course, is the thesis of Lewis (1971).

29. See Paul (1984b).

30. A classic case of this was a woman who, several years before, had angered her affines by unilaterally disposing of her deceased husband's property to people outside the family. When she became ill, no help was forthcoming and she was later found rotting in her bed. Another case was that of a woman resident at the monastery who, suffering from psychosis, had burnt down her house and committed other social and religious transgressions. No one, either monk or layperson, would agree to house or help her and she was later found drowned in the river.

31. Pem is generally not contracted from someone outside one's network of relations.

32. Many healers are required to heal patients living in different communities (e.g., the Rolwaling valley) of whose social dynamics they could not have any knowledge.

33. The lure of tourism is such that few children remain at school beyond 5th grade. Partly for this reason, there are very few Sherpas in professional careers outside of tourism, either in the Khumbu (where all service and Government positions are filled by Nepalis) or Kathmandu.

34. The teachings offered to Westerners by Tengboche Rimpoche on such subjects, and even his accounts of early Sherpa history are unfamiliar to Thame Sherpas.

35. See Chophel (1983). Lichter and Epstein (1983) also note the variation in understanding of such concepts as *bla*, *rlung rta*, *las 'bras* etc..

36. See my Ph.D. thesis (Draper, forthcoming, a) for a detailed discussion of these issues.

37. For example *nerpa* ('spirits of deceased ancestors') might be angry that their efforts to alert the living to their suffering have been ignored, and *klu* ('serpent deities') will continue to cause illness until the pollution of their residing places is removed.

38. One of the reasons for this is that healers must enter into an exchange with other healers for healing to take place when they themselves are sick.

39. It is noteworthy that, since the laity are prohibited from carrying out healing rituals, any cases of illness occurring while people are up in the yersa ('high summer pasture settlements') or outside of the Khumbu involve special difficulties.

40. The conventional anthropological view that Sherpas, and indeed Tibetans as a whole, are divided into patrilineages is, I suggest, quite problematic (see also Aziz 1978). It appears to have derived from the bias of male informants of relatively high status, and represents a misunderstanding of the significance of lineages and the concepts of **ru** ('bone', cf. Tib. *rus*) and **tak** ('blood', cf. Tib. *khrag*) in Sherpa society.

41. See Draper forthcoming, a.

42. See references to 'dharma madness' in Epstein (1977) and Clifford (1984).

43. One may note here the undertones of Gluckman's 'rituals of rebellion'. See also Sierksma's (1966) account of the Tibetan scapegoat exorcism.

44. Cited in *Gesar* vol.3 no.1 (1975):6.

45. Note the considerable discrepancies betweeen von Fürer-Haimendorf's (1964) and Paul's (1979) account of a dumji. In Thame, the dumji is entirely different again.

46. See Ortner (1978a) and von Fürer-Haimendorf (1964) for similar accounts.

47. See von Fürer-Haimendorf (1964), Jerstad (1969), Ortner (1978a).

48. The year before, I was present when another such lake broke, causing extensive environmental damage and loss of valuable farming land.

49. For other accounts of lokpar, see von Fürer-Haimendorf (1964), Paul (1979), Nebesky-Wojkowitz (1956) and Morris (1938). A similar lokpar is used in dumji.

50. The destruction of *gtor ma* with arrows and daggers is found in most 'low' kurim. See Beyer (1973), Stein (1972) and Samuel (1975). Stein suggests that the stabbing of the *gtor ma* releases the power trapped within it for the benefit of the audience. No Sherpas, however, seemed to consider this interpretation relevant.

51. See also Ortner (1975).

52. A similar argument can be mounted against the structurally homologous opposition, so popular in medical anthropology, between 'disease' and 'illness'. In other words, in attempting to take into account the subjective socioculturally influenced nature of response ('illness') to biophysiological dysfunction ('disease'), the latter's status as a legitimate category of objective fact, independent of socially constructed meanings, is reproduced. See Draper, forthcoming, b.

'CHAM: RITUAL AS MYTH IN A LADAKHI GOMPA

Ana Marko

Introduction

THE present paper is based on a performance of *'cham* or sacred dance by a number of Tibetan monks at Spituk Gompa in Ladakh as part of the festival of *Spituk Gustor* (Tib. *dPe thub dgu gtor*) held at the monastery during late January 1987. The performance was attended by some eight hundred lay Buddhists, who arrived from many different villages to reap the benefits of this major component of popular religion.

During *'cham*, the monks display sacred masks representing cosmological forces which have been 'bound' to serve the Dharma. Mythic qualities are attributed to the monks who assume the characters represented by the masks. Thubten Norbu (1982:130-1) remarks that during a *'cham* performance "...the courtyard of the monastery becomes the mandala and all the dancers are transformed into the deities which exist in that particular mandala".

At Spituk Gompa, the mythic quality of the performance is enhanced by two essential rituals: the *gser skyems* (the 'golden drink' offering) on the first day of the masked performance; and the *gtor rgyab* ('casting of the offerings') on the final day. These ritual means enable the monks to remove evil influences causing illness and other misfortunes occurring in the society.

Preparations for 'Cham

One interpretation of *'cham* is that it originated in the dreams or meditations of Tibetan lamas, who translated these experiences into ritual (Ellingson,1979:175). It is only in the context of a public performance that *'cham* has an impact on popular religion. For this to take place, the monks at Spituk Gompa prepare for the performance at least six days before the arrival of lay Buddhists as follows:

1. On the twenty-second day of the eleventh Tibetan month, preparations begin for *drug bcu ma*, the main *gtor ma*.
2. During the eleventh Tibetan month, the *bskang gsol* rituals are performed each morning for the *lha* and 'Jigs byed. These are followed by rehearsals and preparations for '*cham*.
3. On the twenty-seventh day of the eleventh Tibetan month, rituals are performed from dawn, the masks and costumes are given out to monk performers for **Dig**,* the first major day of '*cham* rehearsal and the day prior to the arrival of lay Buddhists.
4. *gSer skyems*, which takes place on the first day of masked '*cham* performance on the twenty-eighth day of the eleventh Tibetan month.
5. The following day is *gtor rgyab*, named after the cutting up of a *ling ga* and the burning of the main *gtor ma*.
6. The day after '*cham* the monks gather in the '*dus khang* ('place of assembly') to assess their individual and collective performances. Those who failed to perform correctly are disciplined by senior monks.

At an early stage of the preparatory period, attention is drawn to the protectors of the *dGe lugs pa* lineage, for the intention behind '*cham* is the ritual disclosure of the protectors or *dharmapāla* and the upholders of the Dharma, as well as those formerly hostile Bon forces now bound by oath to serve Buddhism. By appearing as the characters of the Buddhist cosmos, the monks demonstrate their own ability to serve the Dharma.

Preparations by the monastic community begin on the evening of the twenty-second day of the eleventh Tibetan month. A temporary residence is constructed in the *drug bcu ma gtor ma* and in a combined *gtor ma* for the *dGe lugs pa* protectors, Chos rgyal, the *lha* and rDo rje 'Jigs byed, the *yi dam*. The monks' preparations begin at seven in the morning in the '*dus khang*. The *dbu mdzad* (the monk in charge of the reading of texts) supervises the morning ritual recitation of text, empowering the *gtor ma*. Following the morning ritual, the monks proceed to the '*cham ra* ('dance floor') to practise

* In this article, bold type denotes a Ladakhi term for which the editors have been unable to identify a Tibetan orthography with any certainty.

the dance steps allocated to them. High monastic officials are responsible for keeping order during the activities and ensuring that monks practise their parts.

Authority behind the monastic performance of *'cham* always rests with the *'cham dpon*, who allocates the masked costumes and then himself dances to demonstrate the prescribed movements of the characters. He distributes the costumes on the twenty-sixth day of the eleventh Tibetan month, following a ritual in the *'dus khang*. On the final day before the arrival of lay people, the monks practise and the *'cham dpon* encourages them to perform with greater precision. Monks jokingly address each other by the names of the characters they portray. Some of the older monks have played every character required for a performance of *'cham*, and a certain amount of prestige attaches to playing the role of the major characters for a number of years.

Old masks not in use in the performances are endowed with great power. These are housed with the statues of the *dharmapālas* in the *mgon khang*. At one level, *'cham* is the ultimate disclosure of the cosmological forces represented in the *mgon khang*. Statues of the two main protectors of Spituk Gompa, dPal ldan Lha mo and Mahākāla, who are also among the main characters in the 'cham performance, are housed in the *mgon khang*. During *'cham*, the *dharmapālas* move out from the centre of the *'cham ra*, waving their weapons at invisible spirit realms and in the direction of the lay crowds. Many of the masks and costumes are awe-inspiring, and there appears to be a consciousness among lay Buddhists about how they should react. Thus people are reminded of the dangerous forces commanded by the monastery as they pull back in fear from the protectors.

Before *'cham* can begin, other rituals must be performed. These are highly relevant to the monks in giving them confidence to perform their parts adequately. The statues in the *mgon khang* are unveiled on either the twenty-second or the twenty-third of the month. When the Tibetan trumpets sound the call to monastic assembly, a number of monks head for the *mgon khang* to recite mantras, perform short rituals and unveil the statues. The ritual must be performed many hours before sunrise, while others are performed by the larger assembly in the *'dus khang* until about ten o'clock in the morning, when lay people gather for the performance in the *'cham ra*. Before completing these rituals, the monks have performed a complete *'cham* without masks. The statues in the *mgon khang* are covered again for a year at the end of Spituk Gustor, on the night of the twenty-ninth day of the month.

The following day's ritual activity, outlined above, begins at about three o'clock in the morning. Daybreak is marked by the completion of a ritual which summons the protectors of the monastery, housed in the *mgon khang.* The many elaborate preparations involved here are intrinsic to the masking of each monk's ordinary identity and his acquisition of the persona of a cosmological character.

gSer sKyems

From the first day of Spituk Gustor, a great many lay people wish to obtain *dbang* ('empowerment', Skt. *abhiṣeka*) from Bakula Rinpoche, and he receives them while *'cham* is being performed. People present Rinpoche with *sku 'gyes,* or gifts of money, incense, and oil or butter for lamps, and and then make similar offerings before the altars in each temple room of the *dgon pa.* In the *'cham ra,* juniper branches are burnt, providing incense for the purification of the performance site. The incense, said a monk, is intended to remove any negative thoughts and deeds which members of the lay crowd may have brought into the monastery.

Members of the Indian police force provide a buffer between the unsettled crowd and the inner space of the *'cham ra.* In former times, the more robust monks performed similar tasks. A *'cham* performed in Tibet might have a specially costumed guard "...dressed as a tiger and equipped with a cudgel made of plush with which he belabours any spectator who encroaches upon the stage" (Migot,1957:198). The police at Spituk are armed with batons, which they use to separate the audience from the central ground of the empty *'cham ra.* Disputes between the crowd and police are common, although brief.

Arguments and fights sometimes break out among the audience of *'cham.* During a *'cham* performance at Stok Gompa in 1984, the drunken and abusive behaviour of a young Ladakhi man caused a major disturbance.* The fact that he came from a village distant to

---

* This incident took place the year following my return to Sydney – my account here is based on personal correspondence.

most of the audience further provoked their anger, and they began to throw stones at him. No attempt was made to stop the growing violence, and the man was stoned to death, effectively a human scapegoat. The entire incident is reminiscent in certain respects of the scapegoat complex of Tibetan calendrical rituals.

Returning to the Spituk performance of *'cham*, on the twenty-eighth day of the eleventh Tibetan month, much of the audience waits seated for more than an hour and a half before the performance begins. The crowd stills to the sound of trumpets, and a procession of monks moves from the *'dus khang* along the top end of the steps leading down to the *'cham ra*. There follows a prolonged period of inactivity during which the monks return to the *'dus khang*. There is disappointment among the crowd that the appearance of the masked dancers is further delayed. Finally, a novice comes out of the *'dus khang* and blows a conch shell three times. At the third sound of the conch, the monks inside the *'dus khang* make the final adjustments to their masked costumes and emerge before the crowd as Ha-shang and his children. They perform the *Hatuk* (*Ha phrug*) dance as the *dbu mdzad* begins playing the cymbal.

Ha-shang's appearance is the most prominent part of the first day of the performance in masked costumes. He is portrayed as an old man with a long grey beard, and his friendly profile gains the audience's sympathy before the appearance of the fear-inspiring protectors of the monastery.

A monk describes his understanding of Ha-shang:

> Ha-shang was a very old, wealthy Chinese man. According to legend, he invited the sixteen arahats from India to China. Even Bakula was one of the arahats who went to China. The arrival of the arahats began the spread and growth of the Dharma and prosperity. Because of this, *'cham* begins with Ha-shang and his children, for they stand for Dharma and prosperity. The dance has no story other than to introduce Ha-shang to the people: this is him, he is like this. The *lha* dance because they are pleased that the Dharma flourishes and that the people have come to see them.

Ha-shang signifies long life, prosperity and abundance, and his pleasing character enables the audience to become absorbed in the reading of the surface appearance so enticingly displayed. Both his own clowning and the more prolonged clowning of his children prepare the audience for the later appearance of other comical dancers. Ha-shang and his children also facilitate an important economic exchange: his children throw ceremonial scarves or *kha btags* around the necks of the adult members of the audience, requiring a gift of money in return; and most give an amount ranging from two to twenty rupees. This is an important source of cash for the monastery.

The monks portraying Ha-shang's children frequently lift their masks to reveal their true identity: the process of masking and unmasking is another extension of a comedy positioning an economic exchange. Resistance to the comic exactions of Ha-shang's children has unfavourable consequences. Thus an older woman declines to give any money to the clowning monks, remarking that she needs it for her own upkeep, and her reluctance to give inspires the crowd to gossip about her. The crowd's condemnation confirms their belief that *'cham* is to be valued for the display and surface appearance of the characters: resistance involves reading below the surface.

Lay Buddhists like to spend some time in the non-monastic activities of Spituk Gustor taking place below the monastery. Groups of lay people have pitched tents for food and drink, and there are gambling schools which become sites of great activity, particularly during the afternoon break from *'cham*. Some people confess that they never go up to the monastery at all, and have come solely to make money by working in the stalls, while others spend the entire day gambling and drinking. Snellgrove and Richardson (1980:247) note that in Tibet:

> Although a performance of 'cham is always essentially a serious ritual for those who know its meaning, for the villagers and visiting herdsmen who throng the temples, and surrounding courtyards it serves mainly perhaps as an impressive and colourful spectacle...

This emphasises the unequal distribution of meaning as between the monastic performers of *'cham* and their lay audience.

That humour is important as an instrument in economic exchange suggests that the source of monastic authority is not absolute. Writing on the ritual use of clowning in other cultures, Babcock (1984:103) remarks that:

> Comedy may be a spiritual shock therapy which breaks up the patterns of thought and rationality that hold us in bondage and in which the given and established order of things is deformed, reformed, and reformulated; a playful speculation on what was, is, or might be; a remark on the indignity of any closed system.

In the case of Ha-shang's children, the monastery uses humour to create a playful context for exacting patronage. The *'cham* characters move from the centre of the "closed system" of the *'cham ra* to the periphery, or the space of the lay gathering, denying its autonomy. But much more serious consequences blend with the humour. To advance Babcock's (1984:103) argument in a different direction, at Spituk Gustor there is no real break on a large scale from a prescribed system in which, contrary to Babcock's (1984:103) argument, humour is deployed to re-create lay patronage of the monastery. There are other non-monastically orchestrated moments of humour which operate outside the formal humour in the masked performance of *'cham*, among them the common practice of referring to Spituk Gustor in terms of the quantities of alcohol consumed, and how friends and kin may have stumbled back into the *'cham ra* drunk after a very prolonged absence. As far as lay people are concerned, a successful Spituk Gustor is generally thought to be one where a lot of alcohol is consumed away from the monks performing the ritual.

The humour deriving from the performance of Ha-shang and his children is swept aside by the appearance of new characters in the *'cham ra*. Threatening forces are read from the characters of the *dharmapālas*. Ha-shang and his children have returned to the *'dus khang*, from which there have now emerged two mGon po Nag po Chen po, or Mahākāla. Each act repeats the full circuit of the *'cham ra*, drawing a mixture of admiration and unease from the crowd.

According to a monk, *mgon pos* dance because they are pleased to see people living their lives according to the Dharma, a standard reply dismissing any question about the deeper meaning of *'cham*. In a sense, this monk was commenting on his role as a performer and how he felt about the attending lay audience.

Benevolent mGon dkar also appear, a pair of white *mgon po* manifestations of Avalokiteśvara, associated with wealth. In the white form, mGon po is the "special protector" of Mongolian Buddhism (Getty,1978:161), and also a protector of Spituk Gompa by virtue of its special association with Mongolia. There now appears a pair of Chos rgyal Nang sgrub, members of Chos rgyal's retinue Each exit dance is known by the monks as *log 'cham*, signifying the return of the characters to the *'dus khang*.

A pair of dPal ldan Lha mo perform the dance of the female *dharmapāla*. Chos rgyal, in his male aspect, dances with dPal ldan Lha mo, performing a protective function over the ceremony.

Patterned performance in *tsam*, or pairs, is a constant in the order of appearance of other characters. A pair of Kitapa appear, members of mGon po's retinue. Finally, a *shva ba*, or deer, a benevolent, lively figure, and a *mdzo*, a symbol of strength and vigour, perform the last paired dance. Each pair descends into the courtyard for a performance and then returns to the *'dus khang*. To complete the cycle, the central figure of lCam sring appears, accompanied by Srog bdag pa and gDong dmar ma, male and female members respectively of his retinue. This trio performs the Shindo dance to an extended musical accompaniment.

Fear-inspiring protectors dance together before lCam sríng, holding an arrow and a heart, and they are joined in the dance by the Gri thogs brGyad, the other eight members of his retinue, each holding a sword and a heart, the cosmological weapons used to attack the enemies of the Dharma. They move in the direction of the lay crowd before them, then back to the inner part of the *'cham ra* and again towards the crowd.

In a description from textual sources, Nebesky-Wojkowitz (1956:89-91) traces the legend of the origins of lCam sring from a *yakṣa* father with "copper locks" and a goddess mother with "blood locks". lCam sring's place of residence is a sea of blood surrounding a copper mountain (Nebesky-Wojkowitz,1956:.89). Corpses of men and the carcasses of horses and their blood form a lake surrounded by packed mountains, with the central mountain housing lCam sring's leather castle (Nebesky-Wojkowitz,1956:90). Another textual reference (Nebesky-Wojkowitz,1956:90-1) describes his invocation from the northeastern direction and his residence:

> ...a most terrible cemetery, where the blood of enemies has been spilt and where their flesh and brain, which had been cut to small pieces, are lying scattered around. Black clouds, consisting of the smoke which rises from burning human flesh, are gathering there, and black revived corpses, whose horrible laughter sounds from afar, perform a dance... Tigers, leopards, bear, wild dogs, and many other ugly, ferocious animals roam there, and smelling the stench of blood, which rises from this cemetery, they come to gnaw the corpses... Numerous *yakṣas* as well as "*rākṣasas* and *rākṣasīs* of the four seasons" (*dus bzhi'i srin pho mo*) roam about, searching for enemies and obstacle-creating demons...
>
> In the centre of this place lies a wildly excited lake formed by the blood of men and horses, and in the middle of it is situated a red, four-cornered mountain of copper, on top of which appears, emerging

> from a sun-lotus and standing on the corpse of a man and on the carcass of a horse, the *gNod sbyin sgrol ging bshan pa* (*lCam sring*). The colour of his body is a brilliant red, like that of a ruby, and his limbs are thick and short. His mouth is widely open and in its corners warm blood is bubbling. His tongue is rolled backward, he bares his sharp fangs of copper, and his eyebrows as well as the hair of his face are yellow-red; they are all aflame like meteors and they move with the speed of lightning. (Nebesky-Wojkowitz, 1956:90.)

The text cited by Nebesky-Wojkowitz supplies further detail, including lCam sring's copper helmet and a "garland of fifty freshly severed human heads" (Nebesky-Wojkowitz,1956:90-1). During the Spituk performance of *'cham*, the hearts held by gDong dmar ma and Srog bdag pa symbolise the hearts of the enemies of the Dharma, and the sword is used to cut out their hearts.

All the characters from the first day of *'cham* appear for a full display. While the dance is in progress, a monk reads out a most important section of text designating Dam can Chos rgyal as the *yi dam* and *guru.* Instruments are played, creating a climax before the final dance for the day. With the exception of the *shva ba*, or deer, all the characters return to the *'dus khang.* The *shva ba* remains to perform the *'cham mjug pa*, or final dance. His task is to repeat the main steps performed by each of the characters, in a summation of the performance thus far. This culminates in his ritual cutting of the *ling ga* for a collectively defined end at a later stage. Then four *dur bdag* appear, the guardians of the cremation grounds, completing the cycle. The *zhva nag* or black-hatted dancers then appear, sixteen in number, swooping down on to the dance ground. This is the dance of the tantric practitioners, who represent the removal and defeat of all the enemies of the Dharma. The full array of *zhva nag* depart with equal magnificence, pausing to dance on the steps. They do not remove or change their masks as a rule until they return to the privacy of the temple. A *shva ba* descends to perform a solo dance. Sword in hand, crowned by a mask with antlers, he dances tirelessly for a long time. This role is said to be particularly difficult and only young monks have the energy to execute it well.

During the interval at Spituk, monks are served tea and a meal provided by the *dgon pa'i gzhung* or collective governing body of Spituk and its branch monasteries. Lay people move down to the stalls at the base of the village side of the monastery, and some engage in gambling and heavy drinking. A common view among the monks is that lay people who spend a long time at these festivities can accumulate more bad karma than the merit they can earn by observing *'cham.* Such people are said to begin to exhaust their stores of merit before *'cham* is over.

Guests of the Rinpoche are received for a formal lunch at a large reception area extending from his quarters. This is an all-male affair and the few women accompanying their husbands remain in an adjoining room directly overlooking the *'cham ra.* The official lunch is attended by the highest-ranking government officials and military dignitaries. A number of officials express concern about my presence during winter, at a time when there is a military alert for potential war with Pakistan. A vast permanent military camp stretches below the monastery next to the village, so that military personnel are well represented during the festival. All present are either notable patrons of the monastery, or there for purely political reasons associated with Bakula Rimpoche's former status as Member of Parliament and his present position as a member of the Minorities Commission. Because of the state of military alert, tanks and radar equipment are present on the monastery grounds, providing a frightening reminder of wars with Pakistan and China. One interpretation of *'cham* is that it removes the fear of a human or spirit enemy equally well.

Following a midday interval of almost two hours, the *gser skyems* ritual in the courtyard becomes the main focus of the dance. A *shva ba* opens the performance with a very long dance which eventually becomes the ground for the joint reappearance of all the characters of the first day of *'cham.* Monks read out texts and play instruments amidst the dance characters, who remain in the courtyard to designate Chos rgyal as a fusion of their *yi dam* and *guru.*

The cutting up of the *ling ga* on the first day of *'cham* is a major ritual task. *Dar lcog* is performed by the *shva ba*, who remain for an extended performance in the courtyard. A *ling ga* is kept in a small triangular-shaped wooden base, placed at the base of the *dar lcog* pole for the expiation of forces opposed to the Dharma. The Hebers (1978:270) report on the sacrifice of a human effigy at Hemis Gompa at the turn of the present century, confirming the idea of the expiation of evil forces. An unusual feature in their account (Heber and Heber,270:266) is the use of live animals as part of the scapegoat complex, described in a series of ritual actions:

> ...blood-reddened clay was brought to each group of animals, and, their backs having been bared, they were well smeared with a bit of

> goat's hair dipped into the ruddy mixture. The ponies, now thoroughly excited, were led off at a gallop, and circling the monastery, were brought in at the opposite entrance, were cheered, hooted, and excited with much noise, they tore across the court-yard to re-appear and vanish again. The ponies thus circled the dGon pa altogether three times, the dogs only appearing once more, while the small timid goats were led slowly across once only... .

The animals were kept solely for the annual ritual (Heber & Heber,1978:266) performed along with *'cham.* It is of concern to those present at Spituk Gustor that the monks should continue to perform long and complicated rituals which are mainly beyond lay comprehension. However, in the case of ritual moments such as the display of animals as gifts to mGon po and the cutting of the *ling ga,* there is less doubt as to their immediate benefit.

The aim behind any *dar lcog,* according to my Ladakhi and Tibetan informants, is never merely to destroy spirits and demons but to covert them to Buddhism and thus bring them into the service of the Dharma. The *ling ga* represents all the set-backs and misfortunes experienced by each person in the society. The physical body of the *ling ga* is cut into several parts, purified, empowered and symbolically eaten in order to consume its power. Masked characters lift pieces of the *ling ga* to their mouths, symbolising the consumption of the power of the transformed *ling ga.* The higher purpose of the ritual is to release the mind element represented by *ling ga* into bDe ba can, the transcendent realm of heavenly bliss. The dasha, the remains of the *ling ga,* are blessed by the recitation of texts and then offered to the *lha.*

We have here a case of separation of the mind from the body, much like the monastic goal of detaching the mind from worldly attachment. Lay Buddhists arrive with their kin at the monastery and are clearly not prepared for a lifetime of ascetic practice. The ritual tells us that even what remains of the *ling ga,* the body in the world, becomes pure in the course of the ritual and is offered to the *lha.* Lay spectators, like the cut and transformed *ling ga,* enter into direct communion with the *lha,* and are rendered pure by observing *'cham,* a movement already initiated by their presence at various rituals.

The cutting and transformation of the *ling ga,* a sign that it is subject to the active power of the monastery, is the climax of the first day of Spituk Gustor. The second and final day of the performance make the concerns expressed through the *ling ga* more explicit and decisive.

gTor-rgyab

In reference to the performance of *'cham* in Tibet as part of the New Year celebrations, Tucci (1980:150) states that "The climax of the ritual action is the expulsion of the powers of demonic destruction (*gto zor*)". These types of festival were widely performed in Tibet (Thubten Norbu,1982). One variant of the New Year ritual outside Lhasa was performed by boys, or *gar phru gu* (Hummel,1964-5 :52). Another variant of interest here is briefly mentioned by Hummel (1964-5:52) in reference to the Magars studied by Jest: the *dgu gtor*, a ritual performed to remove demons who are believed to cause illness.

Before sunrise, the monks perform prostrations and other brief rituals inside all the temples of Spituk Gompa. They are lead by either the Rinpoche or a high monastic office holder from temple to temple. Monks beat their drums, which can be heard in the village. The second day of *'cham* begins with a procession of high office holders from the *'dus khang* to the *'cham ra*, led by the Rinpoche and accompanied by musicians. An official called the Tadikpa formally assigns places for the assembly on Ladakhi carpets. Any major money sponsors may approach the Rinpoche, who is now seated on his throne in the *'cham ra*. After an interval, a monk official makes a sign indicating that any other patron may now briefly see the Rinpoche, and thus causes a sudden movement in the crowd – some see this as suggesting that there are insufficient major patrons.

After a period of inactivity and verbal exchanges between monks co-ordinating the activity, a black horse and a black dog with a white chest are brought into the *'cham ra* by a lay assistant accompanied by a monk attendant. These animals, prescribed in the text, are *bskang gsol* offerings to mGon po. As representatives of the animals closest to human society and yet potentially wild and unreceptive to the Dharma, they must be transformed into pure offerings by the recitation of a text before they can be symbolically transferred to mGon po.

The horse attempts to escape, moving wildly and drawing cries from the crowd. An uneasy atmosphere develops among the hundreds of impatient people awaiting the dancers, and the police move across the edges of the '*cham ra*. Monks continue to recite texts before the next appearance of the dancers.

The '*Cham* begins with another appearance of Ha-shang and his children, or *Hatug Ha-shang*. All the *lha* who appeared in the previous day's performance, as well as those who are to appear later, begin the Sershunma or Serjunma dance.

Various female characters, mostly representing violent and potentially threatening powers, eventually clear the way for the dance of the '*cham dpon*, the leader of the '*cham*. '*Cham* is performed only by male dancers, representing both male and female powers – celibate men dance the role of personified cosmological female powers.

This is followed by the performance of *gser skyems* in the dance of the protective *lha*, leading to the final victory, the burning of *gtor ma* at the end of the day.

The dance ground is then taken over by two *shva-ba*, or deer. dPal ldan Lha mo appears with two members of her retinue, one with the face of a crocodile and the other that of a snow lion. A princess of Gyechin appears next, belonging to a *lha* realm and holding a multi-coloured flag in one hand and a *me long*, or brass-plated mirror in the other. A *klu* (Skt. *nāga*) princess appears and like the previous character dances as a member of dPal ldan Lha mo's retinue.*

Before any full *lha* can appear in the dance, the monks read out the *sPyan 'dren* text, the invocation of *lha*. A *gnod sbyin* or female spirit appears first, followed by other wild members of dPal ldan Lha mo's retinue, including a *bdud kyi bu mo*, or daughter of a demon, and a *srin po*, or man-eater in human form. A pact is forged between a high monastic official and a *lha* legitimating the ritual. A climax is reached with the arrival of a number of forms of gShin rje, the Lord of Death, appearing in many different-coloured costumes. These forces of uncontrollable destruction are interrupted by the leader of '*cham* himself sweeping on to the '*cham ra*.

The '*cham dpon* appears alone dressed as *zhva nag*. Beginning his dance on the steps of the '*dus khang*, he offers Chos rgyal a skull, symbolising a blood offering. Holding the offering, he says

---

* Cf. the set of four *sring mo*: *lha'i sring mo, gshin rje'i sring mo, klu'i sring mo, gnod sbyin sring mo* (Nebesky-Wojkowitz, 1956:37) – eds.

"*Arkham*", or "Take", requesting Chos rgyal to accept the offering and approve the many ritual activities which he has to perform. After completing a solo dance performance in the *'cham ra*, he is positioned within sacred space by the arrival of the other *zhva nag*. The main black-hat dancer and ten others sit in a long line extending from the Rinpoche's throne, along a wall lined with Ladakhi carpets.

Lha Chos rgyal then moves onto the dance ground in *yab yum* manifestation with Cāmuṇḍī. First the *yum* manifestation appears, followed by the *yab*. All other *lha* join in for a grand performance of *gser skyems*, intended to appease the protective *lha*. Incense is lit (which has the added benefit of subduing the lay gathering), and music is played during the continuing ritual.

The *pag ling*, a *ling ga* moulded out of *tsam pa*, has already been brought out of the *'dus khang* and placed beside the *dar lcog*, ready to be cut up. The *'cham dpon* dressed as *zhva-nag* leads the cutting of the *pag ling*. The *dar lcog* ritual for the cutting of the *pag ling* is a lengthy business, performed along with a ritual dance, and sections of text have to be recited.

The second day of *'cham* indicates by its name the importance of *gtor ma* in the ritual. The cutting up of the *pag ling*, representing a naked figure of a man with enlarged, swollen genitals, symbolises the removal of obstacles accumulated over the past year. Snellgrove and Richardson (1980:247) describe the performance of *'cham* in Tibet, and its use of *ling ga*:

> The action of the manifested divinities in this ritual dance is directed towards the overpowering and expulsion of evil, usually represented by a small sacrificial model of a human body, known as a linga or 'sign'. Having imbued its 'life force', the dancing performers ritually slay and dismember the human effigy, thus performing a kind of general exorcism of evil for the whole community... .

In the *ling ga* are highly compressed and concentrated negative forces, which can be read as representing aspects of the collective body of all those present for the performance of the ritual. *Ling ga* are often made to represent a highly sexualised human form. Unlike the more abstract *ling ga* used in the first day of the ritual this one is clearly identifiable to the crowd. Nevertheless, those seated furthest away from the central ground of the *'cham ra* are unable to identify the object. In this and other ways, the *ling ga* characterises the continual ambiguity between monastic disclosure of value and the allusiveness of precisely what is disclosed.

The cut *pag ling* separates inherent coarse material, or personified attachment to bodily existence, from the refined potential of the *ling ga*, which is transmitted by ritual to a transcendent realm. Once the *pag ling* has been exposed to these ritual transformations, the remains are taken to the *'dus khang* for further ritual. In a confirmation of Stein's argument, Paul (1979:297) puts forward the view that the slaying of the *ling ga* goes well beyond a slaying of demons. The life force of demons is separated from embodiment of evil, the ritual benefiting the monks in particular (Stein,1957. Paul,1979:297). Life power has to come from a source, the demons, through the ritual cycle of regeneration of life power (Paul,1979:297). By virtue of their asceticism, the monks are favourably placed to accumulate *tshe dbang*, or life force, transferable to the entire community (Paul,1979:297). In my view, the social impact of the ritual attention given to *ling ga* lies primarily in its claim to transform the body, thereby increasing the potency of monks as ritualists in the society. This power does not fundamentally derive from demons, as Paul (1979) argues, but rather from the lay presence at the site where the ritual is performed.

Before *dar lcog* ends, and before the climax of the *'cham*, many of the lay crowd have left the *'cham ra* and monastery. A number of monks and lay people describe this part of the ritual as too long, slow and detailed to hold the crowd's interest. Nevertheless, one part of the ritual cannot fail to capture their interest: the spectacle of the stabbing of a human effigy. Exposed to the earlier dances and approaches of demonic forces represented in certain *'cham* characters, the effigy depicts evil forces, and their inevitable violent end as a transformation.

After the cutting of the *ling ga*, the monks slowly make their way to the *'dus khang*. Only a hundred or so lay people remain, some in the courtyard and along the steps, and others performing prostrations inside the *'dus khang*. There is a sense of strain in having performed *'cham* and ritual for such a long time, a feeling shared by lay people, who are becoming unsettled.

Inside the *'dus khang*, the monks, still dressed in their costumes, perform the zorgyul ritual. A *lcags li*, or image of Chos rgyal, is removed from the *gtor ma*, which is symbolically changed into *zor* and is carried outside the *'dus khang* by a procession of monks. The *zor* contains all the negative powers given form during the ritual and the preparations, thus facilitating the final transformation.

The performance is behind schedule, and after final hurried preparations the *gtor ma* is carried to the *gtor khung* in full procession, led by the *'cham dpon* and accompanied by the chief characters, including Chos rgyal, dPal ldan Lha mo and *shva ba*. The *gtor khung* is now placed outside the *'cham ra*, where the remainder of the ritual must begin facing the setting sun from this site on a hill above the village. Lay people follow behind the monks in procession, stopping at the entrance leading outside the *'cham ra* for the recitation of text.

The burning of *gtor ma*, empowered into *zor*, demands the performance of another section of *'cham* in which *shva ba* figures prominently. This time he dances before the *gtor ma*, as two hired labourers from Bihar gather branches to fuel the fire. Lay Buddhists do not like to come into such close contact with the *gtor ma* empowered as *zor* ready for the final removal of evil spirits, for they fear that evil spirits might enter them instead of the *gtor ma*. The *slob dpon*, or teacher and abbot of the monastery, is handed a bow and arrow, the tip of which is then lit. The *gtor ma* is tossed into the triangular wooden frame of the *gtor khung* to contain its power. Forces of destruction, spirits causing disease in humans and domestic animals, are vanquished and the ritual clears the way for health, prosperity and peace in the village. Benefits spread from the *slob dpon* as a central actor in the personified power of Spituk Gompa, emanating in the four cardinal directions.

The arrow is shot into the *gtor khung*, while small crowds watch from a considerable distance. A *'cham* is performed by the monk with the mask of the Deer, symbolising victory and the removal of destructive forces.

The *'cham dpon* performs the Sunggong dance, ensuring that the evil does not return from the fire. Fragments of *gtor ma* in the fire are pushed firmly into the flames. Another procession leads the return to the *'dus khang*.

In the *'cham ra*, a text is recited for Chos rgyal as six characters dance, representing the *lha*. In the meantime, the *'cham dpon* has gone to the *'cham ra* and the *'dus khang* to make other preparations. Inside the *'dus khang* another ritual is performed around the remaining large *gtor ma*, Shaktor. In the *'cham ra*, the dancers perform Nansol, returning to the *'dus khang* in pairs at the end of each stanza of recited text. A ritual invoking all auspicious things is performed, increasing the benefits already accruing through the many days of ritual activity. The doors are closed to signify tantric ritual in progress.

The idea, common to Tibetan and the Ladakhi rituals associated with the New Year, that the monastery has life-bestowing and life-replenishing powers is on this occasion expressed in a particularly idiosyncratic manner after the *'cham* performance and before the burning of the *gtor ma*. On the second day of the performance, a Rinpoche from Phiang Gompa delivers a short speech to the crowd in the Spituk *'cham ra*. He reminds the crowd of an incident several years ago, when Ladakhis demonstrated against attempts at government-instigated land reforms and other forms of intervention. The Ladakhis attacked and set fire to the police station at Leh and the police opened fire, killing two of the demonstrators, including a monk from Phiang Gompa. In the audience, there is a woman belonging to the household into which the monk-demonstrator was born a generation ago. The Rinpoche asks this woman to come forward with her baby, which, he explains, is an incarnation of the deceased monk, has been given the monk's name and is already promised to the monastery. This stirs the crowd deeply, and they discuss the miraculous nature of the event and how an "ordinary monk" has become a Buddhist hero, incarnating quickly to return to the monastery. A sceptical Ladakhi remarks to me that knowing the past life of a newly born child is more difficult than the crowd seems to think, particularly when the child is not the reincarnation of a Rinpoche. He suggests that promising the child to the monastery might simply have been a token of good intention towards the Dharma. And the child, after all, will be elevated to a senior monastic position as soon as he joins the monastery.

Following the second of the two days of *'cham* before lay people, it is necessary for the monastery to re-establish its separateness from the lay community. Internal monastic disciplinary measures are essential to maintain the sense of the monastery as an exemplary source of vitality and service to those outside through its ascetic practices. Thus, after the second day of *'cham*, monks are required to assemble in the *'dus khang*. The occasion is an entirely internal monastic procedure: the *'cham dpon* will single out and discipline any monk who has not performed adequately over the period of the preparations and performances of *'cham*. Ideally, the disciplining should take place before the full assembly of monks, and individuals selected for punishment should perform prostrations before the entire assembled monastic community and the statues of the *'dus khang*. However, a number of monks report that these formalities do not take place before an entire assembly, and that it is sufficient for those concerned to be aware that they did not perform to standard; or if they have already received a sign from the *'cham dpon*, they may appear before the statues at the *'dus khang*, where they may be required to perform several sets of one hundred and eight prostrations. Their discipline as monks is thus enforced, and their difference from lay Buddhists is emphasised.

Conclusion

'Cham displays, in a very dynamic way, the power relations between the monastery and lay Buddhists. In the annual performance of *'cham*, monks provide immediate representation of the forces and workings of the cosmos through the sacred masks under their control, thus removing some of the ambiguity which surrounds those forces. Ritual, cosmology and performance are brought together at the monastery in a way unparalleled by any other ritual occasion, meeting both the pragmatic needs of the laity and the specialised requirements of the monastic community.

Ritual specifically enhances the mythic attributes permeating *'cham*, and with them the social relationships required for the performance, thus reaffirming a difference in power between lay Buddhists and monks, who command the masks. Lay attendance is an endorsement of these social relationships, as well as an exchange relationship enabling lay Buddhists, through their patronage of the monastery, to obtain the symbolic values attributed to the performance. Exchanges with the monastery, whether in the form of gifts of money to the Rinpoche, temple gifts, or the sums playfully exacted by Ha-shang's children, constitute the lay person as an active agent in the transformation of self and society made available by the performance of *'cham*. Lay people are required to respond to the performance by confronting the masks. Their belief in the Three Jewels, Buddha, Dharma and Sangha, is affirmed.

Whether one participates by observing *'cham* or plays a part as a sacred character of the masks, the interaction is a part of a cosmogonic cycle, and the power and influence of the monastery is reasserted. Power is immanent in the performance behind the masks.

References

BABCOCK, B.A. 1984. "Arrange me into disorder: Fragments and reflections on ritual clowning", *Rite, Drama, Festival, Spectacle. Rehearsals Towards a Theory of Cultural Performance*, Edited by John J. MacAloon. Philadelphia, ISHI.

GETTY, A. 1978. *The Gods of Northern Buddhism.* New Delhi, Munshiram Manoharlal.

HEBER, A.R. and Kathleen M. HEBER, 1978. *Himalayan Tibet and Ladakh.* New Delhi, Ess Publications.

HUMMEL, S. 1964-65. "Boy dancers at the New Year's Festival in Lhasa", *East and West*, N.S. Vol.15, Nos.1-2.

MIGOT, A. 1957. *Tibetan Marches*, Translated by Peter Fleming. London, Richard Clay and Co..

NEBESKY-WOJKOWITZ, R. 1956. *Oracles and Demons of Tibet*, The Hague, Mouton.

NORBU, T.J. 1982. "Festivals of Tibet", *Journal of Popular Culture*, Vol.16, No.1, 126-134.

PAUL, R.A. 1979 "Dumje: Paradox and resolution in Sherpa ritual symbolism", *American Ethnologist*, 6:274-304.

SNELLGROVE, D. and Hugh RICHARDSON. 1980. *A Cultural History of Tibet.* Boulder, Colorado, Shambhala.

TUCCI, G. 1980. *The Religions of Tibet*, Translated by Geoffrey Samuel. London, Routledge and Kegan Paul.

THE MAKING OF GONPA

Norbu Rinpoche from Kardang and Kunga Rinpoche from Lama Gonpa

Elisabeth Stutchbury

Introduction

Issues of modernity, "in culture as lived *local* experience and the understanding of the latter in *global* perspective... about how collective and individual identities are negotiated" (Marcus 1992: 311), are a double-edged sword when applied to the arena of my field work, for Lahul, three high Himalayan valleys populated by an ethnic Buddhist minority in modern day India, is also known in the Tibetan Buddhist world as Karzha Khandroling, 'Karzha land of the *ḍākinīs'* (the land of those who "move through space", the feminine principle of enlightenment), an important power place of spiritual practice visited by wandering yogic practitioners, on the periphery of the Tibetan cultural arena. The people of Karzha continue to negotiate their identity between two globalising perspectives, Indian and Tibetan. These perspectives in their modern manifestations ironically merge, with various emergent possibilities in the process of identity formation.

This paper is a radical revision of the paper originally presented in 1988 in the session, 'Tantra and Popular Religion in Tibet'. Although the focus of both papers is similar, my thinking about the material presented and my treatment of it has matured considerably through the process of 'writing ethnography'. My doctoral dissertation was completed in the interim, and I am currently engaged in the revision of that work for publication.[1] In the process of my research, and more particularly in the process of writing about it, I have grappled with issues of reflexivity, now acknowledged in the discourses about anthropology, and ethnography (eg. Clifford and Marcus 1986; Marcus and Fischer 1986).

My approach throughout this process has been both to give primacy to my experience in the field, and to rely upon my understanding of the nature of existence, derived from my involvement with Tibetan Buddhist spiritual practice, in my efforts to develop appropriate conceptual frameworks and techniques of presentation. Consequently, Abu-Lughod's suggestions in 'Writing Against Culture' for an ethnography which particularises rather than generalises; and her discussion of the dilemmas faced by feminists and 'halfies',* have helped to crystallise my thinking about several issues I faced in writing this ethnography.

In this paper, the processes which create continuity in spiritual practice through time and space, and through which identity is negotiated, are explored in particular detail. I have presented the connections discussed diagrammatically, locating the focus of these connections around one particular yogic practitioner, for this is the manner in which the connections are constructed by the Karzhapa. In the discussion, I have attempted to extend and contextualise these connections in the broader Tibetan cultural arena. These same connections could have been ordered and constructed in a diagram using a linear time frame, more in keeping with a western historical appreciation of the material covered.[2] However, the construction presented is more representative of the ways in which identity was negotiated by the spiritual practitioners with whom I worked (see diagram, p. 189).

In order to elucidate the process through which a small village *gonpa* (*dgon pa*, religious institution frequently glossed as 'monastery') was established in 1912, in Karzha Khandroling (*dKar zha mKha' 'gro gling*), a border region in the Tibetan cultural arena, I focus on the biographical details of one particular individual, Norbu (*Nor bu*, 1883?-1947) from the Khyemches[3] household in Kardang village. This *gonpa* is now known as Kardang Gonpa, and is regarded as the most active religious establishment in modern-day Lahul, a Sub-District of Himachal Pradesh, India. The details of Norbu Rinpoche's life, and thus the founding of Kardang Gonpa, were collected orally from several individuals, some of whom had been disciples of this teacher, and some of his friend and vajra brother,[4] Kunga (*kun dga'*) Rinpoche (1884?-1967), from the Abizhi household. A few years after Kardang Gonpa was founded, Kunga

---

* "People whose national or cultural identity is mixed by virtue of migration, overseas education, or parentage... and the indigenous anthropologists to whom they are related... dilemmas that reveal starkly the problems with cultural anthropology's assumptions of a fundamental distinction between self and other" (Abu-Lughod 1991: 137).

Rinpoche and a few of his disciples established a small hermitage known as Lama Gonpa, above neighbouring Gozzang village.

Both Khyemchespa'i Norbu and Abizhi'i[5] Kunga were disciples of Togden Śākya Śrī (*rTogs ldan Sha kya Shri*, 1853-1919), a great yogi of the Drukpa[6] Kargyu (*'Brug pa bKa' brgyud*) lineage of Tibetan Buddhism, from Kham (*Khams*), East Tibet. The period of political and spiritual ferment in Kham during the nineteenth and early twentieth century is now generally referred to as the *Rimé* (*ris med*) or 'non-sectarian/non-biased movement', and Togden Śākya Śrī is an important figure in the Drukpa transmission lineage associated with this period of change. Information about the way in which lineage connections were made, and about the building of Kardang Gonpa in a border region on the western extremes of the Tibetan cultural influence, informs our understanding of the ways in which the developments in Kham in the nineteenth century affected the larger Tibetan cultural arena, an effect which continues to permeate Tibetan Buddhism today, not only in Tibetan cultural areas, but also in the expanding sphere of Western Tibetan Buddhism.

Karzha and Lahul

The narrow, glaciated valleys of the Chandra and Bhaga Rivers of Lahul have long formed part of the western trade corridors across the inner Himalaya, connecting the subcontinent of India with Central Asia, and the peoples of Lahul have long experienced Buddhist and Hindu, as well as Moslem, social and cultural influences. The situation in Lahul today can thus be viewed as part of an ongoing process of integration and accommodation of various cultural influences which have coalesced in the region. The history of this region has not been thoroughly researched, and there is little historical primary source material, except for the last century and a half, for which we have written sources. However, the following sketch will orient the reader.

The entire western Himalaya was of critical importance in the development of the tantric or *siddha* tradition of the Vajrayāna from at least the 7th century (see Klimburg-Salter 1982). In local oral traditions in Lahul, the region is associated with Padmasambhava (the 'lotus born') or Guru Rinpoche ('precious teacher') as he is commonly called, one of the main cult figures of the Tibetan tradition, revered by all Tibetan Buddhists, as the yogic saint who introduced Buddhism in its tantric form to Tibet in the 8th century. The confluence of the Chandra and Bhaga rivers is identified as one of the eight cremation grounds particularly empowered by Guru Rinpoche on his journey through India, Tibet and the Himalaya.[7] Furthermore, Ghāṇṭapa, one of the eighty-four *mahāsiddhas*, the Indian tantric teachers of the 7th to 11th centuries, is said to have converted the peak Drilburi (*dril bu ri*, 'bell mountain'), which rises above the confluence, into a *maṇḍala* of Cakrasaṁvara (Lauf 1971:366-367; Tobdan 1984:84)

Historical evidence to corroborate these two local traditions is lacking, although art historians attribute a very early date (perhaps the 8th or 9th century) to Guru Ghantal, the temple above the confluence on the pilgrimage route, which is in keeping with the local attribution of this temple to Guru Rinpoche (Lauf 1971). For the famous Drukpa yogi, Gyalwa Gotsangpa Gonpo Dorje (*rGyal ba rGod tshang pa mGon po rDo rje*, 1189-1258), textual evidence in his *namthar* (*rnam thar*)[8] or sacred biography (see Tucci 1971) supports the local oral traditions pertaining to his sojourn in Karzha in the early 13th century *en route* to Oḍḍiyāna.[9] His practice and residence in various caves apparently strengthened the Buddhist cultural strand within Karzha, and Karzha's importance as a place of pilgrimage in the wider Tibetan context is at least partly attributable to Gotsangpa. Gotsangpa's disciple Orgyanpa (*O rGyan pa*, 1230-1293?) also visited Karzha in the thirteenth century. Another Drukpa yogi, Taksang Repa (*sTag tshang Ras pa*), the founder of Hemis Gonpa in Ladakh, inspired by Gotsangpa and Orgyanpa, came to Karzha in the seventeenth century (Lauf 1971; Tucci 1971:369, 377-417). Others, such as Trulzhi Ngawang Tsering (*'Khrul zhig Ngag dbang Tshe ring*, 1717-1794) made several pilgrimages to Karzha (Nawang Tsering 1979: 3-4, 33-35).

Karzha, then, is an important *né* (*gnas*) or power place of pilgrimage within the Tibetan tradition, particularly within the tantric or *siddha* tradition of the Vajrayāna, associated with Padmasambhava and with Cakrasaṁvara, the main *yidam* (*yi dam*, 'meditational deity') of the Drukpa yogic tradition. The evidence suggests that the region has had a long and continuous history of degeneration and regeneration of Buddhist culture, and that it has been visited by numerous wandering yogic practitioners. The textual evidence of the *namthar* of some of the more important lineage masters of the Drukpa verifies Karzha's significance as a place of pilgrimage and practice, and reports aspects of the resurgence of Buddhist culture, although many other visits by practitioners of lesser renown, and probably also by lay folk and traders, are unrecorded.[10]

As previously stated, the historical data available from primary sources is scanty, and a thorough investigation of the region has not been undertaken. Thus the reconstruction of the flow of events is problematic, and a detailed history for Lahul will probably remain elusive (see Roerich 1931: 27-34). Furthermore, although factual details of the political history of the region inform our understanding, a more complete appreciation of the social and cultural processes in the area is largely speculative. For instance, although Lahul may never have been part of Ngari Kor Sum (*mNga' ris sKor gsum*, the Western Tibetan Empire of the 10th and 11th centuries), it is reasonable to regard the entire region of Lahul as part of what is more loosely called Ngari, or 'Western Tibet', a trans-Himalayan cultural zone with considerable Tibetan and Buddhist involvement, until the 16th century. It was then taken over by the Hindu Rāja of Kulu, and so became politically part of what is now India, although this did not preclude further Buddhist cultural influence, particularly in the 17th and 18th centuries. The area is therefore one of the few predominantly Tibetan cultural regions which did not fall into Chinese hands at the time of the 1959 uprising, and thus did not suffer during the Cultural Revolution.

However, as is apparent from Lahul's position on a significant trade corridor through the Himalaya, the region has for several hundred years had important links with the society and culture of the Indian plains to the south. Considerable trade and financial benefits were to be derived from the control of the negotiable passes across the Himalaya. Prior to Independence (1947) and Partition, there was also some Moslem presence in Lahul.

Another significant channel of external cultural influence dates from the mid-19th century. In 1857, Kyelang, across the valley from Kardang, became the centre for the activities of Moravian missionaries, who stayed until 1945.[11] While the missionaries had little success in converting the local population to Christianity, they introduced the metal cooking and heating stove with chimney, Western-style education, and knitting. Their agricultural activities met with acceptance, and they were responsible for the introduction of the potato[12] and other crops. The colonial British administrators did not rule directly in Lahul, but exercised their authority through the *Thakur*, the local rulers. Nevertheless, they had considerable effect in the region, particularly encouraging trade with Tibet (Harcourt 1972 reprint, Huttenback 1961: 482-485). This fascinating era in the history of Lahul, for which written records are available, awaits thorough research.

The most recent resurgence of Tibetan Buddhist influence in Karzha began at about the turn of the century. Several men, among them Kardang Khyemchespa'i Norbu, travelled to East Tibet and received teachings from Togden Śākya Śrī. Later, a new *gonpa* was built above Kardang village to enable these people, and others who were inspired by them, to practise the meditation techniques which they had been taught. These events are the focus of this paper.

The activities at Kardang Gonpa today are best understood as a continuation of the social and cultural process of Buddhist resurgence which began earlier this century. Naturally, the influx of Tibetan refugees into India has further stimulated Buddhist influence in the region, although trans-Himalayan trade through Lahul was damaged by the closure of the Tibetan frontier. There have been no settlements of Tibetan refugees in Lahul, although descendants of Togden Śākya Śrī and associated teachers within this particular Drukpa lineage have had a significant effect upon the practice of Buddhism, continuing their close relationship with the *gonpa*, where they found refuge in 1961. This family group, like may other Tibetan refugees, established residence in the Kulu-Manali valley, several hours journey to the south, across the Rohtang Pass (3, 980 metres, 13,050 ft.).

The British constructed a bridle path across the Rohtang and through Lahul in order to facilitate trans-Himalayan trade. A century later, the Indian Government built a road across the Rohtang, connecting Lahul to plains India, primarily for military purposes. The road work took place in the late 1960's and the route was open to vehicular traffic in the early 1970's. This high-altitude road enabled the Lahuli people to develop the seed potato as a cash crop, which resulted in significant changes in the agriculture and economy of the region. Although the advantages in terms of increased income have been most welcome in this ecologically difficult inner Himalayan valley, the long-term environmental damage is likely to be devastating and irreparable. In addition, Indian cultural influence has increased. For instance, Tibetan dialects, which used to be the *linguae francae* of the area, have since the opening of the Rohtang Road been replaced by Hindi, an indication of changing identity within the region.

The Lahuli people have been enterprising, and many have transformed their material condition from considerable poverty to comparative wealth. Many Lahuli people now not only spend winter in the Manali valley, which is less severe and less isolated, but have settled permanently there, growing apples or operating tourist concerns such as hotels and restaurants.[13] However, they retain their land in Lahul, which is worked with the assistance of itinerant labour during the summer months, when the potato is grown.

It is clear that Lahul has been an important place in the process of cultural interchange through the Western Himalaya. An indication of this is the extent of cultural differentiation – and hence diversity of identity – found in the region. Many of the people from the Chandrabhaga valley, the lowest and southernmost valley of the conjoined rivers in Lahul, regard themselves as Śaivite Hindus, whereas the majority of the inhabitants of the Bhaga valley regard themselves as Buddhist. Some Lahuli people operate as Buddhist in some social contexts, and Hindu in others.[14] The valley of the lower Chandra (called Tinan), the lower Bhaga (Punan or Gar), and the upper Bhaga (Tod, Tib. *sTod*), form the modern administrative unit or Tehsil of Lahul, and it is this region which is known locally and by other Buddhists (Tibetan, Ladakhpa, Zangskapa and Spitipa) as Karzha.[15]

Although Karzha is part of the larger Tibetan Buddhist cultural arena, many aspects of the society and culture provide the people with their particular ethnic identity – the people are not Tibetan nor do they regard themselves as such, although they recognise a deep common bond in their Buddhist practice. They do regard themselves as Indian, at least in some contexts, although they acknowledge that their adherence to Buddhism and many of their social practices set them apart from the majority of Indians, and as already suggested, their identity is changing, and contextual.

The brief description of Kardang village and *gonpa* which follows places Karzha, and particularly Kardang, within the broad comparative framework of the Tibetan cultural matrix. This description completes the background information necessary for the presentation of the social and cultural processes which led to the founding of Kardang Gonpa in 1912, the main focus of this essay.

Kardang Village and Gonpa – The Comparative Context

Despite the increasing influence of Indian society and culture, Tibetan Buddhism continues to flourish in Karzha, and has been used as a conscious means of self-identification during the past twenty years, which have seen many significant changes in the region, notably the growth of a cash economy. However, the pattern of Buddhism in Karzha shows a number of characteristic differences from other, better-known parts of the Tibetan cultural region.[16]

From the literature on Tibet we are reasonably familiar with the large monastic communities of the Gelugpa (*dGe lugs pa*), another of the main lineages or traditions within Tibetan Buddhism. The principal seats of the Gelugpa were near Lhasa in Central Tibet. Gelugpa monastic communities frequently lived in wealthy establishments called *gonpa*, which accommodated thousands of monks. These were landed institutions, collecting taxes from the surrounding villages. The few nuns associated with these communities lived in physically separate, smaller establishments, known as *ani-gonpa*.[17] However, this is but one of the variations of the social manifestation of Tibetan Buddhism to be found.

In contrast to this arrangement, which was characteristic of Central Tibet and persists to the north of Lahul in Ladakh, the people of Karzha practise Vajrayāna Buddhism in small village *gonpas* where both males and females reside. There is close cooperation and interdependence between the *chöpas* (*chos pa*, 'religious practitioner') and the village laity, and the majority of the *gonpa* inhabitants are from the associated village.

During my fieldwork from 1981-1984, Kardang village consisted of twenty-six households, each inhabited by an extended family.[18] In 1992 one house was demolished, as the Abizhi household, which had previously lived in both Kardang and the neighbouring village of Gozzang where they have their fields, had decided to abandon their Kardang residence.[19] The ideal is that each family owns not only its village house but also a small house at the *gonpa*, which is situated some half an hour's walk above the village, at about 11, 000 feet above sea level. During my initial fieldwork there were seventeen small houses at the *gonpa*, and by 1992 another had been built. All members of a family, both male and female, who decide on a religious life normally reside in their family's *gonpa* house. Brothers and sisters, aunts, nephews and so on live together in the one small house, each with his or her own small room, and their families supply them with most of their needs. Most village households also have a small room in which they keep a Buddhist shrine, where daily offerings are made.

There were 28 members of Kardang Gonpa in 1983, thirteen male and fifteen female practitioners. I did not count myself as a member of the *gonpa* community in this census, although in most ways I was regarded as such. (In 1992 the *gonpa* population was a little lower, as several of the older members had died. However, new recruits had also joined). Unlike most of the other *gonpa* members, however, I had not taken the *getsul* (*dge tshul*, 'novice') vows to 'go forth from the life of a householder', that is, to take monastic ordination. My position was similar to that of two other young women from Kardang villages who were in the process of becoming *chomo* (*jo mo*, '*religieuse*'). These women had cut their hair, although they still wore lay clothes. They spent the winters at the *gonpa* practising meditation, but worked in the household's fields and lived in the village for at least some of the summer. They were free to choose whether to take vows and enter fully into the religious life of the *gonpa* or to return again to village life. In Karzha, individuals generally follow their own inclination with regard to the religious vocation, and do not begin spiritual practice until they are at least in their teens. This contrasts with some other Tibetan cultural areas, where households may be obliged to provide sons to the regional *gonpa* as part of a formal tax arrangement, or where the decision to commit a child to the monastic life is made by the parents when their child is still quite young.

Kardang Gonpa has a particular history and position in Karzha society, and today it has the largest membership and is one of the most active and highly regarded *gonpa* in Lahul, although in many ways it is similar to the other village *gonpa* in the region. Ideally, every village has its own *gonpa*, although the smaller settlements of only a few households do not have *gonpas*, and anyone from these smaller villages who wishes to become a practitioner will join one of the nearby *gonpas*.[20]

The Founding of Kardang Gonpa

Having sketched the historical processes and the comparative Tibetan cultural framework which contextualises the events in Karzha at the beginning of this century, I begin the presentation of the material which pertains to the founding of Kardang Gonpa with transcripts collected from two of the most senior lamas (*bla ma*).[21]

Jhampa Mémé and Abhi

Before Kardang Gonpa was built, there were only two *chorten* (*mchod rten*, Skt. *stūpa*) up here. No one stayed up here. There was a small *kothi gonpa*, a village *gonpa*, beside the Lharje family's house, as well as Jabjez (*zhabs rjes*, 'foot,' honorific) Gonpa. When Atsa (*A sar*) Rinpoche came to Kardang, he stayed in the *kothi gonpa*.[22] (Lama Kanjur & Lama Paljor Lharje)

A lama from Zangskar – we call him Jhampa (Chamba?) Mémé[23] – came to Gondhla village and stayed there for quite some time. At that time there were no *chöpa* living there. No-one knows quite how long ago that was, nor for how long he stayed there at Gondhla, living near the confluence of the Chandra Bhaga Rivers, which is an important place for practice, one of Guru Rinpoche's cremation grounds, you know. As there was no-one looking after Jabjez Gonpa in Kardang village, where Gyalwa Gotsangpa left his knee prints,[24] one man from Kardang Kyelapa house suggested that Jhampa Mémé should come and care for this *gonpa*. He agreed on the condition that he was given 40 kilos of barley each year, on which he could live. So he moved to Kardang, and remained there to care for the *gonpa*. Jhampa Mémé had a wife, also a practitioner – maybe she was also a Zangskapa, maybe from Gondhla – we're not so sure.[25] She was called 'Abhi', which we use in Karzha dialect for older female practitioners – like mémé'. (Lama Kanjur & Lama Paljor Lharje)

When Jhampa Mémé died, a *chorten* was built for his cremated remains above the village. Then Abhi spent most of her time practising up there beside the *chorten*. When Norbu Rinpoche returned from Kham, with instructions from Śākya Śrī to build a small *gonpa*, he chose this site where Jhampa Mémé's *chorten* was, where Abhi used to meditate. So at first the *gonpa* was called 'Abhi Gonpa'. Now the *kothi gonpa* is finished in Kardang, and this is Kardang Gonpa. (Lama Kanjur and Lama Paljor Lharje)

At the time when this story was collected, the lives of Abhi and Jhampa Mémé already seemed to be merging into a kind of a mythological distant past without any clear linear time sequence. Some of the factual details had been forgotten, such as whether Abhi was from Gondhla village, in Tinan on the lower Chandra valley, or from Zangskar. The details remembered were used to explain the relationship between Jabjez Gonpa, an important site in Kardang village on the main pilgrimage route in Karzha; the defunct *kothi gonpa*, where those individuals from the village interested in spiritual practice used to spend the winter months in retreat; and the present day Kardang Gonpa, which was built on a site previously empowered by Abhi's meditation and Jhampa Mémé's *chorten*.[26] Other details, such as the payment of 40 kilos of barley per year, bring the story into the present, for that payment continued to be made to Abhi and Mémé's descendants, who inherited the responsibility of caring for Jabjez Gonpa.[27]

In the reconstruction of the history of these events, and the founding of Kardang Gonpa, I utilised the genealogical material collected from the Abizhi household to establish that Kunga Rinpoche, who was born in 1893 (see above), was a fourth generation patrilineal descendent of Abhi and Jhampa Mémé.[28] Indeed, Jhampa Mémé established an important *ngagpa* (*sngags pa*) lineage[29] in Kardang village, passing on the role of caretaker of Jabjez Gonpa, and spiritual ability to the eldest male in each generation. Kunga Rinpoche had only one child, a daughter, who made a *magpa* (*mag pa*) marriage[30] with a practitioner, another disciple of Togden Śākya Śrī. They in turn had one daughter who also made a *magpa* marriage, although in this generation husband and wife were not practitioners. There were six children in the next generation, three of whom are practitioners, two women and one man, who has done his three year retreat and who, unlike the majority of male practitioners in Karzha, wears his hair long in a topknot, in recognition of his connection to Kunga Rinpoche, and the *rus* (lit. 'bone', or patrilineage) of Jhampa Mémé. Although theoretically *rus* passes through the male line, the males in this case have married in for two generations, thus raising questions about *rus* and inheritance through females.

Kunga Rinpoche and Gyalwa Gotsangpa

As mentioned above, Kunga Rinpoche was a disciple of Togden Śākya Śrī, as well as the inheritor of the *ngagpa* lineage of Jhampa Mémé. He was also an important teacher in Karzha until his death in 1967, and was regarded as a reincarnation or *tulku* (*sprul sku*) of Gyalwa Gotsangpa, the Drukpa yogi whose sojourn in Karzha in the thirteenth century is verified from the written *namthar*.[31] Several caves are associated with Gotsangpa, as is the rock in Kardang village known as Jabjez, where Gotsangpa's knee-prints are to be found. These sites are on the pilgrimage routes in Karzha, and it was while I was visiting these sites, doing *khora* (*'khor ba*, 'circumambulation)', that the numerous stories about this yogi's spiritual prowess were told to me. This is one of the main contexts for the oral tradition relating to Gotsangpa, which includes details not familiar in the written namthar, which are rarely used in Karzha.

Abizhi'i Kunga was among the group of Karzhapa, which included Khyemchespa'i Norbu, who travelled to Kham in the first decade of this century, and took teachings from Śākya Śrī. Upon their return to Karzha after Śākya Śrī's death in 1919, Kunga Rinpoche decided not to live in the *kothi gonpa* in Kardang village, nor in his family house, and thus was not the caretaker of Jabjez himself. Rather, he chose to live and practise in other, more remote caves, particularly Gotsangpa Drupdé (*grub sde*), above Gozzang village, which also contains imprints of Gotsangpa's body. A few practitioners built small houses nearby and began to live there also. This is now known as Lama Gonpa, and it operates as a small hermitage associated with Kardang Gonpa. The practitioner Sonam Tenzin (*bSod nams bsTan 'dzin*), another disciple of Śākya Śrī, who made a *magpa* marriage to Kunga Rinpoche's daughter, also chose not to look after Jabjez Gonpa, and spent much time in Nepal.

The process which led to the demolition of the Abizhi house in Kardang village in 1993 had begun, in keeping with Jhampa Mémé's prophecy that his *rus* would last for four generations, and then cease to function as Jabjez caretaker. I had been told of this prophecy in 1983, while gathering Kunga Rinpoche's life story, twenty-six years after his death. However, the significant events which changed the focus of spiritual practice from Jabjez and the *kothi gonpa* in Kardang itself, to the site above Kardang village already empowered by Kunga Rinpoche's *rus*, and the cave above Gozzang village previously empowered by Gotsangpa, had taken place in the first three decades of this century.

Kunga Rinpoche's role in this period of change and transformation was pivotal, due to his inherited *ngagpa* lineage and spiritual power, bolstered further by his recognition as a Gotsangpa *tulku.* These inherited lineal powers (genealogy and reincarnation) were further enhanced through his teaching and transmission lineage, received from another Drukpa yogi, the Togden (*rtogs ldan,* 'rich in knowledge, spiritual insight'), Śākya Śrī from Kham, a *Rimé* master. This teaching and transmission lineage included the *Naro Chödrug* (*Nā ro'i chos drug*), the Six Yogas of Nāropa, a series of complex meditations from the *Anuttara Tantra*, which involve the inner yoga practices of *tsa-lung* (*rtsa lung,* 'psychic veins and inner airs'). These yogas, which use the *Chagchen* (*Phyag chen,* Skt. *Mahāmudrā*) method of meditation, are accomplished in a retreat lasting three years, three months and three days, and were among the principal spiritual practices of Gyalwa Gotsangpa.[32] Although Kunga Rinpoche did not look after the knee prints left by Gotsangpa in Kardang village, and the associated village *gonpa,* he nevertheless entered into Śākya Śrī's and Gotsangpa's practice lineage, actually performing the yogic meditations that Gotsangpa had used previously and with which he had empowered the caves in Karzha.

Kunga Rinpoche was not one of Śākya Śrī's full lineage holders or *thuksé* (*thugs sras,* 'heart son'), as was Norbu Rinpoche. However, he was a significant and powerful teacher in Karzha, and continues to be regarded with devotion by his many disciples. Indeed, as he lived twenty years longer than Norbu Rinpoche, who in any case chose to spend the latter years of his life at Dzonkhul (*rDzong khul*) Gonpa in Zangskar, there are more disciples of Kunga Rinpoche in Karzha than there are of Norbu Rinpoche, although some regard both as their teachers. Just before his death, Kunga Rinpoche told his disciples that he would not return, and no *tulku* has been found.

Norbu Rinpoche and Kardang Gonpa

Although both Abizhi'i Kunga and Khyemchespa'i Norbu were close friends of the same age, who travelled to Kham together with nine other Karzhapa for the first time toward 1909/10 and received transmission and teachings from Togden Śākya Śrī, their life stories contrast in many ways. However, these stories complement each other, and from them I have constructed a reasonably coherent picture of some of the social processes which led to the establishment of Kardang Gonpa and which contribute to its continuing vitality. Although altogether eighteen men from Karzha travelled to Kham, over the four separate journeys made in the ten years between the initial trip and Śākya Śrī's death in 1919, these two are the most remembered. Both became important teachers in Karzha, earning the title 'Rinpoche' or 'Kushog' (*sku shogs,* title of respect accorded to religious practitioners in Karzha). Furthermore, many practitioners, disciples of these men, delighted in telling me about their teachers, and so although I was also told about the other seventeen disciples of Śākya Śrī, their life stories did not emerge from the many conversations.

These other disciples of Śākya Śrī, as well as the men and women[33] who became disciples of Norbu Rinpoche and Kunga Rinpoche, were nevertheless important figures in the process of establishing Kardang Gonpa, and a few years later Lama Gonpa, for in many ways it is those people who actually perform the spiritual practices and constitute the spiritual community who 'make' the *gonpa.* In Kardang, many lay people also involve themselves in spiritual practice, hearing the teachings, sponsoring rituals and attending tantric empowerments. Furthermore, their support is essential for any member of their household to become a full-time practitioner, as they provide most of the day-to-day requirements. Thus the *gonpa* is very much part of village life, and the interaction between village and *gonpa* is fundamental to the continuity of the spiritual community.

However, it was Kushog Norbu who was instructed by Śākya Śrī to build a small *gonpa* when the group of Karzhapa returned to their homeland in 1912, after taking transmission and teachings from the Togden in Kham. Indeed, Karzhapa Norbu Rinpoche became one of Śākya Śrī's three *thuksé* (lit. 'heart son') and lineage holders, disciples fully empowered to transmit the full corpus of teachings received from their master.

Unlike Kunga Rinpoche, who belonged to a *ngagpa* lineage, Norbu came from a family which was not particularly involved in spiritual practice, although his two elder brothers were in the first group of men who journeyed to East Tibet with Atsa Rinpoche to meet Śākya Śrī. Norbu's youngest brother was the only one in that generation from the Khyemches household who did not become a practitioner.

Although both of Norbu Rinpoche's elder brothers were regarded as good practitioners, neither of them became teachers, and they are not remembered in the same way as their younger brother. Several members of the Khyemches household, in the three generations descended from Norbu's younger brother, have been involved in spiritual practice, and there are currently two *chomo* who are members of Kardang Gonpa.

Norbu himself was apparently quite personable, forming a good relationship with the King of Bhutan, whom the group of Karzhapa visited *en route* to Kham: the group had visited several pilgrimage sites in India and Nepal before reaching Bhutan, where they stayed as a guest of the King,[34] who took a particular liking to Karzhapa Norbu and thereafter sponsored all his travel.

> While they were staying with the King in the *dzong* (*rdzong*, 'castle'), the palace attendants would provide the Karzhapa with a *palang* (a large container) of chang which was supposed to last them for three days, but of course it barely lasted them for a day. When the Karzhapa complained to the attendants, they were told that they couldn't be given more as the King had given the instructions. So Norbu Rinpoche mentioned the matter to the King, who then ordered that they be supplied with all the chang and arak that they wanted! Now when the Bhutanese drink, they hold the cup in their lap and cover it with their hand. Rigzin Dorje (Norbu's eldest brother), who was a bit of a joker, would always put his cup on the floor, Karzhapa style. The King used to admonish him saying that he could behave how he liked in Karzha but that while he was there he should at least drink properly as the Bhutanese did! (Lama Kanjur and Lama Paljor Lharje)

Norbu Rinpoche visited the King of Bhutan again on his return journey to Karzha, and requested the full set of the *Kanjur* (*bKa' 'gyur*) scriptures for the *gonpa* which he had been asked to establish. These were donated, and are now kept in the *Chöskhang* (*chos khang*, 'dharma hall') of Kardang Gonpa. Over the years, Norbu Rinpoche attracted many other gifts and offerings, which contributed to the material growth of Kardang Gonpa. However, it was not only royal patronage, but donations received from many ordinary men and women who became his disciples – not only from Karzha, but from many places in the Tibetan Buddhist region – that enabled Norbu Rinpoche to build up the *gonpa* structure. Craftsmen from Bhutan and Zangskar also came to Kardang, largely at Norbu Rinpoche's request, and they contributed their services, making several of the fine paintings or *thangkas* (*thang ka*) and statues housed in the various shrine rooms at Kardang Gonpa. These objects of spiritual devotion and practice today attract many visitors (tourists, both Indian and westerners) to Kardang Gonpa, which has developed a reputation for its fine artworks.

Norbu Rinpoche's charismatic qualities were largely based on his ability as a spiritual practitioner and teacher, and he attracted both material wealth and personnel to Kardang Gonpa.

> Norbu Rinpoche was not a good scholar as far as reading and writing Tibetan texts was concerned, but his actual meditation was extremely good. One time Śākya Śrī gave all his disciples an oral exam concerning their meditation, and Śākya Śrī said that Norbu Rinpoche was like the 'top of the *tsog* offering'[35] and had definitely understood the point of realisation where there is no more meditation, and that there was no going back from this realisation (i.e., it was stable).[36]

> There were three *thuksé* of Śākya Śrī: Drukpa (Bhutanese) Lopon Sonam Zangpo (*sLob dpon bSod nams bZang po*, 1892-1983); Ladakhpa Tripon Pema Chögyal (*Khrid dpon Padma Chos rgyal* 1878-1959); and Kardangpa Norbu Rinpoche. Kunga Rinpoche was not a full lineage holder. Probably all of these three had the same realisation, and so it just depends upon your faith (as to which lineage you follow). (Lama Kanjur and Lama Paljor Lharje).

That Śākya Śrī bestowed on Norbu Rinpoche the responsibility of a lineage holder bears witness to the spiritual accomplishment of this Kardangpa. Furthermore, this responsibility meant that disciples who wished to practice within that particular transmission lineage would travel great distances in order to receive teachings, just as the Karzhapa had made arduous journeys to Kham in order to receive transmission and teaching from Śākya Śrī. Although the majority of the inhabitants of Kardang Gonpa were from the immediate vicinity, especially the village, it is clear from the household genealogies and other information which I collected that individuals from all over joined the Kardang community, sometimes staying briefly and at other times becoming longer-term residents.

Norbu Rinpoche was a man of exceptional ability who was able to inspire the Kardangpa and others to assist him in fulfilling his teacher's instructions to establish a new place of spiritual practice in Kardang. The founding and growth of Kardang Gonpa was made possible because of the strong local community support both from individuals who joined the *gonpa* as practitioners, and materially in the donation of village land for the new *gonpa* site, building materials and labour for the physical structure.

The site chosen by Norbu Rinpoche and agreed upon by the villagers was previously sanctified by the *chorten* of Jhampa Mémé, and Abhi's meditation – by the *rus* of Kushog Norbu's vajra brother Kushog Kunga, as explained. In geomantic terms, the site is also quite favourable, nestled below the peak of Nyimafed Latse (*Nyi ma phyed la rtse*) with a spring on the right, although extensive terracing has been necessary to create the enough level ground for the main *gonpa* building.[37] The initial building has been extended on several occasions, with Norbu Rinpoche overseeing the first additions after his second visit to East Tibet. Kardang Gonpa also lies on the path which pilgrims take to make *khora* around the peak of Drilburi, which is associated with the *Mahāsiddha* Ghāṇṭapa, and visit the caves and rocks previously empowered by Gotsangpa's spiritual practice. Thus as a result of a variety of auspicious circumstances, conditions were favourable for the expansion of the new *gonpa*, which quite quickly shifted the focus of spiritual practice from the *kothi gonpa* and Jabjez in Kardang village, to the new Abhi Gonpa, which soon became known as Kardang Gonpa.

Norbu Rinpoche remained at Kardang Gonpa for some time after Śākya Śrī's death, but then moved to Zangskar, where he stayed at Dzonkhul Gonpa. Two caves there are associated with Nāropa, the Indian eleventh-century *siddha* with whom the Six Yogas of Nāropa originated. He undertook renovations and extensions at Dzonkhul Gonpa, as well as continuing his practice and teachings, particularly of the Six Yogas.[38] The two most senior lamas explained to me that Norbu Rinpoche moved to Zangskar because he felt the people of Karzha did not appreciate that he had developed considerable renown as a teacher and a lineage holder throughout Tibet. However, several practitioners from Kardang visited and stayed with Norbu Rinpoche at Dzonkhul Gonpa, in order to continue their studies, until his death in 1947. It seems that Kunga Rinpoche was better placed in the eyes of the local populace to be a teacher, as he was the inheritor of the most important local *ngagpa* lineage, derived from Jhampa Mémé, even though he was not a full lineage holder. Furthermore, his recognition as a *tulku* of Gotsangpa strengthened his ties with the various sacred sites associated with this yogi.

Unlike Kunga Rinpoche, however, Norbu Rinpoche had a *tulku*, born in Tibet in 1949 to a Drukpa reincarnate, Karag Yongdzin Rinpoche (*Kha rag Yong 'dzin*) and his wife Kutima. Some members of the Kardang Gonpa community helped care for the young reincarnate until he was nine years old, when fighting with the Chinese escalated. Despite their efforts to bring their young *tulku* out of Tibet, permission could not be obtained from the Chinese, and finally under threat themselves, the Karzhapa fled early in 1959, leaving Norbu Rinpoche *tulku* behind. In 1983, the Kardangpa finally received news that Norbu Rinpoche *tulku*, who is still alive although he had been kept in isolation, had not been allowed to pursue a religious career, and is a poor farmer. It is unlikely that he will have the opportunity to travel to his *gonpa* above Kardang village.

Kardang Gonpa and The Oral Traditions of Karzha

There are no written sources in Karzha for these events. During my fieldwork in Karzha in 1981-84, I collected oral accounts of the origins of Kardang Gonpa and of the lives of Kushog Norbu and Kushog Kunga from people at the *gonpa*, and the preceding material is based on what I learned from them. It became apparent when I was collecting these stories that my interest actually triggered an awareness among some of the younger practitioners now at Kardang Gonpa of their own lack of knowledge of the details of these men's lives. They also realised that the few older people who authoritatively remembered the biographical details were dwindling in number, and that soon such information would be lost to them. No *namthar* have been written for Norbu Rinpoche and Kunga Rinpoche, despite the obvious importance of these two men in the locally acknowledged revitalisation of the teachings and practice of the Drukpa Kargyu lineage of Tibetan Buddhism, particularly the advanced *Naro Chödrug*, and the equally obvious devotion of the students of these men, from whom these oral accounts were collected.[39]

It is likely that without my intervention the story of the founding of Kardang Gonpa would within a few generations have become a matter of fragmentary stories without historical context. This had already happened in the case of the lives of Abhi and Jhampa Mémé, who had probably lived through the late 18th and early 19th centuries. Thus my fieldwork in this small inner Himalayan valley, the first of its kind permitted by the G.O.I., played its own small part in the process of renewing appreciation among some segments of Lahuli society, particularly among the Karzhapa *gonpa* communities.[40]

In the past twenty years, with the opening of the road across the Rohtang Pass, there have been significant economic and agricultural changes in Lahul. Other processes are likely to effect the oral storytelling traditions, and thus escalate the rate at which details are forgotten and the stories condensed and fragmented. Not only is the *lingua franca* now Hindi, but in 1992, during my visit, the last house in Kardang village without a television entered the era of modern telecommunications. In 1983, the first video, operated with a generator, had been brought to Kyelang, the District administrative capital, two hours' walk across the valley. Thus in eight years considerable inroads in the Hindi language medium have been made into the Kardang households, the impact of which is still unfolding.[41]

There are several Karzhapa who tell a good story, particularly among the older men, including the two lamas who spent hours reminiscing and retelling stories they had heard about the groups of Karzhapa who journeyed to East Tibet seventy years before. The stories about Gotsangpa are told in much the same way, although he lived eight hundred years ago. In Karzha, where the native language has no orthography, the retelling of such stories is vital. Although Kunga Rinpoche is said to have possessed a copy of a Gotsangpa *namthar*, which is still kept somewhere at Lama Gonpa, only a few practitioners are aware that there is a written source for this popular Drukpa yogi. However, several stories of key episodes relating to his sojourn in Karzha are well known, not only to the *chöpa* but to the laity as well, and most make pilgrimage and visit the sites, remembering and retelling the stories, which in any case are not derived from the texts.[42]

The practitioners at Kardang, and Lama Gonpa have little need to read the Tibetan *namthar* about Gotsangpa, and little interest in doing so. However, they perform the same complex and specialised yogic practices, the Six Yogas of Nāropa, which have been passed on in an oral transmission lineage.[43] In this manner, through practice, the past is brought into the present, and the centuries which have elapsed since Gotsangpa's yogic feats are meaningless. Indeed, this helps us to understand what it means to regard Kunga Rinpoche as a reincarnation of Gotsangpa. This is a practice tradition, rather than one which emphasises scholastic learning, as is clear from the transcript above, which points out Norbu Rinpoche's accomplishment as a practitioner, notwithstanding his poor ability with Tibetan texts. Despite the increasing incorporation of Lahul into the broader twentieth-century Indian context – and perhaps also in part because of it, as I suggest in my book (Stutchbury, forthcoming) – Kardang Gonpa is thriving, with some younger people joining in preference to following college education, and over the past fifteen years several groups of young men in the upcoming generation of the *gonpa* community have completed their three year *Naro Chödrug* retreats, a testament to the vitality of this practice lineage.

Through corroboration with information obtained from household genealogies, examination of the architectural evidence of additions to the *gonpa* structure, conversations about the acquisition of *thangkas* and statues, and many conversations with the practitioners from Kardang Gonpa and Lama Gonpa about their life stories, as well as the oral accounts of the lives of Norbu Rinpoche and Kunga Rinpoche and the founding of Kardang and Lama Gonpa, I have been able to develop some understanding of the dynamic social processes which have operated through this century. In this paper I have attempted a distillation of this considerable body of ethnographic material, which is presented more fully elsewhere. A *gonpa* and its associated hermitage came into being and the focus of spiritual practice shifted from a still important pilgrimage site and small *kothi gonpa* within the village of Kardang. How do these events relate to their broader Tibetan context, and more particularly, what is the significance of the connection with Togden Śākya Śrī, who lived in the second half of the 19th century and early 20th century in Kham, East Tibet?

Gyüd: Continuity and Lineage

The men from Karzha who travelled to Tibet established very important lineage connections with Śākya Śrī. They became his disciples, receiving transmission of spiritual practices, and teachings from him, and also from his more advanced students.[44] Both Norbu Rinpoche and Kunga Rinpoche became teachers themselves, handing on the transmission and teaching lineages they had received, and particularly in the case of Norbu Rinpoche, not only in Karzha, but in Zangskar and in Tibet. As a lineage holder, one who is recognised as having received and accomplished the full corpus of a master's transmission and teachings, Norbu Rinpoche was particularly important in the continuation and spread of Śākya Śrī's lineage, as was Tripon Pema Chögyal, who spent several years in Dingri, and Lopon Sonam Zangpo, who taught in Bhutan.

Although the transmission and teaching lineage is the essential thread for the continuity of a practice lineage – and indeed the word for tantra is *gyüd* (*rgyud*), which carries the meaning of 'continuous', 'uninterrupted' 'thread of tradition' – continuity also occurs through genealogical lineages, for which the closely related word *gyüd* (*brgyud*) is used.[45] Within the Tibetan tradition, the other thread of continuity is the reincarnation lineage of *tulku*, in which a master purposefully transfers his or her 'consciousness' or 'wisdom mind' at the time of death – and through control in the *bardo* (*bar do*), the intermediated state between death and rebirth – into the embryonic union of male and female, to be reborn as another individual (*yang srid*) in whom the same consciousness or wisdom mind can be reawakened with appropriate spiritual practice.[46]

In the case of the lineages received passed on by Togden Śākya Śrī, these threads of transmission and teaching, genealogy, and reincarnation, have become intertwined in various ways, which at times can be quite complex to unravel, for the effect of the interconnections between these lineages is that they also mesh different lineages together. The *tulku* of Norbu Rinpoche, for instance, was reborn as the son of another Drukpa reincarnate. In the present discussion I delineate some of the more important connections which have contributed to the continuity of practice in Karzha throughout the 20th century, a process which is, in itself, a continuity of practice in Kham in the 19th century: *Rimé*.

Process in action

Togden Śākya Śrī

When the group of Karzhapa set out for Kham, probably toward 1909/10, they were accompanying Atsa Rinpoche, who had stayed in the *kothi gonpa* in Kardang village (see above), and taught them the preliminary practice of the *ngöndro* (*sngon 'gro*),[47] which they had completed in retreat over several months. Atsa Rinpoche had been sent to Karzha Khandroling by Togden Śākya Śrī, who had learnt through a dream that he had several disciples there. In the oral stories about Śākya Śrī which were told to me, there is frequent mention of his foreknowledge, insight and ability as a great yogic practitioner.

> ...Then they went to Kham Sutikha to see Śākya Śrī, who had foreknowledge and had told his people to prepare things for his disciples from Karzha who would soon be arriving. After they arrived, Atsa Rinpoche went in to see Śākya Śrī and report to him about these disciples that he had brought from Karzha. He had tested their minds on the journey with scoldings and so on, and assured Śākya Śrī they were good disciples. Śākya Śrī told him not to bother with a long report as he already knew that they were good, just as he knew that they were about to arrive... Śākya Śrī immediately gave all of them the teachings on *Naro Chödrug*, Rigzin Dorje included, although he hadn't done his *ngöndro* in Karzha before leaving, as had the others. (Lama Kanjur and Lama Paljor Lharje)

Śākya Śrī was a *terton* (*gter ton*), a discover of revealed teachings, and somewhat unconventional in his lifestyle. He had been a monk at Drugu (*gru gu*) Gonpa in East Tibet, the seat of Chöje (*chos rgyal*) Rinpoche, a Drukpa Kargyu reincarnate. However, he left, married and became a lay practitioner, living at Kham Sutikha (*su ti kha* or perhaps *siddhi ka*), in a small cave. I have heard many stories about Śākya Śrī which elaborate upon the biographical data contained in his *namthar*, but in the current discussion I focus only on details pertinent to his relationship to Kardang Gonpa and *Rimé*.[48]

Śākya Śrī's wives and children

Śākya Śrī established a *ngagpa* lineage[49] in Kham, just as Jhampa Mémé had done in Karzha. However, the Togden was much more prolific in this regard. According to the official *namthar*[50] and other sources, Śākya Śrī had two wives, six sons and four daughters. The names of the six sons, in order are: Tulku Rinchen Kunden (*Rin chen Kun ldan*), Tsewang Jigme (*Tshe dbang 'Jigs med*), Kunzang Tenzin (*Kun bzang bsTan 'bzin*, also known as Kunlha), Tsewang Rinchen

(*Tshe dbang Rin chen*), Sé (Apo) P'achog Dorje (*Sras 'phags mchog rDo rje*), and Ngawang Lama (Ngawang Chöying, *Ngag dbang Chos dbyings*). The two wives were Ama (*a ma*, 'mother') Adrok and Ama Lochuk; and the four daughters Achi (*a che*, 'elder sister') Lhunchö, Achi Drönkar, Achi Apé and Achi Bola. His youngest son, by his second wife, Ngawang Lama, died when still a young man, and was reborn as the son of Kunzang Tenzin, a son by his first wife. This grandson of Śākya Śrī, Apo (*A pho*) Rinpoche, Yeshe Rangdrol (*Ye shes Rang grol*, 1925-74) is an important figure in the development of Kardang Gonpa, coming there as a refugee in 1961, and later establishing a *gonpa* and family home in Chittyari, Manali. This branch of Śākya Śrī's descendants is central to my research.

There are, however, two other connections worth mentioning, as they illustrate my point about the complexities of the interweaving of lineages. Sé P'achog Dorje was recognised as one of several rebirths, a *tug ku (thugs sku*, 'mind emanation')[51] of Khyentse Wangpo I (*mKhyen brtse'i dBang po*), one of the three central *Rimé* teachers. Although Sé P'achog Dorje in turn reincarnated, no further details of this lineage are currently known to me. This connection is a skeletal indication of the way in which Śākya Śrī's *ngagpa* lineage interconnected with an important *Rimé* reincarnation lineage. Few details of the lived reality of this connection are known – for instance about his teachers and teaching, his disciples and so on. Information about the relationship between the Karzhapa disciples and Śākya Śrī's children is scanty, and yet particular in its content. The relationship between Norbu Rinpoche, as one of the three 'heart sons', and Śākya Śrī's family, was close.

> Śākya Śrī was residing at Kyiphug (*skyid phug*, 'happy cave') in Tsari (*Tsa ri*) when Norbu Rinpoche visited him for the last time. After Śākya Śrī died there were many earthquakes, and rainbows in the sky.
>
> When Norbu Rinpoche learnt of Śākya Śrī's death, he cried a great deal, as is the custom in Karzha. Śākya Śrī's children, who called Norbu Rinpoche *chojo* meaning 'little brother' in Karzha kha, begged him not to cry in this way – especially P'achog Rinpoche, who said that if you really have faith in your Lama then you are inseparable from him wherever you are, even if he is dead. (Lama Kanjur and Lama Paljor)

Achi Bola, Śākya Śrī's youngest daughter, married Drukchen (*'Brug chen*, 'great Lama of Dragon Gonpa') Jigmé Mipam Chöwang (*'Jigs *med Mi pham Chos dbang*, 1884-1930), the Xth hierarch from a primary reincarnation lineage within the Drukpa Kargyu.[52] A practitioner, like other women married to high reincarnates, she was his *sangyum* (*gsang yum*, 'secret consort'), and the mother of Drukpa Tuksé Rinpoche (1916-1983),[53] born three years before his maternal grandfather's death. Tuksé Rinpoche in turn became one of the principal teachers of the XIIth Drukchen, Jigmé Pema Wangchen (*'Jigs med Padma dBang chen*, b.1963), staying in Darjeeling and in Hemis Gonpa in Ladakh, post-1959. In 1974 Tuksé Rinpoche came to Kardang gonpa and taught, after assisting at the cremation of Apo Rinpoche (his mother's brother's son, and his mother's brother's *tulku*), at the *gonpa* in Chittyari, Manali. He gave the *getsulma* ordination to several female practitioners and taught Śākya Śrī's *nyen gyüd* (*snyan rgyud*)[54] to the three young men who were doing their three-year *Naro Chödrug* retreat at that time.

The Transmission and Teaching Lineages of Togden Śākya Śrī

Although the Karzhapa had received the *ngöndro* teachings from Atsa Rinpoche, and they received oral instructions from other advanced disciples of Śākya Śrī during their stay in Kham, it is nevertheless the master Śākya Śrī who is regarded as the key transmitter of the lineage. Those advanced students who gain experience instructing other disciples may in turn become teachers in their own right, as in the case of Tripon Pema Chögyal. Indeed, as the title *Tripon* (*khrid dpon*) indicates, this is the teacher (*dpon*) responsible for giving the oral instructions (*khrid*). Only those disciples who are considered by their teacher to have thorough knowledge and practical accomplishment of a teaching will be asked to teach other students, such assistance forming an integral part of the student-teacher's training.

When the group of Karzhapa first met Śākya Śrī in Kham, a practitioner called Lama Mindrol (*sMin grol*) gave the group the *Naro Chödrug Tsa Tsig* (*rtsa tshig*), the root text teachings. Śākya Śrī transmitted his *nyen gyüd* teachings to Norbu Rinpoche and to Kunga Rinpoche, as well as to another Bhutanese disciple Monlam Rabzang (*sMon lam Rab bzang*). Śākya Śrī did not give these secret oral teachings to any other of the Karzhapa, and they were not transmitted either by Norbu Rinpoche or by Kunga Rinpoche in

Karzha. Thus, for forty years or so, this important practice lineage was not passed on in Karzha. Indeed, I have not been able to establish if the lineage was continued through Norbu Rinpoche at all. Some of the practitioners at Kardang Gonpa and Lama Gonpa did receive these teachings more recently from Apo Rinpoche who received them from Tripon Pema Chögyal; and from Tuksé Rinpoche, as mentioned above.

The process of tracing the precise teacher-disciple connections is complex, as the details about the transmission of the *Naro Chödrug* to the Karzhapa disciples indicate. However, all these teacher-disciple connections have occurred within the fabric of the transmission lineage from Śākya Śrī. Indeed, the process of teaching and transmission is one of intertwining or intermeshing of different lineages, strands within a larger tradition, as a practitioner will often request transmission and teachings from more than one master holding a particular practice lineage – masters who may have received the teachings from a common teacher, for instance.

Dzogchen and *Rimé*

This process of interweaving of lineage strands, creating the union of transmission, is particularly associated with the activity of the great *Dzogchen* (*rdzogs chen*) masters in 19th century Kham, among them Jamyang Khyentse Wangpo (*'Jam dbyangs mKhyen brtse'i dBang po*, 1820-1892), Jamgon Kongtrul Lodro T'ayé (*'Jam mgon Kong sprul bLo gros mTha' yas*, 1813-1899), and Chogyur Lingpa (*mChog 'gyur gLing pa*, 1829-1870), and is evidenced by the collections of empowerments and oral instructions of numerous diverse traditions of the yogic tantric path which had developed in Tibet, such as the *Rinchen Terzod* (*Rin chen gTer mdzod*), a compilation of *terma* (*gter ma*, 'discovered or revealed teachings') in 60 volumes made by Jamgon Kongtrul.[55]

Underlying the synthesis which is seen as typifying *Rimé* is the understanding that the ultimate goal of all diverse practice lineages is the same, whether they employ the meditation methods of tantric transformation in *Chagchen* (*Phyag chen*, Skt. *Mahāmudrā*), or *Dzogchen*, which seeks to unify all transmissions and practice into the state of *rigpa* (*rig pa*), a profound awareness of the nature of mind and thus an understanding of all relative manifestations. The *Dzogchen* masters mentioned above, who were at the forefront of this process in East Tibet in the 19th century,[56] sought out numerous transmissions and teachings from both popular and obscure practice lineages, unified transmission within their own practice, presented the teachings in encyclopedic collections such as the *Rinchen Terzod*, and then passed on these in their entirety.

This period in East Tibet, referred to as the '*Rimé* synthesis', or '*Rimé* movement',[57] may be understood in part as a reaction against the sectarian tendencies of the monastic traditions of the previous centuries, particularly of the Gelugpa, who had come to power in Central Tibet in the 17th century and intervened in Eastern Tibetan politics during the Nyarong (*nyag rong*) troubles of 1862-1865.[58] Whatever the political and social environment was in Kham during the mid-nineteenth century – and more research is needed to develop a more sophisticated view – our understanding of *Rimé* is limited without an appreciation of the principles of the *Dzogchen* method as it translates into the process through which lineage strands are interwoven.

This is an expansive, complex, and as yet largely unresearched topic, which is part of the broader theoretical concern which seeks to explore the process of relationship between ideology and social process. Neither a Weberian analysis giving primacy to ideology, nor a Marxist analysis looking to the material economic base of social processes provides any more than a barely adequate interpretive framework – either perhaps accounts for some of the perceived historical developments, but both fail to account for many others.[59]

Togden Śākya Śrī and *Rimé*

Like the three masters mentioned above, Śākya Śrī was a *Dzogchen* master. He held and practised both *Dzogchen* and *Chagchen* lineages, and taught both, although to some disciples he taught either one or the other method of meditation, and to some he taught both, depending upon their needs and capacities. Śākya Śrī's principle *Chagchen* teacher was the VIth Khamtrul (*Khams sprul*), Tenpé Nyima (*bsTan pa'i Nyi ma*, 1849-1907), although he received the *Naro Chödrug* from another Drukpa yogi. His principal *Dzogchen* masters were Jamyang Khyentse Wangpo and Adzom Drukpa Drodul Pawo Dorje (*A 'dzom 'Brug pa 'Gro 'dul dPa' bo rDo rje*, 1842-1935), recognised by Khyentse Wangpo as a reincarnation of Pema Karpo, the IVth Drukchen. Śākya Śrī also imparted the *Dzogchen* transmission to Adzom Drukpa.[60] Like Śākya Śrī, Adzom Drukpa had several *Dzogchen* masters, and that they passed their transmission to each other is a further indication of the way in which the unification of *Dzogchen* lineages took place.

> Śākya Śrī received the *Naro Chö drug* teachings from Drukwang Tsognyi (*Grub dbang Tshogs gnyis*)[61]... Later on he went to Jamyang Khyentse Wangpo to request the *Dzogchen* teachings, which he also received from Adzom Drukpa, who was a *tulku* of Drukchen. There were two *tulkus*. The Drukchen line continued, and then also Adzom Drukpa, who transmitted the *Dzogchen* lineage. Adzom Drukpa spent most of his life in a tent made out of yak felt, and never went inside a house. Adzom Drukpa and Śākya Śrī lived at the same time, but Śākya Śrī died when he was sixty-eight, and Adzom Drukpa when he was eighty-four.[62] But they were very close friends and Dharma brothers... To some students Śākya Śrī would give the *Chagchen* path, and to others *Dzogchen*, depending on the capacity of the student. (Gegan Khyentse and Elizabeth Harper)[63]

> Most of the Karzhapa received the *Naro Chö drug* teachings...Rigzin Dorje was known as Khyemches Mémé...Rigzin Dorje used to say to us that all the *Chagchen* practitioners were on the slow path, while *Dzogchen* practitioners quickly reach the cloud of light and go immediately to Buddhahood. He used to tease the other Karzhapa like this, as most were *Chagchen* practitioners. (Lama Kanjur and Lama Paljor Lharje)

The *Rus* of Śākya Śrī and Kardang Gonpa

Norbu Rinpoche had told the Kardangpa on several occasions that he had built Kardang Gonpa with the intention that one day the *rus* of Śākya Śrī, a member of his *ngagpa* lineage (*dung gyü d*), would come to Karzha. Whether Śākya Śrī himself had expressed this intention to Norbu Rinpoche, his heart son (*thuksé*), is not known. Perhaps Norbu Rinpoche felt that the Karzhapa might respect the holder of Śākya Śrī's *ngagpa* lineage, as they respected Kunga Rinpoche, the holder of Jampa Mémé's *ngagpa* lineage, and that such a person would be able best to continue the practice lineage. As already indicated, there seems to have been some ambivalence about Norbu Rinpoche's position as a lineage holder in Karzha, which led him to spend the last years of his life in Zangskar.

After Śākya Śrī's death people asked Norbu Rinpoche to teach such things as *Naro Chö drug*, and Norbu Rinpoche became quite well known in Tibet. At first Norbu Rinpoche said he had no realisation and couldn't teach. Apo Tsewang,[64] Śākya Śrī's son, said to Norbu that if he didn't hold the lineage, then who could, and begged him not to refuse to teach. Patta Mémé heard this conversation, and although he previously had more faith in Bokor Betsering, he became very devoted to Norbu Rinpoche and remained so when they returned to Karzha. (Kunga Rinpoche and Lama Paljor Lharje)

The evaluation of Norbu Rinpoche as a teacher and lineage holder is an issue loaded with significance for Kardang Gonpa today, in view of his *tulku's* current predicament as a non-practitioner and poor farmer in TAR (Tibet Autonomous Region).

However, in accordance with Norbu Rinpoche's wish, just two years or so after his *tulku* was detained by the Chinese, Śākya Śrī's grandson, Apo Rinpoche, together with his wife Urgyan Chödron (*O rgyan Chos sgron*) and baby son Sé (*sras*, 'son') Rinpoche,[65] his Tripon Gegan Khyentse Gyatso (*dGe gan mKhyen brtse rGya mtsho*), and another disciple, Imi Tubten (*thub bstan*), came to live at Kardang Gonpa. The group had fled Tibet and spent nearly two years in extremely difficult conditions in Buxa refugee camp in West Bengal, where Sé Rinpoche was born (1961). Sé Rinpoche, Ngawang Geleg Namgyal (*Ngag dbang dGe legs rNam rgyal*) was recognised as the *tulku* of Tripon Pema Chögyal, who had been Apo Rinpoche's main teacher and who had died in Dingri in 1959.

Within two years of the closure of the border with Tibet and the consequent impossibility of receiving teachings in Tibet, Apo Rinpoche's residence in Kardang Gonpa resulted in unprecedented religious activity there. People from Pangi, Kinnaur, Zangskar, Ladakh and as far away as Sikkim and Bhutan travelled to Kardang in order to be present at the *wangs* (*dbang*, Skt. *abhiṣeka* 'initiation, empowerment') which he gave. He discovered some terma (*gter ma*), teachings hidden by Guru Rinpoche, confirming Karzha's significance as a place of practice. In the context of the larger Tibetan cultural arena, at this time seriously disrupted with many refugees in India, this effectively put Karzha, and particularly Kardang Gonpa, 'on the map', with immediate continuity of the transmission and teachings, largely a result of Lahul's political status within India. This interest in the teacher and lineage holder residing at Kardang Gonpa, by refugees and other practitioners from border areas in India, generated greater interest in the path of spiritual practice in Karzha.

Apo Rinpoche and Ama-la Urgyan Chödren had four more children, one of whom died in infancy, and Apo Rinpoche decided to establish a family home and his own *gonpa* in Manali. He continued to travel and teach in Karzha, putting three of his disciples into their three year *Naro Chödrug* retreat before his death in 1974. Tuksé Rinpoche transmitted Śākya Śrī's *nyen gyüd* teachings when he visited Kardang Gonpa after Apo Rinpoche's cremation, and Gegan Khyentse – who had been Apo Rinpoche's *tripon*, and who, like Apo Rinpoche, had received his teachings principally from Tripon Pema Chögyal – took over the responsibility of instruction and guidance. In this way, confidence in Gegan Khyentse's ability as a teacher was established; and in 1981 (coinciding with the beginning of my fieldwork) Gegan was invited to Kardang Gonpa for the summer to teach the *ngöndro* to the newer members of the *gonpa* community, as well as perform numerous rituals and continue the religious instruction of all, preparing a group of practitioners for their three year *Naro Chödrug* retreat. Sé Rinpoche, by then twenty years of age, accompanied him, and took his place during rituals and teachings on the throne his father had used before him.

Since then, the visits and teachings have occurred regularly every year, and several groups of practitioners have received the transmission and teachings on the *Naro Chödrug* and completed their three year retreat under Gegan Khyentse's guidance. Sé Rinpoche is also assuming greater responsibility for teaching and transmission, although initially he had reservations about his ability to teach and is somewhat in awe of his responsibility to his lineage. Like all young Tibetans of his age group who were born as refugees in India, he has been greatly influenced by the myriad of life choices available in India, speaking not only Tibetan and Hindi, but also excellent English. As well as Karzhapa and Tibetan refugees, a significant number of Westerners, some of whom have formed long-standing relationships with both Gegan Khyentse and Sé Rinpoche, seek teachings at Apo Rinpoche Gonpa. In assuming his adult responsibilities in an environment very different from that of his predecessors, Sé Rinpoche faces choices and decisions which will effect the continuity of the practice lineage. The *ngagpa* lineage of

Śākya Śrī has entered its fifth generation, as Sé Rinpoche decided to marry a young women from Kardang village and has two children.

Lineage and Continuity – the Modern Context

As with his father Apo Rinpoche – a third generation member of Śākya Śrī's *ngagpa* lineage and reincarnation of Śākya Śrī's youngest son, who became a lineage holder in his own right, receiving the transmission and teachings from Tripon Pema Chögyal – in Sé Rinpoche we see the complexities of the intertwining of lineages. He is a fourth generation member of Śākya Śrī's *ngagpa* lineage and the *tulku* of one of Śākya Śrī's lineage holders (his fathers' teacher). Furthermore, he has received the full transmission and teaching lineage of Śākya Śrī, in part from his father and from Gegan Khyentse, but principally from Śākya Śrī's lineage holder, Lopon Sonam Zangpo. Sé Rinpoche (b. 1961), together with the present Drukchen Rinpoche (b. 1963), and Dzongsar Khyentse Jamyang Chökyi Gyatso (*rDzong gsar mKhyen brtse 'Jam dbyangs Chos kyi rGya mtsho*) Rinpoche (b. 1961), the rebirth of Dzongsar Khyentse Chökyi Lodro (*Chos kyi bLo gros*, 1896-1959),[66] all received the *Naro Chödrug* teachings from Lopon Sonam Zangpo, and undertook their three year retreat together. These three vajra brothers thus share the lineage of transmission from Togden Śākya Śrī, and all are involved in teaching this lineage and the other lineages they hold, both in India and to Western practitioners. The most senior representative of the Khyentse lineage until his death, Dilgo or Dingo (*Dil mgo / Dis mgo*) Khyentse Rinpoche (1910-1991), a figure in many ways synonymous with *Rimé* and *Dzogchen*, has also been an important teacher for this generation, particularly for Dzongsar Khyentse and Sé Rinpoche. This is indicative of the way in which *Rimé* and *Dzogchen* continue to influence Tibetan Buddhist practice.

As mentioned above, Śākya Śrī's daughter married the Xth Drukchen, and their son, Thuksé Rinpoche, was also an important teacher for the current Drukchen and Sé Rinpoche. Dzongsar Khyentse Rinpoche's connection to the lineages of Śākya Śrī are less well known, but nevertheless significant in the ongoing intertwining of lineages which typifies *Rimé*, which is his *forte* as the predominant holder of the Khyentse lineage today. Dzongsar Jamyang Khyentse also belongs to a *ngagpa* lineage. Both his father, Thinley (*'Phrin las*) Norbu Rinpoche, and his paternal grandfather, H.H. Dudjom (*bDud 'joms*) Rinpoche (1904-87), are significant *Dzogchen* masters. Khyentse Rinpoche's maternal grandfather is Lopon Sonam Zangpo, thus he has a significant genealogical connection with one of Śākya Śrī's lineage holders, although this is through the daughter of Sonam Zangpo, and so this is theoretically not a connection of *rus* (*dung gyüd*).

Both Drukchen Rinpoche and Dzongsar Khyentse Rinpoche have travelled extensively in the west, developing a significant following. Both have transmitted and taught practices from Śākya Śrī's corpus of teachings in Australia and elsewhere.[67] Sé Rinpoche has talked of travelling to the West, and teaching there, having formed close relationships with several western Dharma students, but is also keen to practice and teach in other border areas of India, such as Pangi, where the influences of tourism and a rapidly changing economy are not yet as great as they are in Manali, or in Karzha. Whether he remains in India, or travels abroad, as a full lineage holder his contribution to the continuation of the lineages of Togden Śākya Śrī, and *Rimé*, will no doubt be significant as the process of transmission through generations continues.[68]

Summary and Evaluative Perspectives

What are the processes which create continuity in spiritual practice through time and space? How do these manifest socially, and how do they effect religious social institutions? How important are *ngagpa* lineages and what is their nature? If *ngagpa* lineages are created by the *rus* which is passed between father and son, why is it that daughters within *ngagpa* lineages also feature in the connections with other types of lineages? What is *their* role? How do *ngagpa* lineages connect with transmission and teaching lineages, and with reincarnation lineages? How are we to understand these lineages? What is transmission? What is passed from one generation to the next, and how? What is reincarnation? What are the connections between generations in a reincarnation lineage? Are some types of lineage more important than others in some situations? How? Why? How frequently and in what ways do these lineages coalesce, and with what effects?

As stated in the introduction to this paper, my discussion raises questions rather than providing answers, although I do seek to indicate an approach which provides insight into the cultural and social processes of continuity of lineage as I trace the connections between Śākya Śrī in Kham and Norbu Rinpoche, Kunga Rinpoche and the other recipients of the lineage teachings in Karzha in the 20th century. The strength of the approach I have taken is that it particularises significant events and connections within the overall complex web of continuity of practice tradition, both temporally, and spatially. It is only in examining the particular with reference to the larger context that the process of continuity can be understood. This very condensed presentation of the theoretical implications of the relationship between the *Dzogchen* method employed by the Khampa masters of the nineteenth century, *Rimé*, and social and historical processes will, I hope, stimulate others and contribute in a small way to deepening our understanding.

Whether the way in which the practitioners in Karzha became associated with Togden Śākya Śrī can be regarded as a result of missionary activity on the part of the Togden, is one of several questions of interpretation and perspective which arise from this material. Such a question addresses Śākya Śrī's intention both in sending Atsa Rinpoche to Karzha to gather his disciples there, and his instruction to Norbu Rinpoche to establish a *gonpa*. It seems that one of the principal motives behind establishing Kardang Gonpa was to provide a quiet place out of the hub of village activity in which to meditate and undertake lengthy retreats. Regular communal rituals are performed, although the emphasis on individual practice and retreat continues to be strong. Although Kunga Rinpoche established Lama Gonpa, this was a process whereby a Gotsangpa cave developed into a small hermitage, where individuals practice alone, rather than engaging in communal practices.

In order to assess the overall situation with respect to Śākya Śrī, it is necessary to consider the activities of his three lineage holders, as well as his other disciples, and evaluate the developments in Karzha in this context. This comparative project requires a considerable amount of further research,[69] and the following merely indicates the extent of Śākya Śrī's disciples' movements. Although details are limited, Śākya Śrī appears to have had a significant effect on another border region, that of Kutang in Nepal, where another disciple of his, Sonam Wangyal (*bSod nams dBang rgyal*) taught.[70] Another disciple of Śākya Śrī and then of Tripon Pema Chögyal settled in Sikkim, becoming a well known practitioner, although with a limited number of disciples (Silverstone 1973: 9-10). A little more information about the activities of Tripon Pema Chögyal in Dingri is available, as a result of Aziz's work with refugees from that region. This teacher's desire for quiet places in which to practice led him to move to Dingri in 1934, where he lived in seclusion for a few years, escaping his fame as a teacher (Aziz 1978: 215-216).[71]

> In his determination to minimize management and exclude all but the most devout, Tr'i-pön carefully designed a decentralized network of sanctuaries over the Tzib-ri range and demanded carefully selected followers to lead a simple ascetic life – after his own. Although he could have drawn unlimited funds from his urban devotees in the Tibetan cities to construct the most elegant *gön-pa* and shrines, Tr'i-pön declined and kept his retreats austere and modest. He constructed eleven centres in all; eight for the *dr'a-pa* and three for his female devotees. None has more than thirteen members. By the end of the nineteen fifties his *gön-pa* population numbered a hundred and nineteen. It could have been much higher but the *la-ma* permitted only the most dedicated and disciplined of his followers to remain near him. Many more of his initiates returned from Tzib-ri to their homes in other parts of Tibet (Aziz 1978: 216).

Although the teachers holding Śākya Śrī's lineage seem to have been relatively popular, they do not appear to have been involved in developing a wealthy following with the intention of establishing large *gonpas*, nor in exerting economic and political influence in the areas in which they resided, activities which may perhaps be associated with missionary activity.

Although this material is inconclusive, it seems more productive to investigate the nature of continuity and transmission of teachings, particularly the ways in which these lineages interconnect with the genealogical and reincarnation lineages, in order to appreciate the impetus to the spread of this practice tradition, rather than to interpret the material through a framework that is in some ways alien to the material itself.[72] To put it another way, the idea of 'missionary activity' may apparently satisfactorily explain the spread of a tradition. However, this interpretation does not entail penetrating the surface of the data – the events and the dynamics of the social processes which constitute the founding of Kardang Gonpa, and Lama Gonpa, as they were presented to me. Rather than a conversion from one religion to another, the process in Karzha has been one in which Buddhist practice, particularly of the Drukpa lineage, has gone through periods of strengthening, brought about by the activity of particular individuals.

In keeping with the appreciation of periods of resurgence or revitalisation of Buddhist practice in Karzha, it is clear, however, that whatever Śākya Śrī's motives, the effect of the workings of his lineages in the region have resulted in another phase of strengthened spiritual practice, and the 'making' of Kardang Gonpa and the hermitage, Lama Gonpa.

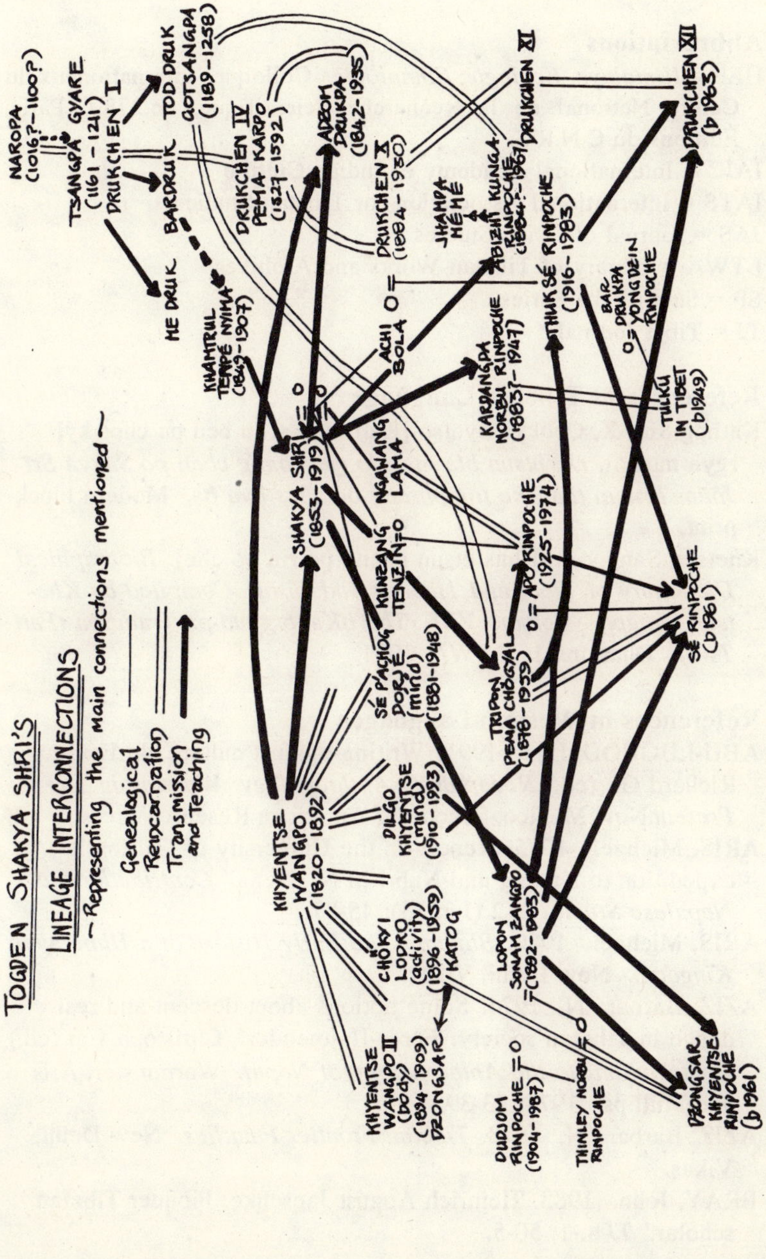
TOGDEN SHAKYA SHRI'S
LINEAGE INTERCONNECTIONS
~ Representing the main connections mentioned ~
Genealogical
Reincarnation
Transmission and Teaching
NAROPA (1016?-1100?)
TSANGPA GYARE (1161-1211) DRUKCHEN I
TOD DRUK
GOTSANGPA (1189-1258)
BARDRUK
ME DRUK
DRUKCHEN IV PEMA KARPO (1527-1592)
ADZOM DRUKPA (1842-1935)
DRUKCHEN X (1884-1930)
JHAMPA MEHE
ABIZHI KUNGA RINPOCHE (1884?-1967)
DRUKCHEN XI
DRUKCHEN XII (b 1963)
KHAMTRUL TENPE NYIMA (1849-1907)
ACHI BOLA
KARDANGPA NORBU RINPOCHE (1883?-1947)
THUKSE RINPOCHE (1916-1983)
BAR DRUKPA YONGDZIN RINPOCHE
TULKU IN TIBET (b 1949)
SHAKYA SHRI (1853-1919)
NGAWANG LAMA
KUNZANG TENZIN
APO RINPOCHE (1925-1974)
SE RINPOCHE (b 1961)
KHYENTSE WANGPO (1820-1892)
SE P'ACHOG DORJE (mind) (1881-1948)
TRIPON PEMA CHOGYAL (1876-1959)
DILGO KHYENTSE (mind) (1910-1993)
CHOKYI LODRO (activity) (1896-1959) KATOG
LOPON SONAM ZANGPO (1892-1983)
KHYENTSE WANGPO II (body) (1894-1909) DZONGSAR
DUDJOM RINPOCHE (1904-1987)
THINLEY NORBU RINPOCHE
DZONGSAR KHYENTSE RINPOCHE (b 1961)

References

Abbreviations

HEE = *Himalaya, Ecologie, Ethnologie.* Colloques internationaux du Centre National de la Recherche Scientifique, no.278. Paris, Éditions du C.N.R.S.

IAIC = International Academy of Indian Culture

IATS = International Association for Tibetan Studies

JAS = Journal of Asian Studies

LTWA = Library of Tibetan Works and Archives

SP = Śata-Piṭaka Series

TJ = Tibet Journal

References in Tibetan Language

Kathog Situ X, Chökyi Gyatso [Kaḥ thog si tu bcu pa chos kyi rgya mtsho]. *rJe btsun bla ma rdo rje 'chang chen po Śākya Śrī Jñāna'i rnam thar me tog phreng ba zhes bya ba.* Modern block-print.

Khetsun Sangpo [mKhas btsun bzang po rin po che]. *Biographical Dictionary of Tibet and Tibetan Buddhism. Compiled by Khetsun Sangpo. Volume VIII. The bKa'-brgyud-pa Tradition (Part Two).* Dharamsala, LTWA, 1981.

References in Western Languages

ABU-LUGHOD, Lila. 1991. 'Writing against culture.' in Fox, Richard G. (ed.) *Recapturing Anthropology: Working in The Present.*New Mexico, School Of American Research Press.

ARIS, Michael. 1975. 'Report on the University of California expedition to Kutang and Nubri in N. Nepal' *Contributions to Nepalese Studies* 2, 2 (Jun 75): 45-87.

ARIS, Michael. 1980. *Bhutan. The Early History of a Himalayan Kingdom.* New Delhi, Vikas.

AZIZ, Barbara N. 1974. 'Some notions about descent and residence in Tibetan society. 'Fürer-Haimendorf, Christoph von (ed.) *Contributions to the Anthropology of Nepal.* Warminster, Aris and Phillips. 1974: 23-39

AZIZ, Barbara N. 1978. *Tibetan Frontier Families.* New Delhi, Vikas.

BRAY, John. 1983. 'Heinrich August Jaeschke: Pioneer Tibetan scholar.' *TJ* 8, 1: 50-5.

BRAY, John. 1992. 'Christian Missionaries on the Tibetan Border: the Moravian Church in Poo (Kinnaur).' in Ihara, Shōren and Yamaguchi, Zuihō (eds.) *Tibetan Studies - Proceedings of the 5th Seminar of the IATS, Narita 1989.* Chiba-Ken, Naritasan Shinshōji.

CHOKYI NYIMA Rinpoche. 1989. *The Union of Mahamudra and Dzogchen: A Commentary on 'The quintessence of Spiritual Practice' The Direct Instructions of the Great Compassionate One' by Karma Chagmey Rinpoche I.* Translated from the Tibetan by Erik Pema Kunsang. Hong Kong, Ranjung Yeshe Publications.

CLIFFORD, James and Marcus, George E. (ed.). 1986. *Writing Culture: The Poetics and Politics of Ethnography.* Berkeley, University of California Press.

DARGYAY, Eva K. 1978. *The Rise of Esoteric Buddhism in Tibet.* New York. Samuel Weiser.

DAS, Sarat Chandra. 1979. *A Tibetan-English Dictionary with Sanskrit Synonyms.* Reprinted. Delhi, Motilal Banarsidass.

GILL, Manohar Singh. 1979. *Himalayan Wonderland: Travels in Lahaul-Spiti.* New Delhi, Vikas.

HANSON, Judith. 1977. *The Torch of Certainty by Jamgon Kongtrul.* Boulder, Shambhala.

HARCOURT, A.F.P. [1870] 1972. *The Himalayan Districts of Kooloo, Lahoul and Spiti.* Delhi, Vivek.

HUBER, Antoni M. 1989. 'A pilgrimage to La-phyi: a study of sacred and historical geography in South-Western Tibet.' M.A. dissertation, University of Canterbury, New Zealand.

HUTTENBACK, Robert A. 1961. 'Gulab Singh and the creation of the Dogra state of Jammu, Kashmir and Ladakh.' *JAS* 20: 477-88.

JÄSCHKE, H.A. [1881] 1975. *A Tibetan-English Dictionary with Special Reference to the Prevailing Dialects.* Delhi, Motilal Banarsidass.

KHOSLA, G.D. 1956. *Himalayan Circuit: The Story of a Journey in the Inner Himalayas.* London, Macmillan.

KLIMBURG-SALTER, Deborah E. 1982. *The Silk Route and the Diamond Path: Esoteric Art on the Trans-Himalayan Trade Routes.* Los Angeles, UCLA Arts Council.

LAUF, Detlef I. 1971. 'Zur Geschichte und Kunst lamaistischer Klöster im Westhimalaya.' *Asiatische Studien* 25: 364-76.

LEVINE, Nancy E. 1981. 'The theory of *ru* kinship, descent and status in a Tibetan society.' In Fürer-Haimendorf, Christoph von (ed.) *Asian Highland Societies in Anthropological Perspective*. New Delhi, Sterling. 1981: 52-78.

MANZARDO, Andrew E. 1982. 'Impression management and economic growth: the case of the Thakalis of Dhaulagiri zone.' *Kailash* 9, 1: 45-60.

MARCUS, George E. 1992. 'Past, present and emergent identities: Requirements for ethnographies of late twentieth-century modernity world wide.' In Scott Lash and Jonathan Friedman (ed.), *Modernity and Identity*. Oxford and Cambridge, Mass., Blackwell.

MARCUS, George E. and FISCHER, Michael M.J. 1986. *Anthropology as Cultural Critique*. Chicago, University of Chicago Press.

MARTIN, Dan. 1985. 'Pearls from bones — relics, chortens, tertons and the signs of saintly death in Tibet.' Typescript (April 1985 version).

MEISEZAHL, Richard O. 1980. *Geist und Ikonographie des Vajrayāna-Buddhismus: Hommage à Marie-Thérèse de Mallmann.* Sankt Augustin, VGH Wissenschaftsverlag.

NAWANG TSERING. 1979. *Buddhism in Ladakh: A Study of the Life and Work of the Eighteenth Century Ladakhi Saint Scholar.* New Delhi, Sterling.

ORTNER, Sherry B. 1989a. *High Religion: A Cultural and Political History of Sherpa Buddhism.* Princeton, NJ, Princeton University Press.

ORTNER, Sherry B.. 1989b. 'Cultural politics: religious activism and ideological transformation among 20th century Sherpas.' *Dialectical Anthropology* 14: 197-211.

RAMBLE, Charles. 1983. 'The founding of a Tibetan village: the popular transformation of history.' *Kailash* 10: 267-90.

ROERICH, George N. [Georges de R.] 1931. 'Problems of Tibetan archaeology.' *Urusvati* 1, 1: 27-34.

SACHERER, Janice M. 1974. 'Sherpas of the Rolwaling Valley: Human adaptation to a harsh mountain environment.' *Objets et Mondes* 14, 4: 317-324.

SACHERER, Janice M. 1977. 'The Sherpas of Rolwaling: A hundred years of economic change.' *HEE* :.289-94.

SAMUEL, Geoffrey. 1993. *Civilized Shamans: Buddhism in Tibetan Societies.* Washington, D.C., Smithsonian Institution Press.

SHAKSPO, Nawang Tsering. 1985. 'Alexander Csoma De Kőrős in Ladakh.' *TJ* 10, 3: 42-47.

SILVERSTONE, Marilyn. 1973. 'Five Nyingmapa lamas in Sikkim.' *Kailash* 1, 1: 9-17.

Sinha, R.

SMITH, E. Gene. 1968. 'Introduction' to Lokesh Chandra (ed), *The Autobiography and Diaries of Si-tu Pan-chen.* New Delhi, IAIC, 1-23. (SP 77.)

SMITH, E. Gene. 1970. 'Introduction' to Lokesh Chandra (ed), *Kongtrul's Encyclopaedia of Indo-Tibetan Culture, Parts 1-3.* New Delhi, IAIC, 1-87. (SP 80.)

SNELLGROVE, David L. and Tadeusz Skorupski. 1980. *The Cultural Heritage of Ladakh. Vol.2.* Warminster, Aris and Phillips.

STUTCHBURY, Elisabeth.. 1991a. 'The Six Yogas of Naropa: A Tibetan system of meditation.' Typescript.

STUTCHBURY, Elisabeth. 1991b. 'Perceptions of landscape in Karzha: Sacred geography and the Tibetan system of geomancy.' Typescript.

STUTCHBURY, Elisabeth. 1993. 'Working with the mind-body connection: The Six Yogas of Naropa' in Lepani, Barbara (ed.) *Revolution of the Mind: Knowledge, Wisdom and Healing.* Sydney, Rigpa Forum.

STUTCHBURY, Elisabeth. forthcoming. *Rediscovering Western Tibet: Gonpa, Chorten and the Continuity of Practice With a Buddhist Community in the Indian Himalaya* State University of New York Press, McGill Studies in the History of Religions Series (ed) Katherine K.Youn g.

THOMAS, Nicholas. 1989. *Out Of Time: History and Evolution in Anthropological Discourse.* Cambridge, Cambridge University Press.

THONDUP RINPOCHE, Tulku [= Tulku Thondup]. 1986. *Hidden Teachings of Tibet: An Explanation of the Terma Tradition of the Nyingma School of Buddhism.* London, Wisdom.

THUBTEN LEGSHAY GYATSHO, the 18th Chogay Trichen. 1979. *Gateway to the Temple: Manual of Tibetan Monastic Customs, Art, Building and Celebrations.* Translated by David P. Jackson. Kathmandu, Ratna Pustak Bhandar.

TOBDAN. 1984. *History and Religions of Lahul: From the Earliest to circa A.D. 1950.* New Delhi, Books Today.

TOPDEN Tshering. 1974. Foreword to *Rare Tibetan Texts from Lahul. Narrative Accounts (rnam thar) of Rgod-tshan-pa Mgon-po-rdo-rje, Chos-rgyal G'yu-sna Legs-pa'i-don-grub, and Sras Guru Chos-kyi-dban-phyug. Reproduced photographically from manuscripts preserved at the Gemur Monastery by Topden Tshering.* Topden Tshering. (Distributed by Tibetan Bonpo Monastic Centre, Dolanji, H.P.).

TUCCI, Giuseppe. 1949. *Tibetan Painted Scrolls.* 2 vols and 1 portfolio. Rome, Libreria dello Stato.

TUCCI, Giuseppe. [1940] 1971. *Travels of Tibetan Pilgrims in the Swat Valley.* Reprinted in *Opera Minora.* 2 vols. Rome, G. Bardi.

VAN DER KUIJP, Leonard W.J. 1989. 'U-rgyan Rin-chen-dpal and his audiences with Qubilai and Shangda in 1292.' Unpub. paper given at the 5th Seminar of IATS, Narita. August 27th September 2nd, 1989.

WYLIE, Turrell V. 1970. *A Tibetan Religious Geography of Nepal.* Roma, Istituto Italiano per il Medio ed Estremo Oriente. (Serie Orientale Roma, 42.)

Notes

1. I refer the reader to my forthcoming book, *Rediscovering Western Tibet: Gonpa, Chorten and the Continuity of Practice With a Buddhist Community in the Indian Himalaya*, and gratefully acknowledge the many discussions with Geoffrey Samuel, and more recently exchanges with Mark Stevenson, which are reflected in this paper.

2. An historical perspective is important in this endeavour, as is a consideration of the way memory operates in oral cultures. See Nick Thomas (1989) who presents the case for ethnography which is situated historically; and Marcus, who argues for a break "with historical determination as the primary explanatory context for any ethnographic present" (1992: 316-317). These methodological issues are discussed more fully in Stutchbury (forthcoming).

3. Many of the words from the Karzha dialect, which has no orthography, are unknown in the Tibetan language, and I offer no transliteration. Italicised transliteration in brackets, following the Wylie system, is used for shared Tibetan words on initial usage.

4. Those who have taken transmission and teaching together, tantric initiations, from the same master are called 'vajra brothers and sisters'.

5. One of the uses of the suffix '-pa' in Tibetan and the Karzha dialect is to denote the person that deals with a place or thing, or the inhabitant who comes from a place (Das 1979 reprint: 775; Jäschke 1975 reprint: 321 eg. Ladakhpa, Zangskapa, Karzhapa. In Hindi, the suffix '-i' is used, thus Ladakhi, Zangskari or Lahuli. Furthermore, in Karzha, housenames precede personal names, with the suffix "'-i" indicating possession eg. 'Norbu from the Khyemches household'. If the context so requires, further identification is made by prefixing the village name, eg. 'Kardang Khyemchespa'i Norbu', 'Kardangpa Norbu'; or the region, as in 'Karzhapa Norbu'.

6. *Druk* means 'dragon', and the Drukpa Kargyu is one of the traditions within the Kargyu, one of the main orders of Tibetan Buddhism.

7. For discussions of the eight cremation grounds (*dur khrod*) of Padmasambhava see Tucci (1949, Vol 2: 542-543, 615); Martin (1985: 6, 30 n.11); Wylie (1970: 21-22); Meisezahl (1980). Tobdan gives the list of *tirtha* associated with Padmasambhava from the *blon po bka' thang* or *blon po bka' yi thang yig* (f46a) which includes Gandhola (*gan dha la*) (1984: 82-83). Tucci points out that the list of cemeteries usually given in the Tibetan tradition differs from the cycle of eight cemeteries given in the Indian tantric literature, though both are arranged to symbolically form a lotus (Tucci 1949 Vol. 2: 615 n. 237). See also Huber (1989).

8. In Karzha, these texts are seldom used, and only a few of the more learned lamas are fluent in the Tibetan language. The language spoken in Karzha, although a dialect of Tibetan, is substantially different, and, as already noted, has no orthography.

9. Oḍḍiyāna, or Orgyan (Urgyan) is probably somewhere near the Swat Valley, in present-day Pakistan. Padmasambhava is said to have been born there (e.g., Tucci 1971).

10. For instance, teachers may have been accompanied by an entourage of assistants and travelled with traders.

11. The mission was initially established in Kardang in 1856, but was moved after a few months to Kyelang, which consequently became the administrative capital for the region. In 1885, the Moravians established a mission in Leh, Ladakh, which became their headquarters, although mission activities continued in Lahul. On the Moravians see e.g. Bray 1983; 1992, and also Stutchbury (forthcoming).

12. Its introduction was significant as it was well suited to the altitude and climate, and thus changed the subsistence patterns of agriculture. An interesting comparison can be made with the Sherpa regions of Solo-Khumbu and the Rolwaling Valley, both in Nepal. The potato was introduced to Khumbu between 1840-1860, the seed coming from the gardens of the British residents in Sikkim. By the 1950s the potato had become the staple food (Ortner 1989a: 30, 158-159). The Rolwaling was first settled by Sherpas around 1860-1870. The potato was introduced there shortly afterwards (Sacherer 1974: 317-324; 1977: 289-293).

13. Because of trading concerns and the severity of winter conditions in Lahul, Lahuli people have long regarded Manali as an alternative place to spend the winter when opportunity permitted, although they resided in Lahul. There are now significant numbers of Lahuli people who rarely visit Lahul, and fewer who remain throughout the winter.

14. Although this may be said of many Lahuli people, the *Thakur*, or ruling families of Lahul, are a particularly interesting example of 'impression management' (cf. Manzardo 1982).

15. There are five linguistically distinct areas in Lahul. My fieldwork centred on Karzha, and particularly in Punan or Gar.

16. For a more thorough treatment of the variations within the Tibetan Buddhist cultural arena, see Samuel, (1993: Part I).

17. Ani (*a ne*), which in the kinship terminology designates father's sister, is frequently used as a term of address for female practitioners.

18. In some cases branches of the extended family had left to take up residence in the Kulu-Manali valley, though this did not necessarily mean that the household had split. The G.O.I. Census figures for Kardang village in 1983 was 188, with 92 males and 96 females, although this figure does not include any household members resident (even temporarily) elsewhere. My investigations indicate that there were somewhere between 75 and 100 non-resident household members.

19. The Abizhi household has a unique position in Karzha, as the male founder came from Zangskar a few generations ago. Because he and his wife, who was probably a Karzhapa from Gondhla (Tinan), were dedicated spiritual practitioners, they became the caretakers of Jabjez Gonpa in Kardang village, a role which was passed down through their male descendants (see below). Kunga Rinpoche, who has been mentioned above, inherited this position, although he did not live in the village and instead established a small hermitage called Lama Gonpa above the neighbouring village of Gozzang. He had no sons and the Abizhi household no longer looks after Jabjez Gonpa (see below).

20. In the 2 *kothi* (administrative units) on the left bank of the lower Bhaga, there were 98 households spread over 10 villages, and 4 *gonpas* (1983 Census).

21. The title 'lama', (*bla ma*, Skt. *guru*) or 'teacher' is earned by practitioners who have completed the three year, three month and three day retreat.

22. Atsa Rinpoche came from East Tibet and was a disciple of Śākya Śrī. See below.

23. The term 'mémé' (*mes mes*) is used in normal conversation in Karzha kha (*skad*, 'language') to indicate any male religious practitioner older than oneself. Its usage in Karzha is similar to that reported by Aris in another border region, Kutang. This is a variation of the standard Tibetan usage, in which 'mémé' is a kin term denoting forefather or grandfather (see Aris 1975: 54, and Ramble 1983: 276). Perhaps 'mémé' carries the connotation of wisdom associated with age. 'Abhi' (*a phyi*) is the corresponding term for the female gender. However, most female practitioners within one's peer group are called 'ani' – father's sister, and males 'ajo' (*a jo*) – elder brother.

24. Gotsangpa's knee prints are to be found in a large rock, around which a *gonpa* has been built, with a shrine and a circumambulatory passage. Appropriate offerings are made there daily by the caretaker, who will also accompany visiting pilgrims when they make their offerings. They may be told the story about Gotsangpa's encounter with a *ḍākinī* (Skt., 'enlightened female energy being', Tib. *mkha' 'gro ma*) which resulted in the knee prints, which explains the site's significance.

25. Tsenku Abhi, the oldest practitioner by several years in 1983, had said that Abhi was from Gondhla, whereas Kanjur Mémé, several years her junior, was uncertain about this.

26. The cremated remains of important teachers are usually placed in a *chorten*, which becomes an object of devotional worship. I discuss *chorten* in some detail in Stutchbury (forthcoming).

27. See also note 19.

28. A century later, the younger members of the Abizhi household are removed by a further four generations from Kunga Rinpoche.

29. Aziz (1974: 24) glosses *ngagpa* as 'hereditary priest'. It is considered that children inherit the *rus* of their father, which can designate a named patrilineage, but also refers to substance, 'bone', inherited from the father. For a comparative appraisal of *rus* in the Tibetan context see Levine (1981).

30. In general, residence is patrilocal. However, when there is no male heir, a man (*magpa*) will marry into a household and take his wife's housename, which is also passed on to their children.

31. As Gotsangpa had no seat or established *gonpa*, this was not a formal recognition involving enthronement. Other Drukpa yogis have been similarly recognised as Gotsangpa *tulkus* – for instance, Pema Chögyal (on whom see below).

32. For a more thorough discussion of the Six Yogas of Nāropa, see Stutchbury (1991a; 1993 and forthcoming).

33. In this discussion I do not emphasise the role of women as practitioners and their contribution to the growth of Kardang Gonpa, which matters are discussed in Stutchbury (forthcoming).

34. Sir Urgyan Wangchuk (*O rgyan dBang phyug*), the first hereditary King of Bhutan, came to the throne in 1907 and reigned until 1926. The current King Jigmé Senge Wangchuk (*'Jigs med Seng ge dBang*

phyug), the fourth in the line, took office in 1972 (Aris 1980: 266-269, 274).

35. The *tsog* (*tshogs*) is the ritually blessed food which is shared after the ritual. In a more familiar idiom, 'the cream of the milk'.

36. As mentioned with regard to Kunga Rinpoche, the Karzhapa do not use texts, such as *namthar*, but instead perform the practices, becoming accomplished practitioners.

37. For more details see Stutchbury (forthcoming and 1991b). Purification rituals are essential to prepare a site for the construction of a *gonpa* or a *chorten*, and a consecration ritual or *rabné* (*rab gnas*) must be performed upon their completion. Norbu Rinpoche and his fellow practitioners performed these ritual, a very necessary part of establishing a *gonpa*. However, in this essay I focus on the social rather than the ritual processes involved in founding a *gonpa*. For a general description of the rituals, see Thubten Legshay Gyatso (1979: 29-35, 73-75).

38. I was told that Norbu Rinpoche established Dzonkhul Gonpa, an indication of the Karzhapa's parochial understanding. Although this *gonpa* has not been dated, it has existed at least since the 17th century. On Dzonkhul Gonpa see Shakspo (1985: 45-46) and Snellgrove and Skorupski (1980: 55-57).

39. *Namthar* have been written for Śākya Śrī's two other lineage holders. Unlike these men, Norbu Rinpoche came from and spent most of his life in areas where there are strong oral traditions, with little reliance or texts. He himself did not record information about his life and spiritual experiences, and among his close disciples there were none with the expertise in written Tibetan and the inspiration to write a *namthar*. The relationship between *namthar* and these oral biographies is explored in more detail in Stutchbury (forthcoming).

40. This is not to suggest that any great significance attaches to my role in this process, although it is important for fieldworkers to be sensitive to the effects of their presence upon the culture being studied. More generally in this particular case, the people of Kardang appreciated that a Westerner chose to live with them, and intended 'to write a book' about them. Previous books written by Indian administrators, such as G.D. Khosla (1956) and M.S Gill (1979), typically misunderstood Lahuli culture, sometimes misrepresenting with open criticism (e.g., Khosla 1956: 208; Gill 1979: 60-62). Generally, Lahulis feel that Indian/Hindu people derogate and denigrate them. However, many Indians value 'Western' things highly (e.g., Levi jeans), whence the appreciation that a 'Westerner' (albeit one from Down Under) chose to live with them, rather than with Hindu Indians, or with Tibetan

refugees. Obtaining research permission for Lahul from the G.O.I. was a difficult and lengthy process, due to the proximity to several international borders. Although others have conducted some research in the general area (eg. Lauf, Lewison, Klimburg-Salter, Sinha), to my knowledge I was the first anthropologist and my association with the region was lengthy.

41. The few people delighted in telling me about a test cricket match they had watched between India and Australia at the Melbourne cricket ground, during which a streaker had run across the pitch. They were very interested to know if we in Australia often behave in this manner during hot weather, and noted that they had not seen me in the crowd.

42. Thirteen different well-known *namthar* for Gotsangpa are listed by Topden Tshering in his printed edition of three manuscripts from Gemur Gonpa in Lahul (1974). He includes another, of unknown authorship, which makes the total number of *namthar* fourteen, indicative of the popularity of this yogi. The *namthar* by Sangye Darpo (*sangs rgyas dar po*), which Tucci (1971) has used, is the twelfth on this list. The full title is *rgyal ba rgod tshang pa mgon po rdo rje'i rnam thar mthong ba don ldan nor bu'i phreng ba.* I have not been able to examine the majority of these, but it is likely that the stories told in Karzha will not be found therein, other than in abridged form.

43. Gotsangpa established the *Tod Druk* (*stod 'brug*, the 'upper Druk') one of three parallel branches within the Drukpa Kargyu. The lineage which Śākya Śrī held and passed on is from another of these three, the Bar Druk (*bar 'brug*, the 'middle Druk'). The originators of these three branches were all full lineage holders of Tsangpa Gyare Yeshe Dorje (*gtsang pa rgya ras ye shes rdo rje*, 1161-1211), the founder of the Drukpa Kargyu tradition. Thus the *Naro Chödrug* has been passed along in parallel transmission lineages.

44. Although the primary connection with a master is made through transmission, or empowerment (*dbang*), the oral transmission or teaching lineage is also important. A master may encourage one or two particular students to explain the teachings in detail to other disciples. See below.

45. See Jäschke (1975: 111-112). Gyvdpa (*rgyud pa, brgyud pa*) is one who transmits knowledge, a teacher. Jäschke was a Moravian missionary who carried out much of the linguistic work for this dictionary (initially published in 1871) in Kyelang, working with the numerous Tibetan travellers who passed through the region, as well as with the local population. He includes both Central Tibetan and Western Tibetan pronunciations and usages.

46. Cf. discussion in Samuel (1993: Chapter 15). P'owa (*pho ba*), the transference of consciousness at the time of death, is the sixth yoga of Nāropa. There is thus an association between these yogas and the development of reincarnation lineages. Although the 2nd (1204-83) reborn as the 3rd (1284-1339) Karmapa is usually given credit for establishing the first reincarnation lineage, there is evidence that tulku of Gotsangpa may predate this; although as previously mentioned, Gotsangpa did not have an established seat. Although individuals such as Kunga Rinpoche are recognised unofficially as Gotsangpa *tulkus*, this seems to less institutionalised (cf. Samuel, 1993: Chapter 25; and van der Kuijp unpub. 1989).

47. On the Kargyu *ngöndro* see Hanson (1977).

48. See Stutchbury (forthcoming) for more information. The web of lineages from Śākya Śrī is an extensive topic for investigation. Tashi Tsering and Geoffrey Samuel are exploring some of these (personal communication).

49. Such a lineage is *dung gyüd* (*gdung brgyud*), meaning 'bone (honorific, cf. *rus*, note 29) lineage'.

50. The *namthar* for Togden Śākya Śrī (1853-1919), "The Flower Garland, the Life Story of Jetsun Lama Dorje Chang, the great Śākya Śrī" (*rje btsun bla ma rdo rje 'chang chen po Śākya Śrī Jñāna'i rnam thar me tog phreng ba zhes bya ba*, abbreviated as 'The Flower Garland') was written by the Katog Situ Xth, Chökyi Gyatso (*kah thog si tu X chos kyi rgya mtsho*). (Situ VIIIth had two rebirths, one who remained at Palpung (*dpal spungs*), and the other who established Katog. Our author was the latter's tulku and a nephew of Khyentse Wangpo (Smith, E. Gene 1968: 22). A xylograph edition was published in Gangtok in 1980. This *namthar* is the source for Khetsun Zangpo's *Biographical Dictionary* (1981 Vol. VIII: 478-500). Chökyi Gyatso used Śākya Śrī's diary as the main source for 'The Flower Garland'. The text was corrected by Dzongsar Khyentse Chökyi Lodro (*rdzong gsar mkhyen brtse chos kyi blo gros* 1896-1959) the activity rebirth of Khyentse Wangpo. The original blocks were carved in Bhutan under the guidance of Lopon Sonam Zangpo, and were sent to Kyiphug, and are assumed to be lost. I obtained a copy of the block print from Apo Rinpoche Gonpa. The involvement of these *Rimé* masters in the production of Śākya Śrī's *namthar* is an indication both of their respect for him as a practitioner, and of his involvement with *Rimé* as a *Dzogchen* practitioner.

51. Aspects of a master which can enter different rebirth individuals include body, speech, mind, activity. The theory pertaining to such multiple rebirths is complex, but theoretical and political aspects aside, the number of rebirths associated with Khyentse Wangpo (cf. Smith 1970: 74) is indicative of the influence of this great master.

52. The other primary reincarnation lineage within the Drukpa tradition was established after the IVth Drukchen Kunkhyen Pema Karpo's death in 1592. There were two candidates for the rebirth, one continuing the Drukchen line and one fleeing to Bhutan in 1616 and establishing the Zhabdrung (*zhabs drung*) lineage and the Lhodruk (*lho 'brug*) or 'southern dragon' tradition of the Drukpa Kargyu.

53. His *tulku* was enthroned in Sikkim in 1988.

54. These *nyen gyüd*, or 'oral lineage' teachings were received in a meditative vision by Togden Śākya Śrī 'directly' from the Indian siddha Tilopa (?988-?1069), who had instructed the Indian siddha Nāropa (?1016-?1100), the originator of the Six Yogas of Nāropa (cf. *terma*). As such, they are regarded as a particularly powerful explication of the practices, and are not frequently bestowed on practitioners. The retreatants had hoped to request these teachings from Apo Rinpoche, their principal teacher, who had died during their retreat.

55. The new edition published by Dilgo Khyentse Rinpoche is in 135 volumes, under the title *Rin chen gter mdzod* or *Rin po che gter gyi mdzod* (see Thondup 1986: 62, 186-88, 254-5 note 225).

56. The union of *Mahāmudrā* and *Dzogchen* was not an innovation of *Rimé*, but had been realised and taught previously by masters who practised both methods, from at least the 13th century. It was greatly developed in the 17th century, for instance by Karma Chagmey (*karma chags med*), (Chokyi Nyima Rinpoche 1989). Thus *Rimé* must also be understood in the context of what preceded it in terms of teaching, transmission and lineage, a point which relates to the three reincarnation lineages of Jigmé Lingpa (*'Jigs med gLing pa*, 1730-1798): Do Khyentse (*mDo mKhyen brtse*, 1800?-1859?); Jamyang Khyentse Wangpo (1820-1892); and Dza Patrul (*rDza dPal sprul*, 1808-1887). (Cf. Dargyay 1978: 197-209; Samuel 1993: chapter 27; and Smith 1970.

57. I am indebted to Namkhai Norbu Rinpoche for generating my interest in this area, with his comments that *Rimé* was not a social or religious movement at the time, but a process which arose out of the *Dzogchen* method. Of course, we are left with the question, 'Why did *Dzogchen* become so popular in Kham during the nineteenth century?'

58. For a discussion of *Rimé*, and the social and political climate in which it arose, see Samuel (1993, esp. chapter 27) and Smith (1970).

59. I have found Samuel's analysis of Tibetan culture and history which contrasts two modes, the clerical and shamanic, to provide a useful framework for thinking about the diversities of religious/social process (Samuel, 1993). My approach, while meshing well with his, has a much narrower focus on particular individuals and events. Cf. his theoretical evaluations in Chapter 28 (Samuel, 1993).

60. The only known biography for this great master came from an invocation written by a female disciple after his death. For more details see Stutchbury (forthcoming).

61. See Khetsun Sangpo (1981, Vol.VIII: 458-477), who gives dates of 1789-1844. Presumably, it is the *tulku* of this lama, or these dates are wrong by a sixty-year cycle.

62. Here the ages are given according to Tibetan reckoning. The dates are Adzom Drukpa (1842-1934) and Śākya Śrī (1853-1919).

63. My thanks are due to Elizabeth Harper, whose translation skills with the Khampa dialect of Gegan Khyentse are greatly appreciated.

64. Two of Śākya Śrī's sons had the names Tsewang, Tsewang Jigmé and Tsewang Rinchen. It was probably the latter who was involved in this conversation.

65. A son born not long after the party fled from Tibet died within a few days of birth; thus Sé Rinpoche is the second child of Apo Rinpoche and Urgyan Chödren.

66. As mentioned above, Khyentse Wangpo had several reincarnations, recognised as different aspects. The principal Body (*sku*) *tulku,* Dzongsar Khyentse Jamyang Chökyi Wangpo II, died at an early age (1894-1909), and the activity (*'phrin las*) aspect, Katog (*kaḥ thog*) Chökyi Lodro became pre-eminent, and has since been known as Dzongsar Khyentse, as is his *tulku.* After his death in 1959, Dilgo Khyentse, a mind emanation (*thugs sprul*) assumed the position of the principal Khyentse lineage holder, a position now passed to the *tulku* of Chökyi Lodro.

67. Dzongsar Khyentse Rinpoche has transmitted and taught Śākya Śrī's *P'owa* (transference of consciousness) in Australia in both 1985 and 1990. In Australia during 1989, Drukchen Rinpoche transmitted and

taught Dorje Phagmo (*rDo rje Phag mo*, Skt. Vajravārāhī) and Cakrasaṁvara practices.

68. Cf Samuel (1993: Chapter 18, and Afterword).

69. Such as that by Geoffrey Samuel and Tashi Tsering, mentioned previously. Sons of Śākya Śrī's daughter are well known practitioners, settled in Orissa. Although technically women do not pass on *rus* or 'bone', there are numerous cases of daughters within a *ngagpa* lineage producing sons who are recognised as reincarnates.

70. Kutang is reported as having had a close connection with both the Drukpa and Nyingma traditions since the 17th century. To my knowledge, a new *gonpa* was not established here, nor have the descendants of Śākya Śrī played a role in this region (Aris 1975). More detailed comparative research would be useful.

71. Pema Chögyal's tendency to eschew populated places in preference for solitude and practice further contributed to his renown as a practitioner, and his desirability as a teacher. There is a brief biography of Tripon Pema Chögyal (1878-1959) in English, along with a photograph, in *Tibetan Frontier Families* (Aziz 1978: 215-217). The information was gleaned from the *namthar*, which was being carved in 1975, and oral accounts. Tripon Rinpoche established himself at Tzibri (*rtsibs ri*), the Gotsangpa site in the Dingri area, in 1934 and most of the material pertains to this later phase of his life.

72. In some areas, particularly those in which *gonpas* were more institutionalised, lamas did establish *gonpas* in border regions with clear missionary and political intent – cf. Samuel (1993: Chapter 8 and Chapter 11). My approach also contrasts with Ortner's (1989a, 1989b) work on the founding on *gonpas* in the Sherpa region of Nepal, the material she collected about these events mirroring her interests in 'cultural schemas'.

Contributors

John Draper's MA thesis (ANU, 1985) deals with religion in Sherpa society. He is currently completing a PhD in Social Anthropology at Sydney University, based on field work in the area of medical anthropology among the Sherpas. He has also worked in recent years for development agencies in Australia and Vietnam.

Hamish Gregor's training is in the field of Hispanic Philology; but he describes himself now as a feral scholar in the field of Buddhist studies.

Span Hanna's narrative derives from a journey to Tibet in 1986. He is currently teaching at a technical college in Hangzhou, China.

Toni Huber completed his MA in Religious Studies at the University of Canterbury, NZ, in 1989 with a thesis on the Tibetan pilgrimage centre of La phyi. He has just completed a PhD in the same department on the pilgrimage centre of Tsa ri.

Ana Marko is completing a PhD in Social Anthropology at the University of Sydney based on fieldwork in Ladakh. She has recently worked as a full-time tutor in Anthropology at the University of Adelaide.

Geoffrey Samuel is Associate Professor of Sociology and Anthropology at the University of Newcastle, NSW. His publications include *Mind, Body and Culture* and *Civilized Shamans.* He is also translator of Giuseppe Tucci's *Religions of Tibet.*

Elisabeth Stutchbury completed her PhD in Social Anthropology at ANU in 1991 with a thesis on the *'Brug pa bKa' brgyud* practitioners of Kardang Gompa, Lahul. She is currently a Lecturer in Anthropology at the University of Melbourne, and will be taking up an ARC post-doctoral fellowship at ANU in mid-1994.

David Templeman is an independent scholar who lives in Melbourne, where he teaches at Collingwood High School. His translations from the Tibetan include *The Origins of the Tārā Tantra, The Seven Instruction Lineages* and *The Life of Kṛṣṇācāryā/Kaṇhā.*